THE ARAB-ISRAELI CONFLICT: PERSPECTIVES

THE ARAB-ISRAELI CONFLICT: PERSPECTIVES

Edited by
Alvin Z. Rubinstein

Contributors
Alan Dowty
Adam M. Garfinkle
Aaron David Miller
Itamar Rabinovich
Alvin Z. Rubinstein
Haim Shaked

PRAEGER

PRAEGER SPECIAL STUDIES • PRAEGER SCIENTIFIC

New York • Philadelphia • Eastbourne, UK
Toronto • Hong Kong • Tokyo • Sydney

Library of Congress Cataloging in Publication Data
Main entry under title:

The Arab-Israeli conflict.

   Bibliography: p.
   Includes index.
   1. Jewish-Arab relations.   2. Israel—Politics and
government.   3. Palestinian Arabs.   I. Rubinstein, Alvin Z.
DS119.7.A6723 1984   956   83-24448
ISBN 0-03-068778-0 (alk. paper)
ISBN 0-03-068779-9 (pbk. : alk. paper)

Published in 1984 by Praeger Publishers
CBS Educational and Professional Publishing
a Division of CBS Inc.
521 Fifth Avenue, New York, NY 10175 USA

© 1984 by Praeger Publishers

456789 052 987654321

Printed in the United States of America
on acid-free paper

In the beginning of what we now call the Arab-Israeli conflict, outbreaks of violence were local, easily controlled, and short-lived. With Israel's independence in 1948, the conflict took on a regional character, with heavy political overtones. Since the late 1960s, it has acquired an intensity and explosiveness that threaten regional and international peace, involve the superpowers in ways that profoundly complicate their relationship, foster polarization and tensions, and pose a challenge to leaderships throughout the Middle East. The Arab-Israeli conflict is the world's oldest regional conflict, its most complex, and certainly its most dangerous.

Despite the wealth of specialized and scholarly studies of the subject, there had been no single book that evaluated the conflict topically and analytically in historical perspective and in a manner that could challenge an intelligent, nonspecialist audience. It was our aim to fill that gap.

This book is composed of six original essays, each devoted to one facet of the overall problem. Together they form a coherent, integrated assessment of the origins, dynamics, dilemmas, and evolution of the Arab-Israeli conflict.

Contents

LIST OF MAPS

THE ARAB-ISRAELI CONFLICT: PERSPECTIVES

1

Genesis

Adam M. Garfinkle

Many people believe that the knowledge of history can set men free, helping them to avoid repeating the mistakes of the past. But history can also become the master of men's souls, diverting their talents into the pursuit of ancient animosities, their futures to be spent taking revenge for the past. The Arab-Israeli conflict, regrettably, seems to support the more pessimistic of these visions.

Everything has a history, and the Arab-Israeli conflict is no exception; but unlike histories of the affairs of man that are far from contemporary concern—the history of Carthage, for example—the history of the Arab-Israeli conflict is as alive and as contentious as the confrontation itself. Each party to the conflict—and there are many—claims its version of history as vindication for contemporary political demands. In histories written under the burden of strong emotion, the "facts" often become tools of advocacy and description blends into myth. When reading extreme pro- and anti-Zionist accounts of the sources of the Arab-Israeli conflict, one sometimes wonders whether the writers are discussing the same events. The wit of the modern cynic applies very well to the Arab-Israeli dispute: everyone may be entitled to his own opinions, but not to his own facts!

Even if it were not for the high emotions surrounding the history of the Arab-Israeli rivalry and the political uses to which it is subject, a simple chronicle of its origins would still be a daunting task. It is not only a political and territorial dispute between two countries, as, for example, was the Franco-German struggle in the nineteenth and early twentieth centuries. Rather, it involves many countries to different degrees, and groups of people not easily identified with any particular country. There is Israel, of course, whose very existence is largely what the entire affair is about. But there are also Jewish communities elsewhere—in the United

States, Canada, Western Europe, the Soviet Union— for whom Israel's survival and security is extremely important. There are the Arab countries, some very near to the conflict politically and geographically, and others far away. All the Arab states profess an interest, but these states have other interests as well, which have led to considerable inter-Arab discord and tension over the years. On many occasions, the policies of the Arab states with respect to the Palestinian issue have been designed more to settle scores with each other than with Israel. And, there are the Palestinian Arabs themselves who have no state at present and who believe that their homeland—Palestine—was taken from them unjustly by the Jews. The Palestinians see themselves as a people victimized by Israel, by the European imperial powers of the past, by the superpowers of the present, by their fellow Arabs, and even by their own self-proclaimed leaders.

Beyond this complicated cast of characters, the Arab-Israeli conflict also differs from many others in that it has had, and may still have, an extreme all-or-nothing nature. Unlike the Franco-German clash noted above, or even U.S.-Soviet competition today, where adversaries take for granted each other's existence, protagonists in the Arab-Israeli arena have not. Until very recently, nearly all Arabs felt that Israel did not have a right to exist, at least not in Palestine, and the ideal solution, from their point of view, was Israel's destruction. On the other hand, there have been many Zionists and supporters of Israel who have denied the existence of a specifically Palestinian Arab people, and who contend that the problem is merely one of accommodating refugees, not one of accommodating national political aspirations.

On top of this, there is yet another layer of complexity, and that involves the legacy of the entanglements of various external forces. What is today Israel—and nearly all of the Arab world, too—was for hundreds of years ruled by the Ottoman Turkish Empire. With its collapse in World War I, political control of the Middle East passed to Great Britain and France, the two greatest colonial powers of the time. Modern Arab nationalism first emerged in opposition to Turkish overlordship, but its subsequent evolution was shaped by the intrusive hegemony of European power. The ideological content of Arab nationalism springs from a collision between changes in European political thinking in the nineteenth century and the local Islamic culture and its political traditions. Arab nationalism, as a result, has taken an ambivalent attitude toward Europe. Most Arab intellectuals admired Europe's power and efficiency, emulated at times its governmental forms, and were influenced deeply by its ideologies. Yet most Arabs resented Europe's exploitation and condescension and rejected overwhelmingly its religions. Inspired by a vision of the legendary Arab empire of the early days of Islam, Arab nationalist intellectuals blamed the European powers for the latter-day reality of weakness, strife, and division among Arabs. They hated the ease with which the Europeans divided the idealized single Arab nation and set its inhabitants against each other for their own imperial convenience.

Zionism, also, is very much a synthesis of European influence and Jewish civilization. It was European culture that for centuries persecuted Jews and set them apart from society, thereby strengthening the already potent religious bonds of Jewish peoplehood. It was European culture, too, after the French Revolution and the Napoleonic wars, that emancipated much of European Jewry and confronted traditional Jewish religious identity with the dilemma of how to come to terms with the secular state and its abstract, universalist criteria for citizenship. Out of Europe's own political struggles and social turmoil of the nineteenth century arose modern Jewish nationalism, Zionism, as one response to these changes and challenges.

While the political doctrines of modern Zionism came out of emancipated Western Europe, these doctrines had their most numerous and firmest adherents in the disappointed Jewish aspirants of the Russian Enlightenment. And so was born the early dominant strain of socialist Zionism—a reborn Jewish society in Israel, based on the modern doctrines of social and economic emancipation.

Thus, Zionism and Arab nationalism—the future antagonists—had at least one thing in common from their past: the struggle to come to terms with Europe—its power, its wealth, its ideologies, and its physical domination. It is one of the many ironies of the modern Middle East that Jewish and Arab nationalists collided with each other in the course of reconciling their own traditions with European culture.

It is interesting to note that while the Arabs lived in the same territories without interruption for thousands of years, their identity—their loyalties—still lay with family, clan, tribe, and religion. For the Jews, however, who lived in exile (*galut*) for these same thousands of years, nationhood was defined and accentuated by religion. National consciousness, it seems, is more dependent on the strength of belief than on physical presence in a territory.

This leads to a final introductory point. There is a religious dimension to the Arab-Israeli conflict. Israel is a Jewish state; Arab opposition to it is overwhelmingly Muslim. Muslim-Jewish relations have a history that goes back to the origins of Islam in the seventh century. In many respects Jews and Muslims have been much less rancorous in their association through the centuries than have Jews and European Christians. Indeed, Jews and Arabs think of themselves, through their respective mythologies, as ethnic and spiritual cousins. Both hold Abraham, or Ibrahim in Arabic, as their forefather, with his son Isaac the seed of the Jews and his son Ishmael (Ismail in Arabic) the seed of the Arabs. Hebrew and Arabic are of the same language family—the Semitic. Islam acknowledges Jewish sources and the evolution of Jewish customs and law has been influenced by Islam. Nevertheless, there are deep-seated prejudices of a historical and theological nature that separate Jew from Muslim.

This is not to say that in every case, or even in many cases, religious prejudices play a dominant, conscious, or explicit role in the conflict—they probably do not. After all, Israel was founded by secular socialists who were not traditionally religious people, and Israel has never been ruled by rabbis. The Arab states around Israel, too, though most are less avowedly secular, have never been ruled by theologians. In practice it is very difficult to separate one kind of motivation from another; human belief systems have many layers, and people cannot be conscious of all the factors that motivate them or of the way that these factors become entwined with one another. Thus, age-old religiously grounded frictions probably do play some role, but not a dominant one and not one that is easy to analyze.

In sum, the sources of the Arab-Israeli conflict include national, territorial, ideological, and religious elements, and these elements have been shaped by the interplay of a great diversity of both indigenous regional and external global actors. The rest of this chapter is devoted to a roughly chronological treatment of the interweaving of these factors, starting with the coalescence of modern Jewish and Arab nationalisms in the late nineteenth and early twentieth centuries, and ending in 1948, when the state of Israel came into being.

1798-1917: THE EMERGENCE
OF NATIONAL CONSCIOUSNESS

Modern Arab nationalism in its many variations is a perplexing amalgam of an ancient, religiously oriented political tradition and a head-on clash with an aggressive, powerful, yet internally tumultuous Europe. This fateful collision may be dated conveniently from 1798, the year that the armies of Napoleon Bonaparte of France invaded and seized what was then a forelorn, hinterland province of the Ottoman Turkish Empire—Egypt. The brief French occupation of Egypt—and the subsequent, more lengthy British intervention—changed the face of Middle East politics forever. In order to understand how this was so, it is first necessary to describe in brief what the French found when they arrived in the Middle East nearly two centuries ago.

The Middle East landscape in the early part of the nineteenth century was characterized by three related conditions: acute political fragmentation and decentralization under the nominal unity of the Ottoman Empire; social conservatism, dominated by the pervasive influence of Islam; and general economic stagnation amid huge discrepancies between the few very rich and the many very poor. Palestine, the northern half of which was administered by the Turks as part of the *vilayet* (or province) of Beirut and the southern part as the *sandjak* of Jerusalem, was no exception.

Except in times of emergency—namely, war—the far-flung Arab provinces of the Ottoman Empire were left to govern themselves. Indeed, some of these provinces on the fringes of the empire were virtually independent. As long as the provinces provided tax revenue when required and military recruits on occasion, Turkish leaders in Istanbul were usually satisfied. On the provincial level, the same sort of loose hierarchical arrangements obtained, and the lives of most people were ordered by traditional authority structures on the village level.

These traditional authority structures were based primarily on kinship groups—families, clans, tribes, villages—and these, in turn, were reinforced by strong religious legitimization. Thus there was, at the village level, close coordination between the political authority vested in the head of the clan or tribe and the religious authority of the Muslim *ulema*, or clergy. The former was responsible for ensuring social stability and maintaining norms, for reconciling internal disputes, and for acting as liaison and advocate for the village at the next higher level of the political structure. The latter was responsible for seeing to the spiritual and ritual needs of the community, overseeing the laws relating to birth, death, marriage, divorce, almsgiving, prayer, and so forth.

The stability of this authority structure was reinforced by the near total absence of social mobility, due to the nature of the traditional economy. Most made their living through subsistence agriculture. Urban centers, such as there were, housed traditional crafts industries, Koranic schools, military garrisons, and an occasional merchant's establishment.

It was not uncommon for a person to be born, live, work, and die without having traveled more than a few miles from home.

Insofar as political identification was concerned, a man identified himself with his family, his tribe, or his village. The only abstract identification was that provided by Islam, and this was abstract indeed. Islam supplied a complete worldview to the devout Muslim, pertaining both to local politics and global, universal affairs as well. It was a worldview in which politics and religion were wholly fused, and in which social structure from the sultan down to the village *muktar*, or chief, was divinely ordained. What was the content of this worldview?

Put simply, the world was a battleground between the faithful, known collectively as *Dar al-Islam*, and the heathen, *Dar al-Harb*. It was the duty of the good Muslim to work to transform Dar al-Harb into Dar al-Islam through the vehicle of *jihad*, or holy struggle. The Muslim world, therefore, was ideally a unity, a community of the faithful. Its political organization—ideally—reflected this unity through the caliphate, an institution dating from the seventh century. The legitimacy of Ottoman rule for the Muslim Arab derived from the respect due its physical power and control and from the position of the Turkish sultan, who was also the caliph, the leader of Islam.

While this simple dichotomy gave structure to the relations between the Muslim empire and its external foes, it did not apply as easily to internal affairs. The Muslim world had expanded so fast and so far between the seventh and tenth centuries that many non-Muslim minorities, and heterodox Muslim deviationists, resided in *Dar al-Islam*. For Christians and Jews a special "protected" status was devised. These minorities were considered "people of the book" (*dhimmi*), their religions being acknowledged forerunners of Islam. They were not to be harmed, and they were allowed an autonomous community life under the direction of their own religious authorities. Politically, however, they were second-class citizens, prevented from serving in the military or owning land, and obliged to pay a special tax, the *jizya*. This basis arrangement dates back nearly to the beginnings of Muslim history, but reached its zenith under the Turks, who refined the *millet system* for minority autonomy to an administrative art. In areas where minorities were numerous and prominent—especially Palestine, Lebanon, and Syria—the *millet system*, an arrangement whereby individual communities were governed by their own religious leaders, created a communal mosaic that persists to this day in Lebanon and parts of Syria.

By the time the French landed in Egypt, Arab realities diverged sharply from ideal Islamic aspirations. The Islamic world was not one, either politically or religiously, having long since disintegrated along regional, ethnic, and theological fault lines. Worse, the Ottoman Empire had long since passed its peak and, since its defeat at the gates of Vienna in 1683, had been thrown back upon itself by the Austro-Hungarian Empire and especially the Russian Empire. Economically, the Arab lands were poor; the grandeur of earlier dynasties, when Arab cities like Cairo, Baghdad, and Damascus had surpassed the major cities of Europe in size, wealth, population, and culture, was gone. Despite imperial decay, poverty, and division, however, the Arab world nevertheless displayed a remarkable social stability, and its ultimate faith in eventual restoration of Muslim power and honor remained, despite the nadir of its civilization.

The frailties of the Muslim world allowed the European powers in the nineteenth century to push back Ottoman boundaries—especially in North Africa and the Balkans—penetrate the economy, and influence the thinking of the entire Muslim world. But rather than adding to the chaos and disintegration evident even in local affairs, persistent defeat in war provided the impetus for Ottoman rulers (and other local potentates) to "modernize" their societies. Moreover, the expansion of European commerce, ideas, technology, and physical presence in the Middle East during the nineteenth century slowly began to break down the pillars of traditional society. Starting first in Egypt under the reign of Mohammed Ali (1801-41), and gradually spreading through North Africa and the Levant, Europeans helped change the economy of the region. Early introduction of cash crops—notably cotton and tobacco in Egypt—some industrialization, and the building of some roads, railways, and canals increased social mobility and gave rise to a new, local middle class dependent on these innovations. Autocratic sultans, kings, and shahs in the Muslim world, trying to protect their own privileges, sought European technical expertise to enhance their power; this led them to send young men to Europe for specialized training, and also to import Europeans for various purposes. This more direct contact with Europe led to the introduction of European political ideas into the Muslim world, particularly by a growing new class of European-educated military officers, lawyers, journalists, and administrators.

The enhancement of the administrative and military capabilities of rulers, on both the imperial and regional levels, led them to seek more direct control over their territories. New police forces, tax collectors, judges, and bureaucrats reduced the former broad autonomy of the village and this created much resentment, particularly among the non-Turkish-speaking, and especially among the Arabs. The reforms of the Turks after the Young Turk revolution of 1908 also upset some Arab Muslim religious authorities, whose privileges were being undercut by the growth of new economies, new social classes, and new ideas promulgated by them. Among these new ideas were those of popular sovereignty and constitutional government. In traditional Islamic culture, the ruler's authority derived from God, not from the people. While a consensus of elders (*ijma*) was in theory required to approve a ruler, his main responsibilities were to promote Islam and lead an exemplary pious life. To the people per se he owed nothing. The notion that the people had political rights of any sort was revolutionary, as was the idea of a constitution to define and protect those rights through a political contract.

Just as unsettling, perhaps, was the European concept of the secular, territorial state in which political and religious authority were separate, and in which citizenship was not determined by kinship ties or religion, but by an abstract code of rights and obligations. Traditionally, borders in the Arab world were not abstract lines drawn on paper maps, but were rather "in the hearts of men," the function of familial and tribal loyalty of a highly personal nature.

These new ideas struck at the very basis of political authority in traditional Arab society, namely, the divine foundations of tribal autocracy. Set against the relative impotence and venality of local leaders, the power of European civilization itself stood as an argument against the old ways. But the main reaction of the forefathers of modern Arab nationalism, men like Jamal al-Din al-Afghani (1839-97) and Mohammed Abduh (1848-1905), was not to reject traditional ways but to reform and reformulate them. These were religious men who spoke and wrote in religious terms, and for whom being an Arab and being a Muslim were virtually inseparable. They hoped to make use of the devices of European power without succumbing to Europe's culture. It was from this conjunction that early Arab nationalism took its dominant characteristic: reformist Islam.

At the same time, the assault by Ottoman Turkey on local Arab autonomy, made possible by European technological and administrative reforms, eventually evoked a distinctively Arab element. This development was a long time coming; a specifically Arab political consciousness had only begun to develop by the eve of World War I. As one student of Arab nationalism, Zeine N. Zeine, put it;

> . . .in the nineteenth century, there was as yet no "Arab Question" in international politics. Indeed, the word "Arab" itself as

a designation for the inhabitants of the Arab provinces of the Ottoman Empire rarely occurs in the books and documents of the period. It was reserved mainly for the Bedouins of the desert and for all the non-town dwellers in the Near East. The general terms "Muslim" and "Christian" were used to describe the two principal classes of inhabitants in this area. As to the great majority of the Muslim subjects of the Sultan, whether Turks or Arabs, they were "brothers in the Faith," i.e., they were Muslims before being Turks or Arabs.[1]

To this description, Zeine adds the following important point:

The world in which the Arabs and Turks lived together was, before the end of the nineteenth century, *politically* a non-national world. The vast majority of the Muslim Arabs did not show any nationalist or separatist tendencies except when the Turkish leaders themselves, after 1908, asserted their own nationalism and ceased to be considered, in Arab eyes, as good Muslims and as brothers in the Faith.[2]

Thus it was the Turks who served as a conduit between unsettling European ideas of political authority and national identification on the one hand and the Arabs on the other. The reforms undertaken by the Ottoman Empire after 1908 were European in inspiration, and the Arabs feared that they portended the "Turkification" of Arab culture. Only after the Turks broke the bond between Islam and political identity did the Arabs follow suit. It was not only the attempt to reduce local Arab autonomy that gave rise to a specifically Arab nationalism, then, but the motives presumed to be behind Ottoman reforms.

The early development of Arab nationalism tended to be strongest in Egypt, where the European presence and influence was more direct and pervasive (the British occupied Egypt in 1882), and among the Christian minorities of Lebanon and Syria, for whom the question of national identity was more pressing and problematic. In Palestine, a relative backwater of the Ottoman Empire, which had a population of no more than 590,000 in 1880 (of which roughly 35,000 were Jews), nationalist activity was almost wholly absent. European penetration had been very limited. In the last dozen years of the nineteenth century, the local Arab community from time to time expressed concern to Istanbul about Jewish immigration into the area, but the local residents remained loyal to the empire even until British armies of occupation entered Palestine in 1917. To the extent that a distinctive political consciousness developed in Palestine at all before World War I, it was partly anti-European (as in Egypt and North Africa), partly anti-Turkish (as in Arabia), and partly anti-Zionist. Anti-Zionist grievances, however, did not translate into an autonomous local political agenda or consciousness. In the early years of this century, the Arabs of Palestine certainly did not think of themselves as "Palestinians." Indeed, they had only just begun to think of themselves as Arabs. They were Muslims from this clan or that family, only with a unique problem.

The concept of Jewish nationhood has been firmly embedded in the experience of the Jewish people for thousands of years, and this experience is rooted historically in the ancient independent Jewish commonwealths that existed two millenia ago in what is today Israel. But modern Jewish nationalism, Zionism, is barely a century old, and its intellectual foundations lie not in the Middle East but in Europe.

After the final destruction of the Second Jewish Commonwealth by the Romans in the year 70, and particularly after the defeat of the Bar-Kochba revolt in the year 135, most Jews left or were exiled from what the Romans called "Palestine"—a name they adopted as a deliberate national insult, for the Philistines had been the Jews' archenemies for centuries. After long years of wanderings and expulsions, many Jews wound up in Europe, where for over fifteen hundred years, because of their non-Christian character in a Christian world, they either chose or were forced to live apart from the rest of society.

The economy of European society was no less feudal and its politics were no less theocratic than those of the Muslim world. Religious intolerance and violent persecution were common fare, and Jewish communities were sometimes expelled en masse from European countries. The Jews of the Muslim world were second-class citizens politically, to be sure, and were denied certain basic rights. But there, unlike Europe, violent persecution was rare and there were no expulsions of Jews from any Muslim domain.

In different ways, the Italian Renaissance of the fourteenth century and the Protestant Reformation of the fifteenth century marked the beginning of the end of the European theocratic state. The French Revolution of 1789 brought its final destruction. The birth of the modern, secular nation-state with the French Revolution, spread by the armies of Napoleon across Western and Central—but *not* Eastern—Europe, emancipated the Jews of one country after another, granting them civil rights and political-legal equality. Jews were free to attend schools and universities, enter the professions, and even to grow wealthy. As a result, most Jews left their isolated quarters, abandoned their distinctive dress and language, and tried to blend into the new, liberal society.

The opening of a new and vibrant European culture to the Jews posed problems for traditional Jewish identity, no less than exposure to Europe posed problems for Muslim Arab society. Emancipation promised enhanced physical security for the Jews and the end of overt discrimination and violence directed against them. It also offered improved social status and the possibility of escaping what had been, more often than not, a grinding poverty. But there was a price for all this, and that was the threat of a dilution of Jewish identity, culture, and social solidarity.

This was not the first time in the long history of the Jewish people that such challenges had arisen, and each time Jewish civilization had adapted itself to new intellectual, economic, and political conditions without losing its own unique character. In Biblical times, Moses and Aaron transformed a mob burdened with the mentality of slavery into a nation during 40 years in the desert (1220-1180 B.C.E.).[3] Joshua and the Judges helped the people adapt to the sedentary life upon the land, and a procession of prophets, from Amos to Malachi, helped guide the nation through foreign occupation, including even the loss of half the people at the hands of the Assyrians in the eighth century B.C.E. The prophet Ezekiel gave a new vision to the people during the first, Babylonian, exile (586-38 B.C.E.) and Ezra and Nehemiah revolutionized Jewish communal and religious life under the restoration sponsored by Persian King Cyrus the Great. The Jewish philosopher, Philo (28 B.C.E.- 50 C.E.) managed to synthesize Jewish tradition with Greek Platonist thought during the period of Roman domination of the land. The Pharisaic revolution during Roman times (165 B.C.E.-73 C.E.) emphasized the personal, ethical aspects of Judaism, making its continuation less dependent upon a hereditary priesthood or any particular locale. In the twelfth century, Maimonides helped Jewish thought come to terms with the Aristotelian scholastic tradition of medieval Christendom and prosper from it. When the leaders of the Jewish community in nineteenth-century Europe confronted the challenge of emancipation, their sense of historical continuity no doubt imbued a certain confidence in their endeavor. Unbeknownst to them, however, this confidence was not well founded, for the challenges of previous centuries involved those of one community against another. The philosophy of the emancipation, however, emphasized the individual; in the new Europe, parochial communities had no status. This carried with it a danger for which the Jewish community was totally unprepared.

There were essentially four types of Jewish response to changes in European society in the nineteenth century, the relative importance and popularity of each depending upon the period of history and the part of Europe in which the drama was played out: assimilationism, reformism, revolutionism, and Zionism.

One response of Jews to the emancipation prevalent in the more culturally modern Western European countries was to assimilate fully into the general Christian cultural milieu. Many intermarried, changed their names, left off all religious observances, and some were even baptized as Christians. Since assimilationism was by definition a denial of Jewish identity, no formal philosophy of assimilation or "school" to promote it arose. For most who chose this path, it seems, abstract convictions played little or no role compared to the sentiment that Jewish tradition and identity were anachronistic, antimodern barriers between themselves and the "good life" of the new Europe in a new, culturally enlightened age.

Leaders of the Jewish community in Western Europe were frightened by the implications of assimilationism and sought to stem it by reforming and reformulating Jewish life in such a way as to conform to modern social and political conditions. The earliest attempts to recast Jewish life so that Jews could simultaneously remain Jewish and participate as active citizens of their country was called the *Haskalah*, or Enlightenment, and it was begun by Moses Mendelssohn (1729-86). The early Haskalah, as it developed after the French Revolution, skirted the question of Jewish nationality, saying little about whether the Jews as such were a nation apart or not. But the matter had not yet arisen in the minds of most Europeans—at least not yet.

In the 1830s and 1840s, however, the abstract universalist ideals of the French Revolution gave way to the rise of romantic nationalism, spurred on by efforts to unify Italy and Germany, by the emergence of new Balkan states, and by the restiveness apparent within the polyglot Austro-Hungarian Empire. It was with the growth of the national question in Europe as a whole that the severest challenge latent in the emancipation truly emerged. When it did emerge, one Jewish response was to recast Jewish identity away from the previously undivided unity of peoplehood and religion. The Reform movement, which arose in Germany in the 1840s, stripped away from Judaism all those aspects that might interfere with the Jews' ability to live fully in secular society—dietary laws, strict Sabbath observance, Hebraic liturgy, parochial education, and, particularly, all references to Jewish national life. As Arthur Hertzberg has put it, Reform Judaism

> defined the religion of the Jew as an ethical creed, the moral heritage of the Bible. The traditional hope for the return to Zion could not be allowed to remain in the liturgy as even a pious dream, for its presence might call into question the unqualified loyalty of the Jew to the state. It was replaced by the doctrine of the "mission of Israel," the belief that the Jews had been dispersed in the world by a beneficent Providence to act as its teachers and its guides toward the ideals of justice and righteousness revealed in the Bible. Nay more, the Messiah was now to be identified with the vision of an individual liberty and universal peace—i.e., with the progressive faith of the first half of the nineteenth century.[4]

While the Reform movement grew in Western Europe, its choices, and even the choice of assimilation, were unavailable to Jews farther east, those living in the Russian Empire (including, then, Poland). In Eastern Europe, where the larger part of European Jewry lived, the effects of the French Revolution and the new political thinking it spawned were modest indeed, at least in the first 60 years of the nineteenth century. There, church and state were as tightly bound as they had been elsewhere in Europe before the Protestant Reformation. Russia's distinctive autocratic tradition and the theocratic Slavic Orthodox Church together propagated a view of the Jews as aliens, heretics, and, increasingly, subversives, bringing to Holy Russia new and dangerous ideas from farther west. Jews continued to live apart, to be poor, to speak a distinctive language and wear distinctive clothing, and to suffer the periodic wrath of the majority population. Moreover, Eastern European Jewry remained traditionally observant for the most part, the choice of trading its religiosity for the attractions of the secular life never having arisen.

For a time in the 1860s, especially under Czar Alexander II, Russia experienced something of a liberalization. The serfs were freed and many of the restrictive limitations on the Jews were relaxed. Jews, Poles, and others began to transmit the culture of the West into Russia, particularly that of "enlightened" France. But Czar Alexander II was assassinated in 1881 and his successors, determined to purify and Russify the empire as the key to imperial power, cracked down on all ethnic minorities, including the Jews.

The new repression in Russia sparked off a number of movements aimed at alleviating the Jewish condition. One reaction was less a political movement than a movement of people, an emigration of large numbers of Eastern European Jewry, mainly to the United States. A second response was that of revolutionism; Jews determined to overthrow the czarist oppression and by changing society, relieve Jewish problems as well. There were many varieties of Jewish revolutionism in Eastern Europe. Some Jews abandoned Judaism altogether and became Marxists, radical socialists, or anarchists. They believed that capitalism was the root of anti-Semitism and that eliminating the former would eliminate the latter. Indeed, many leaders of the Bolshevik party in Russia were Jews by birth, the most famous, perhaps, being Leon Trotsky (whose real name was Lev Bronstein). Other revolutionists jettisoned their religiosity but not their Jewish identities, believing that in a new, revolutionary Russia, Jews could live in their own autonomous area. These were members of the Jewish Bund, and are often referred to as Bundists.

Some Jews in Russia, however, rejected the Marxist project as being either too fanciful or too assimilationist. They thought the Bundists were unrealistic. But they were too exposed to modern thinking to rest content in traditional religiosity, waiting in poverty and fear for the coming of the Messiah. These were the Zionists, who hoped to solve the Jewish problem where it was most acute—in Russia—by applying the romantic nationalist ideology of the day to their own condition. They sought to recreate a Jewish commonwealth in Palestine.

Interestingly, the very first Zionists were not those of Russia in the 1880s, but instead two men who lived in earlier times in buffer zones between "enlightened" Western Europe and autocratic Russia, where the national idea was very strong, but the impetus for assimilationism or reformism was very weak. These men were both rabbis—Yehuda Alkalai (1798-1878) who lived in Sarajevo in the Balkans, and Zvi Hirsch Kalischer (1795-1874) who was from Posen in western Poland. In the 1850s and 1860s they combined the religious vision of the return to Zion with a sensitivity to the plight of Jews amid the rising nationalisms of Europe. They both argued, in essence, that God would not send the Messiah until the Jews started to redeem themselves and their land.

The message of Alkalai and Kalischer, along with that of another remarkable Zionist precursor, Moses Hess, was largely ignored in the West in the 1850s, where the Reform movement gained strength as the emancipation moved even farther eastward. Besides, these were rabbis whose message was garbed in religious language, and this was hardly popular among the "modern" Jews of the West. In Eastern Europe, for those few who were exposed to Alkalai, Kalischer and Hess, these were times of liberalization and hope in Russia—no time for impossible, utopian fantasies.

Zionism came alive in the 1880s and 1890s, owing to two events, one of which, as noted above, was the return of repression in Russia. Leo Pinsker wrote a book in 1882, entitled *Autoemancipation*, which was the first full, nonreligiously dressed exposition of modern Zionism. Within Russia, small clubs were formed—Hovevei Tzion, Hibbat Tzion—to promote Jewish national consciousness, the revitalization of the Hebrew language, and emigration to the Holy Land. Zionism in Russia in the 1880s and 1890s grew steadily, but relatively speaking, it was a small movement confined to intellectuals who had been glancingly exposed to the cultural ferment farther west in Europe.

Zionism's main impetus, ironically, came from a partly assimilated western Jew, Theodore Herzl (1860-1904). Herzl was born in Budapest and educated in the German cultural milieu of the Austro-Hungarian Empire. He worked as a journalist and in 1894 happened to be a Paris correspondent for a major Viennese newspaper. There he witnessed the infamous Dreyfus trial. A Jewish army captain, Alfred Dreyfus, stood falsely accused of spying for Germany, and his trial, one of many manifestations of rising "scientific" anti-Semitism and racism, had a profound effect on Herzl. Hearing the shouts of the mobs, "A bas les Juifs" ("Down with the Jews") and "A la mort les Juifs" ("Death to the Jews"), helped Herzl reach certain conclusions about what was happening to enlightened European society and the role of the Jews in it. Herzl conceived a project for the solution of the "Jewish problem"—the rebirth of Jewish national life in the land of Israel. In 1896 he published a book outlining his idea and his project—*Der Judenstaat* (The Jewish State)[5]—and the next year, under Herzl's leadership, the First Zionist Congress met in Basel, Switzerland.

Whereas the pleas of Alkalai, Kalischer, and Hess had fallen on deaf ears in the 1850s, this was not the case in the 1890s. The optimism of the Jews of Wesern Europe in the first half of the century gave way first to doubt, and then to quiet despair, as universalist, liberal creeds were overshadowed by exclusivistic nationalisms tinged with racism and anti-Semitism. Most of the Jews of Western Europe kept faith with reformism as the answer to the Jewish problem, and Herzl's revivification of the (pre-emancipation) link between Judaism as a religion and Jews as a nation was, to put it mildly, unpopular and unappreciated. But a small number in Western Europe followed Herzl, and a few wealthy benefactors aided his ambitious project.

Herzl's real success came not among his own Western European Jewish fellows, but among the downtrodden Jewish masses of the reactionary Russian Empire. And here Herzl was more a catalyst than an originator, for Pinsker had already led the way, and by the time Herzl's life was transformed by the Dreyfus trial, there were already hundreds of Zionist "clubs" in Russia. An effort had also been made—ultimately successful—to found agricultural settlements in Palestine under Turkish rule. Between 1882 and 1897 more than 20,000 Jews immigrated to Palestine, many of them dedicated Zionists. This was known as the First *Aliyah*, or Ascent. The settlements of the First Aliyah were important for many reasons, but they were not self-sufficient economically. Had it not been for the generosity of a few wealthy European Jews, notably Baron Edmund de Rothschild, these first attempts would have withered away completely. Nevertheless, when Herzl turned his not inconsiderable talents to Zionism, a beginning had already been made.

Herzl provided two critical elements. First, he organized the Zionist Congress, which for the first time brought Jews of Eastern and Western Europe together and allowed them to plan and commiserate together. And second, Herzl's argument unified the basic condition of Jews in all of Europe and stressed that the Jews were one people in a political sense, a notion that was all but absent from the religion-oriented self-image of European Jewry at the time. If the Jews of Russia suffered active persecution and pogroms, so too, one day, might the Jews of France and Germany. Herzl's main point, and perhaps his simplest one, was that ultimately the decision to let Jews become an integral part of secular European society did not rest with the Jews but with the non-Jewish Europeans. Zionism was an expression of deep pessimism about the future of European liberal civilization; it predicted that, in the end, the gentiles would answer no.[6]

As the Zionist movement evolved and grew in the early years of the twentieth century, it faced many problems, not the least of which were its unpopularity among the majority of financially comfortable Western European Jews, the antipathy of the orthodox religious establishment in Eastern Europe, Turkish obstruction of Jewish settlement efforts, financial weakness, and internal dispute. Nevertheless, the obviously worsening plight of Russian Jewry, the growing popularity of Zionism among the Jewish masses of Eastern Europe, and the personal efforts of Herzl and, after his death in 1904, Dr. Chaim Weizmann, kept the movement alive.

The Zionist movement changed its emphasis and tone, and acquired a more specific social and political ideology, as it passed into the hands of Russian Zionists like Weizmann. Herzl had tried to use high diplomacy to accomplish his ends, meeting with the heads of state of Ottoman Turkey, Germany, and Italy and even Pope Pius X, and he never lost faith that the majority of the Jews in Western Europe would eventually be brought to see the light. He did not oppose settlements in Palestine, but he did not believe that working from the ground up, so to speak, would ever achieve a homeland. For this, a diplomatic breakthrough with the great powers was necessary. This approach came to be known as "political" Zionism.

As far as social philosophy was concerned, Herzl had never been moved by socialist ideologies or any other kind of ideology, and very little is known of his views—if he had any—as to how a Jewish state would be governed, should one ever come into being. He was also not much concerned about the revitalization of an authentic Jewish culture. He knew little, for example, of the efforts of Eliezer Ben-Yehuda to renew the use of the Hebrew language and thought that a Jewish state would be multilingual, like Switzerland. The Zionists of Russia, however, were greatly affected by the ideological winds sweeping through the decrepit Russian Empire and many were convinced socialists. The second Aliyah of 1905-14 was the one that really shaped the character of Israel-to-be and the dominant chords of Zionist ideology.

By the turn of the century there were over 50,000 Jews in Palestine, but only about 5,000 were to be found in the 20 or so rural Zionist settlements of the First Aliyah. Nearly all of them depended on outside assistance or charity of some sort. After the failure of the Octobrist Revolution in Russia in 1905, however, and the dawn of the grimmest oppression yet under the czar, Russian Zionists put off their local organizing to come to Palestine. Even those who were not socialists were attracted by the romantic call to pioneering and propelled by the fear of what awaited them in Russia. Between 1905 and 1914 more than 30,000 Jews came to settle on the land (though many of them did not stay there). They believed that labor upon the land could revitalize the soul of the Jewish people and create the new Jew. In Europe, Jews had not been farmers, had not been able to defend themselves, had not really spoken their own language. In Palestine, Jews would be agriculturalists, would bear arms, would speak Hebrew, and would normalize the Jewish social structure through Hebrew labor at every level of society, from the highest to the lowest. Dedicated to self-help and a vision of social justice, the new pioneers disdained charity and outside aid. They refused to hire local, cheap, Arab labor, for this was, in their view, to exploit them and distort the new Jewish economy. In contrast to the political Zionism of Herzl, the Zionism of these socialist-minded pioneers, or *khalutzim*, as they were called, became known as "practical" Zionism.

In 1909 the *Yishuv*, or "Settlement," as the Zionist efforts were known, started the first socialist-inspired collective settlement, or *kibbutz*, later named Deganya, near the Sea of Galilee. By 1914 there were 14 such settlements, and a Jewish city, Tel-Aviv, had taken root as well. In 1914 there were half a million Arabs in Palestine and 85,000 Jews, of which approximately 12,000 lived in rural areas.

The success of the Second Aliyah gave confidence to the Jews of Palestine and confidence, too, to the Zionists in Europe (and now America) who would soon join it. Its success also implanted in European governments the notion that a Jewish homeland in Palestine was a practical and serious proposition. Hard work and sacrifice had made possible, finally, Herzl's dream of a diplomatic triumph. This triumph was achieved by the personal charisma and talents of Chaim Weizmann, the sympathy for Zionism among the British aristocracy—this being a legacy of their classical education and the religious imagery of the Church of England—and World War I.

When war erupted in 1914, Britain and Ottoman Turkey found themselves on opposite sides. The British attempted to use any means, fair or foul, to turn the non-Turkish inhabitants of the empire, many of whom had been at the edge of rebellion even before the war began, against their increasingly harsh and capricious masters in Istanbul. In the course of this effort, the British made many promises, some of them mutually exclusive, to the Arabs and to the Jews. In return for aiding the British war effort against the Turks, London promised the Arabs political independence. The promise to the Jews, brokered by Dr. Weizmann, who as a chemist had aided the British war effort, was the Balfour Declaration of November 1917. The declaration, which took the form of a letter from Lord Balfour, a member of the British war cabinet, to Lord Rothschild, president of the British Zionist Federation, read, in part:

> His Majesty's government views with favor the establishment in Palestine of a national home for the Jewish people...it being clearly understood that nothing shall be done which may prejudice the civil and religious rights of existing non-Jewish com-

munities in Palestine, or the rights and political status enjoyed by Jews in any other country.

THE ISSUE IS JOINED: 1917-33

The Balfour Declaration was rightly seen by the Zionists as a political windfall; it cemented a relationship between the Zionists on the one hand and the greatest of the victorious allied powers, Great Britain, on the other. The fact that a Jewish legion, fighting within the British army, had helped in the final military seizure of Palestine from the Turks also gave added confidence to the movement, this despite the fact that the Jewish population of Palestine had dropped from 55,000 to 35,000 during the war, owing to deportation, emigration, combat fatalities, starvation, and disease.

The Arabs had some reason to rejoice, as well. During the war, the British had promised the *Sherif* of Mecca, Emir Hussein ibn Ali, that if the Arabs would rise up in revolt against the Turks, they would after-wards be rewarded with political independence.[7] Sherif Hussein was the head of the Hashemi family and, at the time, ruler of the Hijaz, a slice of the Arabian peninsula bordering the Red Sea, which held within its sandy borders the holiest places of Islam—Mecca and Medina. Hussein had great ambitions to enlarge his domain both in Arabia, at the expense of other tribal chieftains, and farther to the north, at the expense of the Turks, his nominal overlords. He cut a deal with the British in 1915, in which Britain recognized and supported "the independence of the Arabs in all regions within the limits demanded by the Sherif (namely, the entire Arab rectangle, including Syria, Arabia and Mesopotamia)," with the exception of "portions of Syria lying to the West of the districts of Damascus, Homs, Hama and Aleppo." Depending on the meaning of "Syria" as a geographical designation, this exception could include Palestine, as the British later held, or it could not, as the Hashemites later argued. In any case, the Arab Revolt, led by Hussein's second son, Faisal, and T. E. Lawrence (Lawrence of Arabia), caused the Turks much trou-ble, and when the dust settled in 1918, Faisal and a ragtag Bedouin army were ensconced in Damascus with British aid.

Faisal's main problem in Syria was the French, who coveted control of the area and who were promised as much in a secret wartime arrange-ment with the British, known as the Sykes-Picot Agreement. Faisal tried, in 1919, to enlist the support of the Zionists against the French and a "treaty" of cooperation was agreed upon. But the Zionists chose not to oppose British wishes, and those included French domination in Damascus in return for British control of Palestine. Thus, the alliance between Faisal and Weizmann was short-lived.

Meanwhile, the growth of the Yishuv, the shock of the Balfour Declaration, the severance of Palestine from Turkish rule, and the glory of an Arab king once again in Damascus galvanized the Arabs of Palestine into political action. They openly sided with Faisal in Syria against the French, their British supporters who were suspected of trying to weasel out of their wartime promises, and the pro-British Zionists. Indeed, they now thought of themselves, though somewhat vaguely, as Syrians and wished overwhelmingly to be a part of Faisal's domain, centered in Damascus. This was reinforced by a barrage of propaganda aimed at the Arab population of Palestine by Faisal and his minions. In March 1920, French displeasure notwithstanding, Faisal declared himself king of Syria, which included, to his mind, Palestine and Transjordan, as well.

The French would have none of "King" Faisal and in the summer of 1920 they forcibly deposed him. Hearing of Faisal's plight, Sherif Hussein (who had his own hands full at the time with the expansionist al-Saud tribe based in Riyadh[8]) dispatched his third son, Abdallah, to come from the Hijaz to his brother's aid in Syria. Paris was suspicious of Faisal and the Hashemites, believing them to be part of a British scheme to deprive France of the mandate for Syria. The San Remo Peace Conference of 1920 had resulted in the creation of a series of mandates in former Turkish territory, and for the first time defined the borders of these areas. France was given Syria. The Palestine mandate, which included all of what is today Israel, the West Bank and Gaza, *and Jordan* (or Transjordan, as it was then known), was given to Britain. So was the mandate for Mesopotamia (Iraq).

But ruling Mesopotamia proved a problem for London. Britain was weakened by the war, despite its acquisition of new lands, and was over-extended militarily and financially. It could not afford to rule Iraq directly, but finding a suitable local *emir*, or prince, through whom London could control the territory, had proven difficult. In the spring of 1921, just as Abdallah and his Bedouin army reached Transjordan, British Colonial Secretary Winston Churchill was in Cairo trying to solve Britain's Iraqi problem. Transjordan, though nominally part of the Palestine mandate, was understood by the British to fall within the Arab domain, not the Jewish. But Faisal in Syria had never made a serious attempt to administer the northern part of Transjordan adjacent to Syria; in the southern part he tried not at all. The sudden homelessness of Faisal, the presence of Abdallah and his army in Transjordan, the problems of Iraq, the sensitivities of the French in Syria, the admitted Arab character of Transjordan, and wartime promises made to Sherif Hussein suggested a remedy to Churchill. Faisal would be made king of Iraq, Abdallah would administer the eastern portion of Britain's Palestine mandate—Transjordan. The Hashemites, as leaders of the Arabs, would thus dominate Arab national politics, the French would be happy, and the Zionists would still be free to settle western Palestine.

The next year, in July 1922, Transjordan was formally separated from the Palestine mandate in the "Churchill White Paper," and further restrictions were placed on the Jewish national home. This "clarification" of the Balfour Declaration, designed to dispel heightened Arab fears over Palestine, stated: "When it is asked what is meant by the development of a Jewish National Home in Palestine, it may be answered that it is not the imposition of a Jewish nationality upon the inhabitants of Palestine as a whole but the further development of the existing Jewish community." Restrictive limitations were also placed on Jewish immigration to conform to the "economic capacity of the country."

The Churchill White Paper was a blow to the Zionists and was seen as such, yet their situation in 1922 was still much better than it had been five years before. Fearful of arousing British ire, Weizmann and the Zionist Executive approved the document. But an Arab delegation rejected it in full, for the principle of Palestine as the Jewish national home remained intact. This Arab delegation was one of the first exclusively Palestinian Arab delegations ever constituted. After Faisal's defeat at the hands of the French, Arab politics in Palestine underwent a dramatic reorientation. The inability to join hands with Faisal in Syria, the special nature of the threat posed by the Yishuv, the administrative chaos caused by the absence of Turkish rule, and the need to compete with the Zionists and others in the administration of the mandate under the British gradually contributed to the evolution of a distinctive Palestinian Arab national consciousness and political agenda.

By 1923 six Arab congresses or meetings had been held in Palestine and these were dominated by a few notable families from Jerusalem, particularly the al-Husayni family. While there eventually emerged a number of different Arab political parties, each one formed around a particularly wealthy and prestigious family group, a basic consensus of Palestinian Arab opinion, nevertheless, did emerge. Even by 1921 its basic outlines were clear.

The British, under League of Nations rules for mandatory authority, were obliged to lead their mandates toward independence, joining the many newly independent European states created by the peace settlement.[9] To this end the British in 1922 planned to hold general elections for a legislative council. This council was to be apportioned according to religious affiliation—Muslim, Jewish, Christian. The Palestinian Arab nationalists rejected this and other proposals, because they were thought to legitimize a Zionist political share in the governing of Palestine. They also forced Arab members to withdraw from other British-devised advisory councils, foiling all early attempts made by the British to create a basis for communal power sharing. Instead, the Palestinians insisted on the formation of a national government based on simple majority rule, an arrangement that would entirely favor the Arabs. They also insisted on the abolition of the principle of the Jewish national home, an end to Jewish immigration, a return to Ottoman as opposed to British law, and demanded that Palestine not be separated from neighboring Arab states.

Arab demands remained remarkably constant and uncompromising through the entire mandatory period (1920-48). The only real difference of importance was that while, in the 1920s, the Arabs imagined that they might expel the Zionist settlements from Palestine entirely, by the late 1930s and 1940s they strove to minimize the growing size and strength of the Yishuv and prevent Jewish political autonomy.

Ultimately, of course, the Palestinians failed even in this more modest goal. There were many reasons for this. First, the Palestinian Arabs were themselves divided, not so much in philosophy or ultimate aims, but on tactics and personalities. The Palestinian parties, as one scholar has described the situation, were derived from a "pyramidal family and clan network, which built on relationships of support and protection from the village level through local potentates to leading families at the district level." This "offered the means of rapid articulation of opinion and mobilization of all levels of society.... However, this structure made it difficult to unify the national movement."[10] The leading families had parallel power bases, from city to village, and parallel economic interests, primarily in the ownership of land. The al-Husayni and Nashashibi families were particularly powerful and particularly resentful of each other.

In 1920 Musa Kazim al-Husayni was mayor of Jerusalem, but he was arrested by the British for his outspoken radicalism and his fomenting of anti-Jewish riots in Jerusalem that year. He was replaced by Raghib an-Nashashibi, who was less outspoken and determined to work "on the inside" with the British against the Zionists. Raghib an-Nashashibi's different tack with the British and his redirection of patronage and protection to members of his own clan angered the al-Husaynis. Meanwhile, a younger relative of Musa Kazim al-Husayni, Haj Amin al-Husayni, became *mufti*[11] of Jerusalem in 1921, and the next year, head of the newly formed Supreme Moslem Council, an organization set up to control all Islamic educational, legal, and religious affairs. This provided the al-Husaynis with their own patronage network.

Competition between the al-Husayni and Nashashibi families grew very bitter as time passed, leading to assassinations and much internecine violence. After 1934, especially, when Raghib an-Nashashibi formed his own political party and allied himself with the Hashemite Abdallah in Transjordan, the feud intensified. The al-Husaynis were rabidly anti-British and the Hashemites, of course, ruled at British pleasure, supported by arms and subsidies from London. Raghib's alliance with them smacked of treachery to the al-Husaynis, who knew that the Hashemites had never abandoned their original claims to Palestine. Later on, the al-Husaynis made common cause with Nazi Germany, on account of their being both anti-British and anti-Jewish. This, in turn, enraged Abdallah, who remained loyal to Britain.

There were also two other divisions in Palestinian Arab society that hurt the national effort. One was the economic gulf that separated the rich landowning elite of the cities and the masses of peasants in the countryside. The peasants resented their wealthy absentee landlords, for, while they ranted in public against the Zionists, some sold land in private to the Jewish National Fund at handsome profits. This cleavage helps explain why nearly all of the episodic violence fomented by the Arabs in Palestine against the Jews and the British was a product of the irregular urban militias of the mufti. Only on a few occasions did the peasantry join the violence—in 1921 in Jaffa, in 1929 in Hebron and Jerusalem, and in the 1936 and 1938-39 general strikes.

A second division was that between Muslim and Christian Palestinian Arabs. Although the Muslim population was eight times the size of the Christian population, the Christians were relatively more educated, more wealthy, and more numerous in the politically central urban areas. Christians feared Muslim domination; Muslims resented disproportionate Christian power and wealth. The Christian Palestinians were particularly nervous at the way Haj Amin al-Husayni made use of his Muslim religious credentials as mufti to preach opposition to the mandate and the Zionists on *religious* grounds. Making use of the universally known Muslim credo, "The world of the infidel is a unity" (*al-kufru millatun wahida*), Husayni would group together the Zionists who were Jews and the British who were Christians, and urge the expulsion of both.

A second reason for the failure of Palestinian nationalism lay in the mandatory policies of the British, especially in the first 15 years of the mandate. The British, especially in the 1920s, supported Jewish immigration to Palestine and remained loyal to the basic premise of the Balfour Declaration, which had been incorporated verbatim into the League of Nations mandate. British authorities refused to recognize formally local Arab political coalitions, such as the Arab Executive (1920-34) and the Higher Committee (1936-47), because they opposed the basic principle of the mandate. Moreover, on a different level, British administration of Palestine made it more efficient than it had ever been. New roads, railroads, telegraph lines, and the like aided the expansion of the Zionist Yishuv, especially in rural areas, far more than it did the relatively stagnant rural Arab economy.

The major reason, however, for the Arab failure in Palestine was the growing strength, spirit, and confidence of the Zionist movement in Palestine itself. The Third Aliyah, 1919-23, swelled the ranks of the Yishuv. Coming mainly from Eastern Europe, mostly for ideological reasons, they totalled 37,000 immigrants, more than replacing the losses of World War I. In these years also, the Jewish Labor Federation, the Histadrut, was founded (1920), as was the Haganah (1920), respectively the seeds of the strong Israeli labor union system and the armed forces. Owing to the ideological character of the Third Aliyah, the political strength of socialist, or Labor, Zionism, increased.

The Fourth Aliyah, 1924-32, followed directly after. It was made up largely of Polish Jews escaping Poland's economic doldrums and the rising anti-Semitism under the proto-Fascist government of Marshal Pilsudski. Between 1924 and 1928, 70,000 Jews made their way to Palestine. There had been 84,000 Jews in Palestine in 1922; by 1929 there were 154,000. These immigrants were not, as a rule, Zionist ideologues, but rather merchants, artisans, and laborers. They tended to live in urban areas, not in rural collective settlements. Consequently, it was during this period that Jewish cities, like Tel-Aviv, began to grow large and that Jewish industry took firm root. In 1921 Tel-Aviv had only 3,600 residents and in 1924, it had 16,000, but by 1929 it had 46,000. It was during this period, too, that the Jewish Agency, the forerunner of the Israeli government, came into being (1929).

The Arabs of Palestine were alarmed at the steady growth of the Yishuv, but because of their internal divisions and the policies of the mandatory authorities, they were unable to stop it through formal political means. As the aims and interests of the Arab and Jewish communities in Palestine continued to diverge during the 1920s, violence erupted. In 1929 a minor religious dispute arose in Jerusalem between Jews and Muslims. This dispute was manipulated by the mufti, however, resulting in rioting in Jerusalem and Hebron, which left 133 Jews murdered. Arab deaths—mainly at the hands of British police—totalled 87. Subsequently, the Jewish quarter in Hebron was abandoned. Coincident with this violence, there was a change of government in Britain; the Conservatives, led by Stanley Baldwin, were voted out of office in July 1929 and the Labourites under Ramsey McDonald were installed. The British Labour Party had never developed much enthusiasm for the Zionist cause and, upon reviewing the violence in Palestine, issued in October 1930 a policy statement—the Passfield White Paper—which repudiated major elements of the Balfour Declaration.

The White Paper was based on two reports—the Shaw report and the Simpson report. The former stated that the reason for the Arab violence was their "feeling of animosity and hostility toward the Jews consequent upon the disappointment of their political and national aspirations and fear for their economic future." It urged tighter controls on Jewish immigration, the protection of Arab tenants from eviction by Jewish landowners, and it proposed that mandatory authorities inform the Jewish Agency that it was not empowered to share governance in Palestine. The Simpson report claimed that the land available to the Arabs was less than had been supposed and that Arabs were being driven off the land by Jews. The truth was that the Yishuv then owned only 6.3 percent of all Palestinian land considered arable. Moreover, Jewish economic activity had led to a dramatic rise in Arab living standards and to *Arab* immigration to Palestine. Nevertheless, the Passfield White Paper admonished that "it is useless for Jewish leaders... to press his Majesty's government to conform to their policy in regard... to immigration and land." It warned the Arabs, too, to drop their demands for majority rule on a national level, but it concluded: "There remains no margin of land available for agricultural settlement by the new immigrants with the exception of such undeveloped lands as the various Jewish agencies hold in reserve." Jewish immigration was to be suspended as long as there was unemployment in Palestine.

By early 1931 the Passfield White Paper had been enveloped in a storm of protest mounted by the opposition Conservative Party and was repudiated. The entire episode, nevertheless, shook the faith of many of the leaders of the Zionist Yishuv in the permanence and reliability of British support, and it seemed to show that the Arab resort to violence got results.

The violence of 1929 and the Passfield White Paper had little or no effect, however, on the growing strength of the Yishuv. Adding greatly to its ranks was the Fifth Aliyah, 1933-1939, which consisted mainly of Jewish refugees from Germany and central Europe. Adolf Hitler came to power in 1933. Most German Jews, who had long since denied their Jewish nationality, at first did not take Hitler's anti-Semitic tirades seriously. Some did. Jewish immigration to Palestine in 1933 was triple that of 1932. Between 1933 and 1939 about 190,000 Jews entered Palestine, the majority from Germany and Central Europe. There undoubtedly would have been more had it not been for the transformation of Arab and British policies in Palestine after 1933. It is these changes that must now be considered.

CRISIS IN PALESTINE: 1933-1945

Zionism, as it developed in its early days in Europe, was woefully ignorant of real conditions in Palestine. Indeed, Herzl had triumphantly pronounced the slogan, "For a people without a land, a land without a people." When Herzl's associate, Max Nordau, pointed out that there were Arabs in Palestine, a half million of them, Herzl is said to have remarked, "I did not know that." The relative absence of politically inspired violence in the early days, and the real cooperation and friendship that often developed between Jew and Arab on the local level, seemed to presage no serious difficulties, however.

With the Balfour Declaration, the coming of the mandate, the growth of the Yishuv, and the evolution of Palestinian national consciousness, this benign view changed dramatically. After the 1921 Arab riots in Jaffa, it became clear to most Zionists that there was a serious problem with the Arabs, perhaps even an irreconcilable one. Some Zionists were acutely sensitive to the dilemma, like Judah Magnes, the founder of the Hebrew University; Martin Buber, the philosopher; and Ehad Ha'am, the Jewish essayist and cultural Zionist. But the mainstream of the Zionist movement never tried very hard to understand Arab sensitivities or come to terms with Arab political demands. The unrelenting, uncompromising attitudes of the Arab elite certainly contributed to this situation, as did the very presence of the British as intermediaries, for this made it possible to abjure direct efforts. The prevailing view was that once Jewish immigration reached a certain level, the "backward native" population would accept the Jewish national home as a fait accompli. Some doctrinaire socialist Zionists even imagined that the Arab peasant would one day thank the Jews for liberating them from their upper-class Arab oppressors.

It was not to be. The radical Palestinian Arab nationalists, emboldened by the rise of Hitler and their alliance with him, believed that in the European struggle to come, the Palestinian Arabs could rid themselves of both the British and the Jews. The British, for their part, felt the need to maintain their position in the Arab world in the face of mounting German and Italian challenges in the area. As a result, the Arabs began a massive general strike in 1936, punctuated by much violence. And, in response, British policy by 1939 had essentially repudiated its promises to the Jews contained in the Balfour Declaration and the statute of the League of Nations mandate.

The violence of 1936 repeated the sequence of events of 1929, but on a much larger scale. There was Arab violence and a British response aimed at placating Arab wrath, which included restrictions on Jewish immigration. But there were also major differences. First, the scope and explicitly nationalist character of the Arab revolt were greater by far than in 1929. Second, it was not the Labour Party that was in power in Britain, but the Conservatives under Stanley Baldwin himself, the same party that had assailed the Passfield White Paper; but this time the shift in British policy, owing to broader international considerations and faded memories of the Balfour Declaration, was not repudiated. And third, the consequences were far more ominous, for the harbinger of the Holocaust could by then be dimly discerned by those pessimistic—or realistic— enough to admit its possibilities.

Part of the reason for the Arab revolt of 1936 was the conjunction of increased large-scale Jewish immigration from Europe—especially Germany—with the dramatic growth of right-wing Arab nationalist parties that took fascist Germany and Italy as their models and patrons. Another was the fact that all around Palestine, Arab sovereignties were coming into existence. Iraq had been granted (nominal) independence in 1930; Syria, Egypt, and Lebanon in 1936. Even Abdallah in Transjordan ruled as an independent monarch by most appearances—why not Palestine? The Palestinian Arabs clearly sought the end of the mandate, particularly as they still constituted an overwhelming majority of the population.

The immediate catalyst but not the real cause of the 1936 strike was a spasm of intercommunal violence. In April Arab bandits (who cared little about Zionism or politics in general) robbed a bus and killed two

Jews. In an act of revenge two Arabs were murdered near Petah Tikva. In response to this, Arab militants led by Sheik Farhan al-Saada began attacking Jewish property, destroying crops, and killing Jewish civilians at random. But the real source of the strike can be traced to none other than Haj Amin al-Husayni. By 1936 the mufti had parlayed his positions into considerable wealth and power, building an extensive patronage system. After the initial spate of violence, Husayni convinced several Palestinian leaders to form an Arab Higher Council with himself as its leader. This they did, and for the first time the mufti monopolized the leadership of the Palestinian Arab movement. Al-Husayni was determined to use his power; what had begun as an undirected, episodic affair soon took on a deliberate, organized form.

The British at first underreacted to the Arab violence of 1936 and then overreacted, enabling the strike to widen and deepen, moving from the Jerusalem elite to all strata of Arab society throughout the country. By the time the strike was ended some six months later, over 300 people had been killed—most of them Arabs.

It was not the mufti's organizational skills that gave the 1936 strike its character, but a shift in the character of Palestinian Arab society itself. First of all, between the end of World War I and 1935, the Arab population of Palestine had increased 67 percent to 960,000. Palestine was the only place in the Middle East, and one of the only places on earth, that had not been savaged by the Great Depression, and this was due primarily to the infusion of Jewish capital. Jewish payments for land, food, services, building materials, rents, and the like greatly stimulated the Arab economy, including that of the upper classes. Additionally, the expansion of projects under the mandate called for Arab workers and middle-class artisans, administrators, and middle men. Economic growth sponsored opportunities for Arabs in business, medicine, law, journalism, and also education, for school attendance among the Arabs had increased sevenfold in a decade and a half. As one scholar has put it, these conditions were "the classical ingredients for a burgeoning nationalism: rising literacy, a growing middle class, larger numbers of white-collar workers and professionals."[12]

After the violence had finally subsided, the British established another commission of inquiry and issued another report. It was the Peel Commission report of 1937 and its conclusions were revolutionary. It undermined the original basis of the mandate, reasoning that 400,000 Jews and nearly a million Arabs could never come to terms with each other in a single political entity. It suggested partition, and drew a map accordingly (see Map 1). The Galilee, with the exception of Nazareth, and the north coastal plain would be a Jewish state. The Arab state would include everything else, save for a wide corridor from Jerusalem to Jaffa, which, with the Nazareth enclave and bases on the sea of Galilee and at Aqaba, would remain in British hands. The Arab state was to be joined, though it was not specified exactly how, with Abdallah's realm in Transjordan.

The response to the Peel Plan was mixed. Al-Husayni rejected it outright, as did the Arabs of Syria and Iraq, because it granted the unthinkable: Jewish sovereignty in any part of Palestine. Publicly, Abdallah and the Nashashibis opposed it as well, but privately it was known that they favored the plan so long as Raghib an-Nashashibi would rule under Abdallah at the expense of the al-Husaynis. The Zionists were divided, as they had been increasingly since the early 1930s, when Vladimir Jabotinsky had bolted from the Zionist Executive in protest over Weizmann's pro-British attitude and his plan gradually to increase the Jewish population to a majority before seeking statehood. Weizmann was in favor of the Peel proposal, preferring sovereignty in *any* part of Palestine and control over Jewish immigration to any other then available option. Jabotinsky and his revisionists opposed any further division of the original Palestine mandate. (Jabotinsky had never accepted the 1922 partition that had created Abdallah's realm in Transjordan).

David Ben-Gurion, then chairman of the Jewish Agency's Palestine Executive, had another idea. He wrote at the time: "We shall smash these frontiers which are being forced upon us, and not necessarily by war." Ben-Gurion hoped for an agreement for open borders reached directly with the Arab state, increased immigration thereafter, and, in the end, the complete fulfillment of Zionist aims. "This Jewish State now being proposed to us is not the Zionist aim," Ben-Gurion said, "for it is impossible to solve the Jewish problem in such a territory. But this will be a decisive step in bringing about greater Zionist aims. In the shortest possible time it will build up the real Jewish strength that will carry us to our historic objective." In the end, the Jewish Agency proposed further exploration of the partition idea; it did not reject it and it did not approve any particular set of borders.

It did not matter what the Zionists decided, for total Arab rejection led to an upsurge of new violence in 1938, this time directed more against the Jews than the British. It did not stop for well over a year. During this period three important developments took place. The first was that by mid-1939, the British government had decisively repudiated both the mandate and the notion of partition. With Nazi activity in the Middle

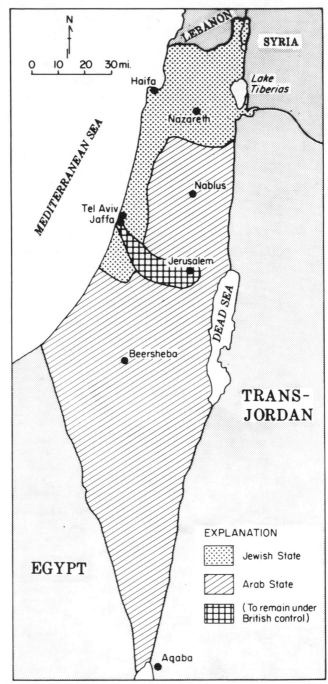

Map 1: The Peel Commission Partition Plan, 1937 (accepted by the Jews, rejected by the Palestinian Arabs).

East increasing and war a possibility, the British decided to hold on to Palestine and to appease the Arabs.

London's new attitude toward Palestine did not appear all at once, however. Between the Peel Plan and the outbreak of war in Europe in September 1939, the British made two more attempts to solve their Palestine problem: the Woodhead Commission Report and the London Round Table talks. The Woodhead Report of November 1938 diluted the Peel Plan, offering several new partition alternatives, all of which further reduced the size of the Jewish state. The Zionists responded with a plan of their own, but the Arabs again rejected the entire concept. Next followed the London Round Table talks of February 1939, which both Arab and Jewish delegations attended. The Arabs refused to sit in the same room with the Jews. The British pressed the Zionist delegation to accept severe restrictions on Jewish immigration for a number of years and thereafter base immigration quotas on Arab consent. In the face of what was happening in Europe, and in the light of Zionist support for *illegal* Jewish immigration to Palestine already, Weizmann refused.

If anything, the situation was becoming increasingly bleak. In July 1938 at Evian, France, an international conference on refugees was held, with 31 countries in attendance. None of the governments present, except the Dominican Republic, was prepared to adjust its own immigration quota to help the Jews of Europe, and this at a time of virulent and overt anti-Semitism in Germany, Austria, Poland, Hungary, and Romania. Clearly, the worst fears of the early Zionists about the evolution of "enlightened" European society and the Jews were being confirmed. At the Round Table talks, Weizmann was told by the British that the Arabs were more important to Britain in present circumstances than the Jews, and it was implied that London might give the Arabs what they wanted— an independent state and the end of the mandate, leaving the Jews' fate to the Arab majority.

The Arabs, for their part, demanded an end to Jewish immigration in its entirety, and the curtailment of land sales to Jews in return for a treaty protecting "reasonable British interests in Palestine." At one point, the British agreed in principle to the main Arab demand, an independent state under majority rule, and discussion turned to special protection and rights for the Jewish minority. The Arabs refused to acknowledge any such rights. In the end there was no agreement and the British dictated their own terms. Jewish immigration would be limited to a total of just 75,000 during the next five years; land transfers were to be curtailed immediately. On the other hand, the idea of an independent Arab state was dropped, at least for the time being. A White Paper containing these strictures was issued in May 1939, less than four months before the beginning of World War II in Europe. Both the Jews and the Arab Higher Committee rejected the White Paper, the former because it curtailed any growth of the Jewish national home, the latter because it prolonged the mandate.

The second significant turn of events was the emergence of a strong Jewish defense capability and the proven ability of the Yishuv to expand its territorial presence. During the violence of 1938-39, much of it directed against Jews, the Yishuv nevertheless managed to build 55 new settlements, and not a single older settlement was abandoned. These were paramilitary settlements, erected usually in a single night, called "stockade and tower" settlements. The Haganah's ability to cope with the violence directed against the Yishuv was an important confidence builder. A crucial element of that ability was the creation of "Night Squads" made up of Jewish soldiers and commanded by British Captain Orde Wingate.

The third significant development was the worsening of the rift between the al-Husayni and the Nashashibi clans. After the Woodhead Commission Report of 1938, the Arab rebellion lost momentum, as it appeared to some Arab nationalists that British policy might now be moved further in their direction through peaceful means. Al-Husayni disagreed, leading a prominent member of the Nashashibi clan in November 1938 to openly oppose his leadership. With this, al-Husayni directed a wave of violence and assassinations against the Nashashibis and their followers, and also took aim at Emir Abdallah himself and his court.

By the time war came in September 1939, Palestine was in chaos. Relations between Jews and Arabs had clearly reached a point of no return, and both opposed the British mandate for different reasons. In the Zionist community, there was division between the Jewish Agency under Weizmann and Ben-Gurion and the revisionists led by Jabotinsky. In the Palestinian camp, division was even greater, more bitter and more violent. Finally, the Hashemites in Transjordan were increasingly active in the politics of Palestine, taking sides in the Palestinians' fractious affairs, cooperating with the British in hopes that London would elect to rule Palestine through the Hashemites, and even making direct contact with the Zionists.

In the war itself, the Palestinian nationalists sided with Nazi Germany and the Axis powers. Haj Amin al-Husayni took up residence first in Rome and then in Berlin, engaging in propaganda exercises for Germany. In 1942, with German troops in Egypt, al-Husayni called on the Arabs to rise up against the Allies "in the name of God and his Prophet." The

Jews, on the other hand, supported the British against the hated Nazis and hoped by doing so not only to protect themselves, but to regain favor with Britain. Hope for reversing the British stand taken in the White Paper was buoyed considerably by the accession to the prime minister's office of Winston Churchill, a friend of the Zionist movement and Jewish aspirations in Palestine. Despite Churchill's efforts, however, immigration restrictions remained in force throughout the war as six million European Jews perished in Nazi concentration camps. The Jewish Agency resolved to fight the White Paper as if there were no war, and to fight the war as if there were no White Paper. The British left off consideration of Palestine's political future in order to concentrate on military matters.

Within the Yishuv during the war, a number of important developments occurred. First, the economic and physical growth of the Yishuv continued apace despite the curtailment of immigration. New settlements were founded, urban population and industry increased, and the Yishuv's self-defense capabilities were built up as well. Second, Ben-Gurion's prominence over the now-aging Weizmann rose steadily. Whereas Weizmann favored gradual movement toward a Jewish majority and opposed pressures aimed at quick statehood, Ben-Gurion took the opposite approach. The latter also favored reducing Zionist dependence on Britain in favor of a closer relationship with the United States, as was manifest in the Biltmore Platform of May 1942. As the war progressed, Ben-Gurion's views became increasingly dominant. Third, there emerged some small splinter groups of Jews who were far more militant, and anti-British, than Ben-Gurion. Operating outside the authority of the Jewish Agency and the Haganah, these groups, especially Lehi and Etzel—better known, respectively, as the Stern Gang and the Irgun—increasingly adopted terrorist tactics.[13]

Even the Jewish Agency, however, had grown impatient with Britain, especially over immigration matters. The longer the war went on, and the more terror and death European Jewry faced, the more bitter and frustrated the Zionists became. While the Jewish Agency opposed terrorism and tried, with mixed results, to stop it, it did encourage and aid illegal immigration during the war. Thus, when the war ended in 1945, Jewish attitudes were decidedly anti-British in varying degrees. Prime Minister Churchill himself, once a strong friend of the Zionist cause, was deeply shocked when the Stern Gang in 1944 assassinated his friend, the British minister of state for the Middle East, Walter Edward Guinness, the first Lord Moyne.

In August 1945 Churchill was turned out of office by the British electorate in favor of a Labour government whose election platform now stated support for a Jewish state in Palestine. Most Zionists by then had given up on the Conservatives as mere verbalizers and had put their trust in Labour. Ideological affinities played a part in these hopes; Ben-Gurion said: "The British workers will understand our aims." But this was not to be. The new British foreign minister, Ernest Bevin, had been sympathetic to the Zionists before, but now Britain, its resources exhausted by the war and its geopolitical position in jeopardy, again placed its bets on the Arabs. The Arab League was formed in 1945 at British instigation. Bevin opposed partition, and tried to get the United States, the new world power, to handle both the question of Jewish refugees from Europe and the political future of Palestine.

The United States was reluctant to get involved in the refugee matter directly. The State Department was clearly hostile to Zionist aims by 1945, believing that Washington's interests lay in siding with the Arabs over Palestine. Washington initially preferred to place Palestine in an international trusteeship under the newly formed United Nations. But President Harry Truman thought differently. At the Potsdam Conference of July 1945, Truman pressed the British to allow 100,000 Jews into Palestine immediately, but he was unsuccessful. He did not accept the State Department's view that U.S. support for the Zionists would "provoke a mass Arab uprising," to the detriment of the United States. A few years later Truman's attitude would prove a decisive benefit for the Zionists.

TOWARD A JEWISH STATE: 1945-47

The Zionist response to Britain's pro-Arab tilt and London's inability to act decisively on Palestine's political future was to repudiate the mandate just as Britain, since 1939, had repudiated the idea of the Jewish national home. The Zionists, in essence, made war on Britain in Palestine, and did so with singular success. The aim was clear: to force Britain to accede to a Jewish state in part, if not all, of Palestine. Only in this way, it was felt, could the pressing emergency of the Jewish refugees—hundreds of thousands languishing in displaced-persons camps in Europe and in Cyprus—be solved properly. Zionist efforts were infused with confidence because their military capabilities had proven successful in 1938-39 and had been bolstered by participation in the war, fighting alongside the British as the Jewish Brigade, in Europe and the Middle East. Zionist determination was raised by the imperative of saving the remnant of European Jewry, the more so as the truth about the dimensions of the Holocaust in Europe became known, in the early months of 1946.

In that year the British again turned to the United States to help them work out a solution for Palestine. Another commission was established—the Ango-American Commission of Inquiry—and testimony again taken from both sides. The Arabs of Palestine, still weak, disunited, and viewed suspiciously by the Allies for their wartime collusion with the Axis, were represented by Azzam Pasha, secretary general of the Arab League. They were aided by anti-Zionist bureaucracies in both the British Foreign Office and the U.S. Department of State. Ben-Gurion and Weizmann spoke for the Zionists. Ultimately, the commission proposed the continuation of the mandate—which pleased the British—and the acceptance by Britain of the entry into Palestine of 100,000 refugees—which did not please the British. The commission recommended that immigration in the future be neither subject to Arab veto nor allowed to produce a Jewish majority. Clearly, the commission report was irresolute on the basic issues and ambiguous even on those matters it chose to address. In a fitting response the United States accepted the report; the British rejected it. This greatly annoyed President Truman, who had agreed to the joint effort in order to help London out from under its political burden. When the British turned down the report, it left Truman looking somewhat foolish and this, in turn, put further distance between the British and American policies over Palestine.

Throughout 1946 the spiral of violence and counterviolence between the Jewish resistance and the mandatory authorities rose. Some Jewish terrorist activities carried out by the Irgun, such as the bombing of the King David Hotel on July 22, were both gruesome and spectacular. The British suffered many casualties and were clearly demoralized by their inability to stop the Jewish effort. Moreover, the Haganah's campaign of illegal immigration by sea was beginning to register important successes— not physically, for few of the ragtag vessels were able to land in Palestine, but psychologically. Photographs of ships filled to the brim with Jewish survivors of Hitler's "Final Solution" being turned away from Palestine appeared in major British and American newspapers. Public sympathy, even in Britain, turned against the British government, as remorse and guilt over the Holocaust seized world opinion.

These developments spawned Britain's final effort to solve the Palestine problem once and for all—the Morrison-Grady Plan. This plan proposed an intricate scheme for transforming the mandate into a United

Nations trusteeship and divided Palestine not into separate Jewish and Arab sovereignties, but provinces. The Negev desert and Jerusalem were to remain in British hands. The Jewish "province" in this plan was roughly 17 percent of the country, smaller even than provided by the proposals of the Peel Commission and the Woodhead Commission. The plan did provide, however, for the entry of 100,000 Jewish refugees into Palestine within a year, if the plan were put into action. For this, both Jewish and Arab agreement was necessary; the report was optimistic about their approval.

The Palestinian Arabs refused to attend the meetings held to discuss the Morrison-Grady Plan because the mufti was still considered persona non grata by the British and was not allowed to lead the delegation. The Zionists rejected the plan; it provided too little sovereignty, too little territory, and the 100,000 refugees was by then an out-of-date figure, for the problem was now greater. The United States, too, rejected it. President Truman considered it a plan for a new ghetto and a betrayal of the Jews. When the meeting did take place on September 10, only the British and representatives of the Arab states were in attendance. As if this alone were not enough to doom the enterprise, the Arabs insisted on a unitary state under majority rule. There would be some rights for the Jewish minority, but citizenship would be extended only to those who had lived in Palestine for at least ten years. This made a solution to the refugee problem impossible.

The Morrison-Grady Plan and subsequent patchwork attempts to adjust it in various ways failed completely. There was a deadlock. Meanwhile, British rulership of India had come to an end in 1947, and the geostrategic significance of Palestine was somewhat reduced as a result. With the British still taking casualties at the hands of Jewish forces, London gave up. On February 14, 1947 Bevin announced that Britain was turning the whole matter over to the United Nations.

At first, the British turned to the United Nations for advice only, and announced that London was not bound to any particular U.N. decision. But the level of violence escalated immensely in Palestine during the latter part of 1947, and the British increasingly were disposed to wash their hands of the whole matter, whatever the United Nations decided.

In May 1947 an 11-nation investigation board was established to look into the problem. It was called the United Nations Special Committee on Palestine, UNSCOP for short. Its members were from Australia, Canada, Czechoslovakia, Guatemala, India, Iran, Holland, Peru, Sweden, Hungary, and Yugoslavia. While they deliberated and took testimony, a spectacular event occurred. In early July a barely seaworthy vessel, a Chesapeake Bay ferryboat to be specific, set out from France with 4,500 Jewish DPs—displaced persons—bound for Palestine. The British navy picked up the ship almost immediately and "escorted" it across the Mediterranean until it reached a full British armada 12 miles off the coast of Palestine. There the British attempted to board the ship, intending to send its passengers to Cyprus to join some 26,000 other Jewish DPs. But the ship, now renamed the *Exodus*, resisted; hand-to-hand fighting broke out. The British resorted to tear gas and machine guns; three Jews were killed. Meanwhile, the ship's radio had been broadcasting an account of events to Haganah radio on shore, which lost no time in transmitting it around the world.

The British commenced to ram the *Exodus*, threatening to sink it with all on board. Only at this point did the *Exodus* surrender. Bevin, humiliated by the incident, decided to send the passengers back to their port of origin on British naval vessels. This meant first France and ultimately DP camps in Germany. This indeed took place. The entire episode was reported extensively in the world press; UNSCOP sent a delegation to inspect the refugee camps in Germany and Austria. There they found over a quarter of a million Jews "who measured their very existence against the hour of departure for Palestine."[14]

On August 31, 1947 UNSCOP finished its work. In its recommendations it laid down 11 principles, the most important being the principle of partition: the mandate would end, separate Jewish and Arab states would arise. The British were lukewarm about the proposal. The Zionists accepted it. While it did not solve everything, it did provide for sovereignty and unlimited immigration at least for the immediate future. The Arabs of Palestine and the Arab states were horrified by the plan and rejected it with passion. But, each for its own reasons, the Soviet Union and the United States stood in favor.

The partition plan called for a Jewish state made up of the coastal plain from Acre, just north of Haifa to just south of Tel-Aviv, the eastern part of the Galilee region adjacent to the Sea of Galilee, and the Negev desert. The Arab state was to consist of northern and western Galilee, the hill country of Judea and Samaria down to Beersheba, and the southern coastline encompassing Gaza. Jerusalem and its environs were to be internationalized. On November 29, 1947 the General Assembly approved the plan by a vote of 35-13, giving it the necessary two-thirds majority. The date set for implementation was August 1, 1948, subsequently moved up by the British to May 14.

Long before May 14 it was obvious that there was going to be a war in Palestine between Jews and Arabs at the very least, and probably outside Arab intervention as well. The al-Husaynis were back in power and the Arab countries roundabout (save Transjordan) supported him fully. Bevin and the British military were certain that the Jews would, in the words of one British army officer, "get their throats cut." Hoping to maintain residual British interests in Palestine after the termination of the mandate, London looked forward to an Arab military victory. As they prepared to evacuate Palestine, the British clearly were partial to the Arab war effort, diverting considerable stocks of weapons and ammunition to them.

By March 1948 hostilities within Palestine were in full gear and, as predicted, the Jews were suffering high casualties. It was not conventional warfare and it was not organized warfare. There were atrocities and counteratrocities, such as the Jerusalem road massacre of Jewish doctors and nurses and the Irgun attack on the village of Deir Yassin. Neither side operated under a unified command. As the violence, confusion, and fear of war mounted, there were sizable movements of population; some expected to return home, some not.

The Haganah at first adopted an ambitious posture of defending all the far-flung Jewish settlements in Palestine rather than concentrate forces along the more easily defended seacoast. This succeeded, in part because the mufti's forces proved to be completely inept, leading to the disgrace of the al-Husayni family. Meanwhile, the Jewish Agency did all it could to prevent all-out war with the Arab states, especially in trying to reach an accommodation with King Abdallah in Transjordan. When these efforts failed, and as the prospect of an invasion by the Arab states loomed—an invasion which put the very lives of the entire Yishuv at risk—Ben-Gurion decided to launch an offensive aimed at capturing strategic positions throughout Palestine, including some outside of the Jewish state as defined by the U.S. partition borders. The campaign was a success; on May 14, the last day of the mandate and the day that Ben-Gurion proclaimed the independence of the state of Israel, Jaffa fell to the Haganah, 70,000 of its Arab residents fleeing eastward.

This was not the end, but only the beginning, of trouble. The next day, May 15, the armies of seven Arab countries invaded Israel.

NOTES

1. Zeine N. Zeine, *The Emergence of Arab Nationalism*, 3rd ed. (Delmar, N.Y.: Caravan Books, 1973), p. 33.

2. Ibid., p. 127.

3. B.C.E. means before the common era; C.E. means the common era. These designations are more neutral religiously than B.C. and A.D., and more appropriate, for this subject.

4. Arthur Hertzberg, *The Zionist Idea* (New York: Atheneum, 1969), p. 23.

5. Actually, the best English translation of *Der Judenstaat* is "The Jew-State." Herzl purposely chose the idiom of the anti-Semite to demonstrate his pride at being Jewish.

6. No Zionist of the late nineteenth century actually predicted anything as monstrous as Nazi Germany's concentration camps, but some came close. Bernard Lazare wrote in 1899: "Today the Jewish question is raised more powerfully than ever. From every side a solution is sought for it. Truly it is no longer a matter of knowing whether anti-semitism is or is not going to win seats in Parliament; it is a matter of knowing what is to be the fate of millions of Jews...." See Lazare's *Job's Dungheap* (New York: Schocken Books, 1948), p. 67.

7. "Sherif" literally means "guard," but the importance of the title is that it can be used only by someone who claims direct descent from the Prophet Muhammed. Sherifian status is very prestigious in the Muslim world.

8. Ultimately, the Hashemites lost the Hijaz to Abdul Aziz ibn Saud in 1924. It is now part of Saudi Arabia.

9. These included Poland, Czechoslovakia, Hungary, Finland, Latvia, Lithuania, Estonia, and Yugoslavia.

10. Ann M. Lesch, "The Palestinian Arab Nationalist Movement Under the Mandate," *The Politics of Palestinian Nationalism* in William Quandt, Paul Jabber, and Ann Lesch, eds., (Berkley: University of California Press, 1973), p. 17.

11. Mufti is a religious title, comparable, roughly speaking, to bishop.

12. Howard M. Sachar, *A History of Israel: From the Rise of Zionism to Our Day* (New York: Knopf, 1979), p. 179.

13. Lehi is a Hebrew acronym standing for "Freedom Fighters for Israel," *Lohamei Herut Israel* in Hebrew. Etzel is another acronym for "National Military Organization," or *Irgun T'vai L'umi* in Hebrew.

14. Sachar, p. 283.

2

Seven Wars
and One Peace Treaty

Itamar Rabinovich

The Arab-Israeli conflict has, unfortunately, been predominantly a military conflict. Its history has been governed and punctuated by seven wars, fought between 1948 and 1982. During the first 25 years of this period, all efforts to resolve, regulate, or stabilize the situation failed, and the cease-fires, armistices, and other arrangements made at the close of each Arab-Israeli war became preludes to the next encounter.[1]

A change in that pattern occurred in 1973 when the concluding phase of the October War developed into a settlement process that culminated in the Egyptian-Israeli peace treaty of March 26, 1979. The peace has lasted, contrary to many predictions, for over four years now and survived the seventh Arab-Israeli war, which ironically was to some extent its product. The Egyptian-Israeli peace, however, remains separate, partial, and precarious, and its prospects and impact uncertain.[2]

This chapter seeks to provide a concise account of the seven Arab-Israeli wars fought in the past 35 years:

- The de facto civil war that was waged from the adoption of the U.N. partition plan on November 22, 1947 to the official end of the British mandate on May 14, 1948;
- The first full-scale war from May 15, 1948 to the signing of armistice agreements on January 1949;
- The Suez War of October 1956;
- The June War, 1967;
- The war of attrition, fought from December 1968 to July 1970;
- The October War, 1973;
- The war in Lebanon, June 1982.

Without imposing a rigid framework on the narrative, several recurrent themes will be given particular attention: the circumstances in which each war began and ended; the length of each war and, closely related to it, the international environment in which it was fought; the size and nature of the coalition that fought on the Arab side; and the war's distinctive military characteristics. The political dimensions of the Arab-Israeli conflict will be dealt with briefly through the analysis of the transition from one war to the other and the assessment of the significance of the Egyptian-Israeli peace treaty of 1979 and the Lebanese-Israeli agreement of 1983.

THE FIRST ARAB-ISRAELI WAR, 1948-49[3]

The war of 1948-49 transformed the Arab-Jewish struggle in and over Palestine into an Arab-Israeli conflict. The different names given to it by Israelis and Arabs reflect not only partisan viewpoints but also the divergent perspectives from which it was seen at the time. The Israelis refer to it as the War of Independence or the War of Liberation, thus emphasizing the importance they attached to the revival of independent Jewish statehood in the ancestral homeland. For the Arabs it was the Palestine War, the war in which part of Palestine was lost and the notion of an Arab Palestinian entity destroyed. The term "disaster" used by Arab writers to depict the events of 1948-49 reflects their larger impact on Arab society and politics.[4]

There were two distinct phases to the war. The first began after the November 1947 U.N. resolution on the partition of Palestine into an Arab and a Jewish state, with an internationalized Jerusalem (see Map 2). The resolution was accepted by the Jewish community, but rejected by the Arab community. The result was an escalation of Arab-Jewish fighting into a virtual civil war. The British mandatory government, about to end its rule in Palestine, was reluctant to stop the fighting and incapable of doing so. Until May 15, 1948 the two feuding communities tried to predispose the outcome of the full-fledged strife that was bound to follow the evacuation of British forces. The Palestinian Arabs, aided by semiregular "volunteers" from neighboring Arab countries, sought to occupy isolated Jewish settlements, while the Jewish side sought to fend off these attacks and to consolidate its territorial holdings. As a result, much of the fighting during this phase was mainly over the control of roads and in mixed (Arab-Jewish) cities.

A new phase began after May 15 with the invasion of Palestine by five Arab regular armies—those of Egypt, Jordan, Iraq, Syria, and Leba-

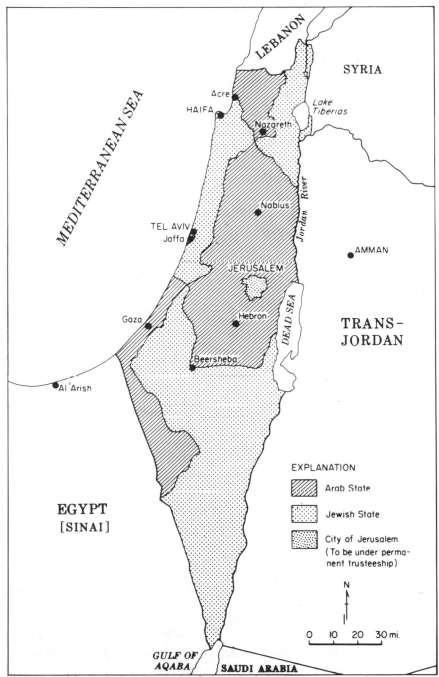

MEDITERRANEAN SEA

LEBANON

SYRIA

Acre

HAIFA

Lake
Tiberias

Nazareth

Jordan River

Nablus

TEL AVIV
Jaffa

AMMAN

JERUSALEM

Gaza

DEAD SEA

Hebron

TRANS-
JORDAN

Beersheba

Al 'Arish

EGYPT
[SINAI]

EXPLANATION

Arab State

Jewish State

City of Jerusalem
(To be under perma-
nent trusteeship)

N

0   10   20   30 mi.

GULF OF
AQABA   SAUDI ARABIA

Map 2: U.N. Partition Plan, November 1947

43

non—in support of the Palestinian Arabs, who were clearly incapable of holding out against their better-organized adversary.

The Arab intervention was the result of genuine support for the Palestinian Arabs, but it was also prompted by particular interests and intra-Arab rivalries. Most notably, the Egyptian royal house pushed its intervention in order to prevent the Hashemite states, Iraq and Transjordan, from expanding their territory and influence.[5]

This phase of the war lasted eight months, in the course of which a dramatic change occurred. Initially, the Israel Defense Forces (IDF), now a formal army, were hard put to contend with the simultaneous invasion of several regular armies, some of which were relatively well equipped and trained. During this period Jerusalem was besieged, the Egyptian army advanced toward Tel-Aviv, and the Syrian and Lebanese armies invaded from the northeast and north.

By December 1948 it was clear that Israel had won the war and was on the verge of routing at least some of her adversaries. The Egyptian army was pushed back in the south and the Israeli army advanced well into Sinai, which it had to evacuate under international pressure. In the north, the IDF pushed the Lebanese army back to its border and captured part of south Lebanon, which Israel evacuated as part of the 1949 armistice agreements. The Syrian army was forced to retreat to a line corresponding, more or less, to the pre-1948 international boundary, though in several places it held on to small pockets of territory lying west of the border. As part of the subsequent armistice agreement these became "demilitarized zones," a source of periodic tensions in the 1950s and 1960s.[6] Fighting between the IDF and the Jordanian Arab Legion was at times particularly fierce and difficult and at other times was tempered by the efforts of King Abdallah and the Israeli government to reach an understanding. The war ended with Jordan in control of what became known as the West Bank. While Israel accepted the principle of dividing Palestine (west of the Jordan River) between herself and Jordan, she failed to capture parts of the West Bank, particularly in the Jerusalem area, which she deemed vital.[7] The Iraqi army played a minor role in the war, despite Iraq's major role in the process that led the Arab League to intervene in the war. In this her leaders had been motivated as much by a quest for hegemony in Arab politics as by genuine commitment to the Arab cause in Palestine. But as her own ambitions and the larger Arab effort were increasingly thwarted by internal bickerings and objective difficulties, Iraq all but withdrew from the war.

Iraq's conduct offers an important insight into one of the reasons that account for Israel's success and the Arab states' failure. Israel was a small new state with a new and ill-equipped army fighting on several fronts. But she did enjoy the benefit of coherent leadership, whose impact was magnified by David Ben-Gurion's ability to integrate military and political elements into a comprehensive strategy. By contrast, the potential and initial advantage of the Arab states were sapped by rivalry and inability to mount a concerted offensive.

As the war continued, other factors came to bear. Although a new state, Israel was predicated on social and political structures that had been developed during the previous decades. Its society and population could thus be mobilized for a sustained effort. The Arab states, some of them newly and some of them only formally independent, were hampered by many of the social and political ills that were subsequently recognized as characteristic of the new states in the Third World. Thus in both Egypt and Syria the army felt that its performance was undercut by the incompetence and corruption of the civilian government.[8]

Later in the war, Israel obtained arms (primarily from Czechoslovakia acting on behalf of the Soviet Union) and turned some of its early military disadvantages into advantages. It exploited the advantages of short supply lines and of the ability to shift forces with relative ease from one front to the other. Consequently, while outnumbered by the combined Arab armies, Israel was able to obtain a number of important gains through the concentration of its forces.

The Soviet Union's (indirect) assistance to Israel was one reflection of the international dimension of the war. Most of the Arab participants were tied to the West or under Western influence, and the Soviet Union was the external power knocking on the region's gates. By helping Israel Moscow hoped to disturb the status quo. Israel, however, was a pro-Western state, and the clear-cut symmetry of later wars, when Soviet and Western clients fought one another, was missing from this first round. Under these circumstances the war did not become yet another manifestation of the Cold War. This goes a long way toward explaining why, in contrast to the subsequent Arab-Israeli wars, it could be fought for such a long time.[9]

The war's consequences were momentous. The existence of the state of Israel in an area larger than the one allotted to it by the U.N. partition resolution was reaffirmed and consolidated. The Arab Palestinian state envisaged by that resolution did not come into being. The territory allocated to it was divided among Jordan, Egypt, and Israel. Concomitantly, the Palestinian refugee problem was created. For the Arab world, military defeat at the hands of the Jewish state came as a humiliating shock, a telling testimony to its inability to cope with the challenge of the West. In time, military coups brought down the corrupt governments that had botched the Arab intervention.

It was not immediately perceived that the war, far from deciding the conflict, actually contributed to its exacerbation and perpetuation. The war was terminated in 1949 by a series of armistice agreements between Israel and four of the Arab belligerents. (Iraq, which does not share a border with Israel, refused to join the talks.) The assumption at the time was that the armistice agreements would provide the mechanism for the transition to normal peaceful relations. Soon afterwards, however, the full depth and complexity of the Arab-Israeli conflict became widely recognized.

THE SINAI-SUEZ CAMPAIGN WAR, OCTOBER 1956

During the early 1950s a process that Nadav Safran defined as "the festerization of the conflict" took place. The mutual antagonisms of the parties were translated into a series or cycle of political, economic, and military acts—the Arab boycott, the closure of the Gulf of Tiran and the Suez Canal to Israeli shipping, armed infiltration across Israel's border, and a succession of ever-expanding Israeli retaliatory raids against targets in Jordan, the (Egyptian-held) Gaza Strip, and Syria.[10]

The escalation of the conflict in the early 1950s bred the notion of a "second round." In its Arab version it would be a full-scale war designed to undo the consequences of 1948-49 and destroy the Israeli state. In its Israeli version it would be a limited war, calculated to strengthen Israel's strategic position (seen as inadequate in view of the Arab states' hostility and improving military capacity), anticipate an Arab attack, or acquire strategic superiority.[11]

In October 1956 Israel, in collusion with Britain and France, attacked Egypt. Several factors combined to determine the war's timing and nature. One was Egypt's evolution under Gamal Abdel Nasser's regime into a regional power, the leader of a revolutionary brand of pan-Arab nationalism and a friend of the Soviet Union. As part of this process Egypt undertook to lead the Arab struggle against Israel. Its growing influence in Jordan and Syria magnified the impact of Britain's evacuation of the Suez Canal zone and the 1955 Czech(Soviet)-Egyptian arms deal and threatened, from Israel's point of view, to endow Egypt with significant strategic advantages.

Nasser's attack on the remnants of Britain's and France's colonial empires in the Middle East had two important effects on the Arab-Israeli military equation. A French-Israeli alliance was formed, and France supplied Israel with the weapons systems that enabled the IDF to make a qualitative leap forward. Later the notion of a combined Anglo-French and Israeli attack was born. Britain and France sought to save their positions in the region by destroying Nasser's regime and the radical Arab nationalism he came to symbolize. Israel's aims were more modest—to eliminate what was perceived as an imminent threat and to establish a new balance in the Arab-Israeli strategic relationship. Despite the asymmetries of aims, there was sufficient overlap for Israel, Britain, and France to collude against Nasser. Israel thus had the benefit of a defensive aerial umbrella (crucial in Ben-Gurion's thinking) and international political support (which turned out to be a broken reed).[12]

The threat to Israel came from two sources. One was the wave of raids by organized Palestinian groups from the Gaza Strip and the West Bank against targets at Israel's very heart. Israel's retaliatory acts escalated the conflict, but failed to solve the problem. The other was Nasser's success in creating a tripartite military pact between Egypt, Syria, and Jordan. In a closed session Prime Minister Ben-Gurion explained how he viewed the pact's significance:

> These three states surround our small state from three sides. The Jordanian army might cut our territory in two—it is not wider than 15-20 kilometers in the center. The Egyptian and Syrian airforces can reach the population centers in a matter of minutes and bomb them thus disrupting the mobilization of the reserves on which all our security rests. Since we do not maintain a large regular army, a coordinated attack by the three neighboring countries under a unified Egyptian command could leave us defenseless.

Unlike 1948, in 1956 the decision to launch the Sinai campaign was taken by Israel and not by the Arabs. The Israeli leadership believed it was waging a defensive, not just a preventive war, that the Arab side had taken belligerent steps and was about to intensify the pace. The Arabs and much of the outside world took a different view of the matter (largely colored by Israel's association with colonialist European powers). (The 1956 war was praised in Israel in 1982 by a government that sought to show that it had not been the first to decide to launch war.)

Israel's Sinai campaign can be seen both in its own terms and in the context of the large operation of which it was a part. Realizing that they were operating within severe time constraints, Israeli military planners aimed at three goals: to reach the Suez Canal, to destroy the Egyptian army in the Sinai, and to capture Sharm el-Sheikh, the point at the southern tip of the Sinai Peninsula dominating the Straits of Tiran. By reaching the Suez Canal they would pave the way for the British and French to launch their own military operation. According to the Israeli plan, a paratrooper force was dropped near the Mitla Pass, one of the two passes in the hills just east of the canal. The bulk of the Israeli forces advanced on land, and, having stormed the major Egyptian positions, joined the paratroopers and reached the Suez Canal. A separate column advanced along the western shore of the Gulf of Eilat and captured Sharm el-Sheikh. The operation took only four days. Israel's complete domination of the skies was an important element in a desert area. Equally important, none of Egypt's Arab allies joined the war, so that Israel's effort could be concentrated on one front.

In stark contrast to the swiftness and success of Israel's military campaign, the Anglo-French operation and the broader scheme into which both had been fitted failed abysmally. The scheme was thwarted by the two superpowers, but despite the more dramatic style of the Soviet intervention, it was Washington's pressure, exerted both on its European allies and on Israel, that forced them to renounce their plans. Nasser remained in power and had no great difficulty in turning military defeat into a political victory. Israel evacuated the Sinai and the Gaza Strip in 1957 in return for security arrangements made by the Eisenhower administration. The Sinai Peninsula was to be demilitarized and to be held by a limited Egyptian force so as to minimize the danger of a surprise attack. U.N. forces were to be stationed in the Gaza Strip, along the Sinai border, and in Sharm el-Sheikh to help prevent armed infiltration, to monitor the border, and to guarantee Israel's freedom of navigation in the Straits of Tiran.

In addition to these arrangements, the Sinai campaign had a number of other important consequences. By demonstrating Israel's impressive military capacity it contributed to the consolidation of her regional and international standing. This was a significant prelude to the establishment of her relationships with Turkey, Iran, and Ethiopia and to the breakthroughs it achieved in the late 1950s in many African and Asian countries. But in the Arab world and in other parts of the Third World the campaign, and particularly the collusion with Britain and France, reinforced Israel's image as a Western bridgehead in the midst of an alien environment.

Of particular importance were the lessons drawn by Nasser from the events of 1956. He was impressed by Israel's military might and resolved not to be drawn, by his own actions or those of others, into another war with Israel before Egypt's—or the Arabs'—decisive advantage had been guaranteed. Such an advantage would rest on three elements: an Egyptian and Arab military buildup, a sufficient measure of Arab cooperation to permit the formation of a single Arab front around Israel, and Israel's international isolation.[13]

THE SIX-DAY WAR, JUNE 5-10, 1967

Nasser's determination not to be drawn into a premature war with Israel held for ten years. In the spring of 1967 a convergence of developments produced a crisis that led to an unplanned war.[14] Among these developments the following were of particular importance:

The Soviet Union's feeling that the United States was trying to topple the Syrian Baath regime and isolate Nasser led it to extend an unusual degree of support to Syria and to feed the Egyptians false information concerning an Israeli plan to attack Syria.

The escalation of intra-Arab rivalries, notably those between Syria and Egypt and between them and Jordan, created a dynamics of "overbidding" in their policies that radicalized the Arab-Israeli conflict. For example, by accusing Egypt of "hiding behind the skirts" of the U.N. forces that had served as a buffer between Egypt and Israel since the end of the Suez War, Jordan pressed the Nasser regime to undo the security arrangements made in 1957.

As was subsequently revealed, Nasser had in the early 1960s lost his control over the Egyptian armed forces and was dealing with military and occasionally national security affairs through his deputy, Abdel Hakim Amer. In the spring of 1967 the Egyptian military wanted an activist policy and told Nasser that should this policy lead to a showdown with Israel, it could check an Israeli offensive in the Sinai until a cease-fire was arranged.[15]

Israel's performance during the crisis and in the months preceding it was affected by the lack of experience and confidence displayed by Levi Eshkol, David Ben-Gurion's successor as prime minister and minister of defense. The absence of a dominant figure to inspire and direct Israel's national security policy contributed to the escalation of the Arab-Israeli conflict and to the attenuation of Israel's deterrence vis-à-vis the Arab states.

In addition, two factors had a particularly powerful impact on the radicalization and escalation of the Arab-Israeli conflict between 1963 and 1967. One was the emergence in Syria of a regime that turned a radical policy toward Israel into an explicit instrument of its domestic and regional policies.[16] The other was the revival of the notion of a Palestinian entity as a major issue in the conflict and the appearance of the PLO (still dominated by the Arab states) and its genuinely Palestinian rivals on the Middle East stage. These Palestinian groups did not bring the 1967 war about, as is sometimes erroneously argued, but they did contribute to the exacerbation of the conflict and established a presence which in the aftermath of the war assumed a great importance.[17]

The actual course of events that led to the outbreak of the Six-Day War unfolded in the following fashion. In the winter and spring of 1967 the Syrian-Israeli cycle of violence, which had begun in 1964, threatened to get out of hand. The Soviet Union informed Egypt that 15 briga. __ were deployed in northern Israel, about to launch an offensive against Syria. Nasser responded with a two-pronged policy—he openly remilitarized the Sinai and sent his officers to Syria to check the Soviet report. By the time he discovered that there was no Israeli military concentration, he had already realized that the remilitarization of the Sinai had restored his standing as the leader of Arab nationalism. In the next few days Israel was hard put to respond to Nasser's challenge, and the Johnson administration was reluctant to act to enforce the arrangements made by the Eisenhower administration a decade earlier. Inexorably, the crisis acquired dynamics of its own, independent of its original cause.

A further escalation occurred when Egypt demanded that the U.N. forces be removed from its territory. In all likelihood Nasser expected his demand to produce a lengthy and complicated procedure at the United Nations. But surprisingly, Secretary-General U Thant responded immediately by ordering the evacuation of the U.N. forces and none of the great powers intervened to halt the process. The most important outcome of this development was the vacuum created at the Straits of Tiran. On May 23 Nasser imposed a blockade, providing Israel with a clear-cut *casus belli*. Even without the closure of the Straits, however, war would have been difficult to avoid. Israel's military strength is based on its reserves. Once these have been mobilized, and the Israeli economy paralyzed, a time limit is placed on the crisis—either the potential threat had to be removed or war is bound to break out.

War did break out 12 days later. During that period several developments reinforced what increasingly appeared as the unfolding of a Greek tragedy depicting an inevitable deterioration toward war. All efforts by the United States and other Western powers to devise a political solution to the crisis failed. In Israel, a National Unity Government was formed to cope with the crisis and the defense portfolio in the new cabinet was given to Moshe Dayan. In the Arab world, Egypt's preeminence was enhanced and institutionalized through the formation of a unified command for the Egyptian, Syrian, and Jordanian armies. The stationing of Egyptian commando units on the West Bank illustrated the practical ramifications of effective Arab military cooperation and coordination.

By early June the U.S. government reached the conclusion that there was no political solution to the crisis and that an Israeli military action was inevitable. Without formally endorsing such action, the Johnson administration communicated its views to the Israeli government through informal channels. Given the close relationship between the Soviet Union and Egypt and Syria, the American reassurance was an important element in the Israeli cabinet's decision to launch war on June 5.

The Israeli military leadership sought to achieve a number of purposes: to retain an element of surprise (against difficult odds); to deal with what was perceived as the major threat, namely, the Egyptian military buildup in the Sinai; to accomplish that within a short period of time (given the anticipated Soviet pressure); and to limit the scope of the war.

Accordingly, the opening phase of the plan consisted of the following elements:

A surprise attack on all major military airfields was launched at an unorthodox late morning hour. It met with complete success and the Egyptian and Syrian air forces were practically neutralized.

While taking this initiative, Israel announced that it was in fact responding to an Arab attack spotted on Israel's radar screens. This political smoke screen was very effective in sustaining international political support for Israel's action during its critical phases.

On land, the Israeli army attacked the Egyptian positions in the Sinai and the Gaza Strip. Based on swift advance by armed units enjoying effective and close aerial support, the Israeli forces achieved an early decision in the Sinai.

Having destroyed the Syrian airforce, Israel did not attack that country on land. This was not considered as crucial an issue, and Defense Minister Dayan was reluctant to provoke the Soviets, who, he thought, had a special commitment to and interest in Syria. The Syrians, in turn, having played such a prominent role in producing the crisis, were not at all eager to play a commensurate role in the war. They shelled Israeli positions and settlements and staged a local attack, but they did not throw their army into the war.

Israel transmitted a message to the Jordanian government to the effect that should Jordan refrain from joining the war, Israel would not attack it. But in sharp contrast to the Syrian president, King Hussein, who had been a reluctant partner in the prewar coalition, acted with unexpected loyalty once the war started. The Jordanians took over (the neutral) Government House in Jerusalem and shelled the environs of Tel-Aviv and its international airport. In response, Israel attacked and captured the whole West Bank including East Jerusalem.[18]

The decision to capture the West Bank was grounded in strong emotional drives as well as in strategic considerations, which the events of May and June clearly reinforced. It was expedited by two other factors—the participation of the nationalist Herut party in the National Unity Government and the early victory achieved in the Sinai.

The decision to capture the Syrian Golan Heights was much more complicated. Defense Minister Dayan objected to an offensive against Syria, but a powerful lobby militated against his view. There were those who argued that it would be foolhardy to let those who had instigated the crisis emerge unpunished and that if Syria remained undefeated and in control of the Golan Heights, the pattern of the previous 25 years along the Syrian-Israeli border was bound to continue and serve as a source of conflict and instability. This point was pushed with great vigor and effect by representatives of the upper Galilee settlements who carried some influence with the Labor Party.

On the night of June 8/9, Dayan changed his mind and ordered an offensive against the Golan Heights. By June 11, when a cease-fire was imposed by the Security Council acting under Soviet pressure, the whole of the Golan Heights, including the town of Kuneitra, had been captured. The conduct of Syria's military and political leadership during this period has been severely censured within the Baath regime and by the regime's Syrian and other Arab critics. They have argued that the hilly terrain could have been defended more effectively against an army that was fighting on two other fronts; and that the elite brigades of the Syrian army were not dispatched to defend the nation's territory, but rather were kept near Damascus to defend the regime.

Radio Damascus came in for particular criticism for having announced the capture of Kuneitra several hours before it was actually taken by the Israelis. This resulted in panic and flight by civilians and military alike. In all likelihood the purpose of the announcement was to pressure the Soviets to expedite the imposition of a cease-fire by the United Nations.

The war of June 1967 was a watershed in the history of the Arab-

Israeli conflict. It exacerbated the dispute by putting the arms race and military buildup on an entirely different level and by aggravating the bilateral discord between Israel and the Arab states whose national territory it came to control. A mood of despair and humiliation prevailed in an Arab world that had suffered a devastating defeat that could no longer be blamed on corrupt *anciens régimes*.[19] The involvement, intervention, and competition of the two superpowers in the Arab-Israeli conflict also assumed new proportions.

Of particular importance was the renewal of the war for Palestine. The question of Palestine was reopened, because for the first time since 1948 one authority was in control of all of Palestine west of the Jordan River. In Israel possession of the West Bank generated a wave of mystical nationalism that reinforced the attachment to a territory whose strategic value had been demonstrated by the war. In the Arab world the PLO, having won its autonomy, became an important actor, oftentimes overshadowing the Arab states.

But there were other sides to these developments. First, the might and skill displayed by the IDF persuaded many Arabs that Israel could not be defeated by them in war. Second, the territories held by Israel, or at least some of them, were seen as bargaining chips that might introduce an element of flexibility into the Arab-Israeli stalemate.

But in 1967 the stalemate could not be broken. It took six years and another two wars before an Arab-Israeli settlement process could be started.

THE WAR OF ATTRITION, DECEMBER 1968- AUGUST 1970

The stalemate following the Six-Day Way reflected one of the fundamental asymmetries of the Arab-Israeli conflict. Israel could defeat three Arab states in six days and take control of large territories in the Sinai, the West Bank, and the Golan Heights, but it could not inflict a total defeat on the Arab world or use its military victory to dictate a peace settlement (see Map 3).

Israel's position, which was then supported by the United States, was that the territories captured in June 1967 (with the exception of the West Bank) should be used as pawns in order to obtain a peace settlement. The experience of May-June 1967 showed, it was argued, that security arrangements devoid of a political underpinning could not be relied upon. But the Arab position, as articulated at the August 1967 Khartoum Summit Conference and on other occasions, was diametrically opposed to this view. In Arab eyes, Israel was the aggressor and should be punished rather than rewarded. The Arab states, knowing that Israel could not force its terms on them and counting on the support of the Soviet bloc and a large number of Islamic and Third World states, sought to force Israel to return the territories captured in June 1967 without any substantive concessions on their part.[20]

In the summer and fall of 1967 Arab efforts, supported by the USSR, concentrated on the United Nations—first in the General Assembly and then in the Security Council. But since Israel's fundamental position was supported by the United States, they could not make any headway. The best they could manage was U.N. Security Council Resolution 242 of November 1967, phrased in such general and vague terms as to make it almost meaningless.

A year later Egypt realized that the stalemate was detrimental to its cause. Nasser also felt that the process of military reconstruction and buildup, begun in the immediate aftermath of the war, was nearly completed. Though no explicit decision to launch it was probably made, a "war of attrition" against Israel was started by Egypt, with some participation by Jordan, Syria, and the PLO.[21]

The concept of a war of attrition rested on the assumption that Israel was either not interested in launching a full-fledged war or not capable of responding to the challenge. This being the case, there were a number of advantages to be drawn from engaging Israel in a series of limited hostilities along the cease-fire lines. The mood of humiliation and despair in the Arab world would be altered by the very fact that the defeated armies of 1967 were once again fighting. It was also important to "keep the pot boiling" so as to demonstrate to the international community that the stalemate in the Middle East could not be tolerated. Yet another purpose was to exert direct pressure on Israel—to inflict casualties (an issue of great sensitivity in Israel) and to exact an economic price by compelling Israel to maintain large forces along long and remote borders and the cease-fire lines.

The main front lay along the Suez Canal. At the outset the Egyptians used to advantage their superior artillery power by shelling the Israeli forces on the canal's eastern bank, In response, the Bar Lev line was built to offer shelter from artillery barrages. Egyptian squads also crossed the canal to attack Israeli outposts or ambush vehicles moving between them.

As the toll exacted by Egyptian shelling and ambushes increased, Israel changed the rules of the game without crossing the line that separated limited from full-blown war. This it did by relying increasingly on the superiority of its airforce. The planes were employed first along the canal—primarily against Egyptian artillery positions and later for "deep raid" bombings in an attempt to force a strategic decision. Commando raids were also launched against Egyptian targets far from the Suez Canal.

By the end of 1969, the Egyptian leadership realized that it could no longer stand the pressure of the Israeli airforce. To prevent Egypt's capitulation, the Soviet Union agreed during Nasser's secret visit in January 1970 to undertake responsibility for defending the skies of Egypt. Soviet ground-to-air missiles and planes and the crews to operate them were brought to Egypt and deployed in phases. In the spring of 1970 they were already taking an active part in the fighting. Several Israeli planes were shot down by Soviet missiles and four Soviet jets flown by Soviet pilots were shot down by Israel over the Sinai in late July.

The significance and repercussions of these developments extended well beyond the Middle East. They finally led U.S. Secretary of State William Rogers to come out with a plan that eventuated in a new cease-fire agreement in August 1970.

An American initiative brought the War of Attrition to an end. It was successful because the chief protagonists, Egypt and Israel, were eager for a way to stop the fighting. Egypt paid a terrible price for a war meant to inflict attrition on its enemy—heavy casualties and the destruction of the Suez Canal cities, with thousands of refugees adding to the congestion of Cairo. Israel suffered many casualties, economic dislocation, cracks in the national consensus, and above all, the frightening prospect of direct clashes with the Soviet Union.

The Palestinian resistance became increasingly prominent. The PLO backed by various Arab governments, exacted permission from King Hussein to permit it to turn Jordanian territory first into a base for operations against Israel and then into an autonomous territorial bridgehead, a state within a state. PLO operations against Israel brought the familiar cycle of punitive and preemptive raids, shellings, and countershellings. These fell into four categories: raids, shelling, and mining along the Jordanian and occasionally the Lebanese border; attempts to turn the West Bank into a base for guerrilla warfare; sabotage inside Israel proper; and violence against Israeli and Jewish targets outside of the Middle East. These activities, besides being part of the overall Arab effort, played a crucial role in building up the PLO's position in the Arab world and in familiarizing the international community with both the PLO and the Palestinian issue.[22]

The PLO overplayed its hand in Jordan and its attempt to resist the

August 1970 cease-fire triggered the Jordanian civil war the following month and resulted in its expulsion from Jordan. But in the atmosphere of the time, the Lebanese government could ill afford to oppose the PLO's establishment of extraterritorial bases in its territory. These served as the foundation for the substitute for the Jordanian base and were developed in the 1970s.

Various accounts of the Arab-Israeli conflict's military history do not consider the War of Attrition a war in the full sense of the term. Though largely a matter of definition and terminology, there is, in any event, no denying the important impact that the war and the fashion in which it was terminated had on the course of the conflict.

The price Egypt paid and the failure of this effort to force a decision on Israel contributed to a change of Egyptian policy in the early 1970s. But that change occurred only later; it was first obscured by the October War. Seen from the perspective of that war, the ending of the War of Attrition had important ramifications for the opening round of the next war.[23]

THE OCTOBER WAR, OCTOBER 5-22, 1973

The October War (often referred to by the Egyptians as the Ramadan War and by the Israelis as the Yom Kippur War) was conceived and initiated by Anwar al-Sadat, who became Egypt's president after Nasser's death in September 1970.[24] Sadat's plan rested on a number of assumptions: that the patterns established after the summer of 1970 operated in Israel's favor and that the Soviet-American detente threatened to freeze the status quo; that the key to changing the status quo lay in Washington rather than in Moscow and that Egypt's (and the Arabs') interests were with the West; that the energy crisis of the early 1970s resulted in a dramatic increase in the Arabs' influence in the international arena and that it could be used to force on Israel a settlement congenial to the Arabs; and that a limited military operation was crucial to set such a process in motion.

The military operation envisaged by Sadat consisted of an Egyptian crossing of the Suez Canal and control of its eastern bank, for which Egypt could amass enough strength to secure a local advantage. A simultaneous Syrian offensive in the Golan Heights would open a second front, closer to Israel's population centers, and would tie down considerable Israeli forces. Ground-to-air missiles and antitank weapons supplied by the Soviets would greatly diminish, if not eliminate, two of Israel's most important military advantages. Furthermore, since Israeli doctrine held that Israel had to defeat any attempt to obtain a bridgehead on the east bank of the Suez Canal before a cease-fire was imposed, failure to achieve that would be defined as a defeat in Israel's own terms and a victory for Egypt.

Surprise was conceived as a particularly important element in the Egyptian-Syrian plan. Israel kept relatively small forces along the Suez Canal and Golan Heights fronts. Its concept of defending them rested on the assumption that an efficient intelligence service would provide ample warning, so that reserve forces could be mobilized in time. Deception became an essential element of the Egyptian-Syrian plan.

Egypt's plan of deception met with an unusual success, to a great extent made possible by the failure of the Israeli leadership to heed the warning signs that were made available to it by its own intelligence services. Consequently, when the Egyptian and Syrian offensive was launched in the early afternoon of October 5, 1973 (that year it was the Jewish Day of Atonement, Yom Kippur), it encountered an Israeli military machine that was only partially mobilized and largely out of gear.[25]

The initial thrust of the Egyptian and Syrian offensives proved effective and successful. The Egyptian army crossed the canal, captured most of the fortified Israeli defense line (the Bar Lev Line), and dug into defensive positions a few kilometers east of the canal. In the different circumstances of the front on the Golan Heights, the Syrian army swept the thin Israeli defensive line with armored columns and recaptured most of the Golan. Israel's initial efforts to regroup and counterattack revealed the effectiveness of the ground-to-air missiles and antitank weapons supplied by the Soviet Union to the Egyptian and Syrian armies. By October 8 the scope of the Arab success and the severity of the challenge presented to Israel were fully apparent.

Under Prime Minister Golda Meir, the Israeli leadership, which had now completed the process of mobilizing the reserves and grasped the significance of the changes that had affected warfare in the Arab-Israeli arena since 1967, developed a strategy to deal with the reverses sustained thus far. It decided to address first the Golan front, where the threat to Israel proper was more serious and where the prospects for swift success seemed brighter. Israel's counterattack was, indeed, successful. Syria's forces were pushed back to the original cease-fire line and then beyond it into an area that became known as "the salient."

This turn of events revealed a cardinal weakness of the Egyptian-

Syrian military alliance—lack of good faith and little coordination beyond the agreement on a simultaneous attack. Syria's war plan was clearly based on the assumption that after two or three days a cease-fire would be imposed. This would have left Syria in control of much of the Golan Heights. When the Soviet Union tried to secure a cease-fire, however, it encountered opposition from Egypt. The Egyptian army felt secure in its new position and President Sadat was in no hurry to end the war.

But as the Syrian army was being pushed back, Syria increased its pressure on Egypt: if the Egyptian government wanted to continue the war it ought to alter its passive stance and take to the offensive. It was indeed under this pressure that on October 14 the Egyptians launched a major attack that was repelled by the Israelis.

Israel's success served as a prelude to the move that on October 16 changed the tide of the war. By that date the debate had been decided within the Israeli leadership as to the strategy to be employed in the south. Rather than seek to defeat the Egyptian forces east of the canal, the Israelis would cross the canal and establish a presence on the Egyptian mainland. It was a hazardous move, but held the promise of considerable advantages: surprise, throwing the Egyptian army out of balance, and a presence on the other side of the canal in case of a cease-fire. The Israeli decision was facilitated by the beginning of the American airlift resupplying the IDF. Following a debate within the Nixon administration, the airlift was undertaken to counter the Soviet Union's resupply of the Egyptian and Syrian armies.

After a precarious beginning the Israeli crossing proved to be a great military success. Six days later the Israeli forces on the canal's western bank were about to encircle the Third Egyptian Army and were at the gates of the city of Suez. By attacking the ground-to-air missile sites, they freed the skies for the Israeli airforce so that an offensive against the Egyptian forces on the eastern bank of the canal could be undertaken.

As the Israeli military effort concentrated on the Egyptian front, the progress of the Israeli forces on the Golan front slowed down. With a very large number of casualties already sustained, Israel was anxious to avoid incurring a stiff price in an arena considered less than crucial. The resistance put up by Syrian troops defending the road to their capital and the arrival of Iraqi, Jordanian, and other reinforcements on the Golan front meant that any effort to inflict a strategic defeat on Syria was bound to be very costly for Israel.

The reinforcements that arrived on the Golan front were a manifestation of the unusual mobilization of the Arab world during the October

War. The Egyptian-Syrian military alliance and the concept of a limited war designed to impose a settlement on Israel were supported by a large group in which Saudi Arabia played a leading part. It assumed a dual role—as an intermediary between "the Arab point of view" and American policy, and as a chief actor in the first effective employment of the "oil weapon." An Arab oil boycott was put into effect against Israel's friends and supporters. Other Arab states, such as Libya and Iraq, which had been critical of the concept of a limited war, also felt compelled to extend their support in the heady atmosphere created by the initially successful war.

Egypt and Syria did not invite Jordan to join the war effort. They were willing to deny themselves that considerable military advantage for two main reasons—distrust of King Hussein and a decision not to include him in the projected settlement plan. In their scheme of things the PLO and not Hussein was designated the claimant for the West Bank.

On October 20 time began to run out for Israel. The Soviet Union, despite the expulsion of its military advisers from Egypt in July 1972, invested great effort to save Egypt from a decisive military defeat. The United States, in turn, faced complex choices. The war and the oil embargo reinforced a shift in U.S. policy, which had been taking shape since 1972, away from Israel toward a more "evenhanded" policy. In contrast to the situation in 1967, Egypt was no longer squarely in the Soviet camp but was apparently seeking to shift its orientation. If this was the case, reasoned Washington, the war should not be allowed to push Egypt back into the Soviet orbit but rather should be used to draw Egypt into the American orbit.

American diplomacy was managed by Secretary of State Henry Kissinger. It sought to achieve several divergent ends: to meet Soviet threats in kind; to give the Soviet Union a sense of participation in, rather than exclusion from, the diplomatic process, but to retain a clear American ascendancy; to prevent Israel from achieving a full victory over Egypt.

The result was Security Council Resolution 338 and the October 22 cease-fire that was finally imposed on October 24. It is still an open issue whether the nuclear alert announced by the United States was directed solely against the Soviet Union or was also meant to frighten Israel into accepting the cease-fire and stopping short of achieving a clear-cut victory over Egypt.

The October War thus ended inconclusively. On the Golan, Israel emerged with a net gain of some territory; in the south, it was in control of sizable territory on the Egyptian mainland, its advanced position being no more than 60 miles from Cairo. But Egyptian forces were in control of most of the west bank of the Suez Canal. Israel also had a number of other factors to take into account: a huge number of casualties, a comparatively large number of POWs, the decline of the government's domestic standing, the high economic and financial cost of the war, a weakening in Israel's regional and international position, and the obvious rise of the Arab world's international influence.

THE ARAB-ISRAELI SETTLEMENT PROCESS

Perhaps the most important consequence of the October War was that it ended the stalemate that had prevailed since 1967. Several factors combined to produce the change. Most immediate was the war's inconclusive outcome. Each of the three chief protagonists had powerful motives for participating in a process that at the outset had rather limited goals—to prevent a reeruption of hostilities and to resolve some pressing problems. The United States emerged from the war as the "honest broker"—the power that resupplied Israel in the middle of the war and saved Egypt from defeat at the war's end. For the first time since 1948, it also reached the conclusion that its interests required a sustained effort to bring about a settlement of the Arab-Israeli conflict.

Washington's determination to pursue a settlement was aided by the conclusions and lessons that both Israelis and Arabs drews from the October War. Israelis could be encouraged by the fact that a war that had begun with a severe debacle ended on the verge of a decisive victory. But there were other aspects to be considered: the nearness of defeat during the war's first days, the terrible price paid, the growing dependence on the United States, the increase in Arab power and influence. It was the first war in which the Arab side used ground-to-ground missiles—an ominous warning that the Arab-Israeli cycle of violence was reaching a dangerous level.

The Arab participants could draw a discouraging conclusion: if Israel had not been defeated in October 1973, when the Arabs had enjoyed almost the ideal opening conditions, it was not very likely to be defeated in the foreseeable future. For Egypt, a somewhat different question presented itself in very acute terms: could Egypt continue to pay the price of bearing the main brunt of the Arab world's conflict with Israel? It took six years of a great national effort to prepare the successful crossing of the Suez Canal. Could and should Egypt continue her participation in the Arab-Israeli conflict at the same level at a terrible price to the quality of public and private life? Or should Egypt take advantage of the opportunity to regain the Sinai and let the Arab world in its entirety meet the real costs of continued conflict?

The question was pinpointed by another consequence of the October War—the quadrupling of oil prices and the accumulation of enormous financial resources in the oil-producing Arab countries. Thus, as Egypt became more impoverished and dependent on financial transfers from the rich Arab governments, its position of leadership in the Arab world was progressively eroded. There was a discrepancy being created between the claims made on Egypt in the name of the Arab cause and her ability to lead, or benefit from, that cause.

A change occurred in the Arab position on the question of an Arab-Israeli settlement. The completely negative position of the 1967 Khartoum summit meeting, which declared that there must be no negotiation with Israel, no peace with Israel, and no recognition of it, was replaced in Algiers in November 1973 by a different formulation. The Algiers Summit, held shortly after the October War, endorsed the general notion of a political settlement with Israel, provided that two conditions were met: first that *all* territories captured in 1967 be returned; and second, that the legitimate rights of the Palestinians be restored. The vagueness of the second condition proved useful when partial settlements were negotiated, but was a serious stumbling block when a comprehensive settlement was discussed.

While adhering to this general Arab position, Egypt was willing to go further in order to regain the Sinai. In 1974 both Egypt and Syria signed disengagement agreements with Israel. The distinctiveness of the Egyptian position emerged when Egypt alone signed a second agreement on the Sinai. In 1977, when Sadat felt that Syria and the PLO were following an obstructionist course that would prevent Egypt from regaining the whole of the Sinai, he went to Jerusalem and conducted direct negotiations with the Israeli government, thereby creating tension between the specific Egyptian position and the general Arab position.[27]

The opening of negotiations with Egypt, with a view toward resolving the conflict and establishing a normal peaceful relationship, confronted Israel with more than one dilemma. Egypt was the single most important Arab state—but did she represent the Arab cause, could she carry the rest of the Arab world or a large part of it, and could she act alone if the other Arab states refused to follow? Furthermore, it was soon evident that while Egypt and Israel seemed capable of resolving their

bilateral conflict, they could not come to an agreement on the Palestinian issue. The vagueness of the Arab position on this matter (as pointed
out above) was reiterated by Sadat in his Knesset speech and in closed
sessions. It would have been difficult for any Israeli government to accept that position, and it was clearly unacceptable to the Likud
government.

The Camp David accords of September 1978 and the Egyptian-Israeli
peace treaty of March 1979 were made possible by skirting and postponing
a decision on the Palestinian issue through the autonomy plan. The first
Arab-Israeli peace treaty was thus signed. But signing a peace treaty when
the underlying conflict had not actually been resolved had its effects.
Egyptian-Israeli peace remained precarious, partial, separate, and controversial. It did not resolve the Arab-Israeli conflict, but rather determined the agenda and the timetable for the continued conflict. As the
Egyptian-Israeli peace treaty was being implemented in the years 1979-82,
the struggle over the Palestinian issue continued in the West Bank and
in Lebanon.[28]

The struggle was conducted in the context of a clear-cut Israeli
advantage. Egypt's (temporary?) departure from the ranks of the Arab
confrontation states created what Syria angrily called "a strategic gap"
in Israel's favor. Other factors served to reinforce the same trend—the
Iran-Iraq war, the recrudescence of the Syrian-Jordanian rivalry, and the
decline in the influence of the oil-producing Arab countries. But the
effects of the Israeli advantage of the late 1970s and early 1980s were
dimmed in Israeli eyes by two factors: awareness that sooner or later
would come a moment of truth over the future of the West Bank, and
a feeling that its advantage was transient, that later in the 1980s the
balance was bound to shift in the other direction. This tension between
a sense of power and advantage and a sense of impending doom was an
important component of the background to the 1982 war in Lebanon.

THE WAR IN LEBANON, JUNE-SEPTEMBER 1982

The war waged by Israel in Lebanon in the summer of 1982 was significantly different from all previous Arab-Israeli wars. It was a long one,
lasting almost three months. It was the first war fought primarily between
Israel and the Palestinians since the early part of the 1948/49 war. Except for the 1956 Sinai campaign, it was the only Arab-Israeli war whose
timing and scope were determined by Israel. And in a fashion more

ambitious than during the Sinai campaign, it sought to achieve political aims and to implement a political plan. It was also the least unexpected of the Arab-Israeli wars; during the six months that preceded it, the international and Middle East media offered numerous predictions of when it would take place and what was its anticipated scenario.

The Israeli war plan sought to achieve four aims: to destroy the PLO's military infrastructure and presence in south Lebanon and so eliminate its capacity to shell northern Israel, which the PLO had demonstrated so effectively in July 1981; to preempt the possibility (argued by a part of the Israeli national security establishment) that Syria would launch a war or a war of attrition a year or two later; to help reconstruct the Lebanese state and reestablish an effective central government, by helping Israel's ally, Bashir Jumayyil, become the head of this government; and to improve its posture in the next phase of the Arab-Israeli settlement process by destroying the PLO's autonomous territorial base in Lebanon (in the south as well as in Beirut) and by forming a normal relationship with a second Arab state.

The war passed through five phases:

First, during the initial thrust, Israel attacked with two columns. The first, reinforced by landings from the sea, advanced through the western sector toward Beirut. The second advanced through the mountainous central sector toward the Beirut-Damascus Road. In the east, the Israeli forces did not attack the Syrian forces and Israel's stated position was that she would not fight the Syrians if they refrained from attacking Israeli forces.

Second, during the fourth and fifth days of the war, fighting did develop between Israel and Syria. The Syrian forces in Lebanon tried to walk a tightrope—to engage the Israelis in a limited fashion that would enable them to claim they had extended support to the PLO and yet fall short of provoking the Israelis. In this they failed, particularly since Defense Minister Sharon believed that the Syrian army ought to be evicted from the southern half of Lebanon. The Syrian ground-to-air missiles in eastern Lebanon were destroyed from the air, many Syrian airplanes were shot down, and a large Israeli column began to push the Syrian forces from the southern part of the Bekaa Valley. Realizing that it was not receiving any support from the Soviet Union or the Arab states, Syria pressed for and obtained a cease-fire on June 11.

Third, by that time Israel's forces had reached the environs of Beirut and established a tenuous link with the "Lebanese forces" (Bashir Jumayyil's militia). It had also become apparent that Israel's war aims were far more ambitious than the creation of a 25-mile security area in south Lebanon. Criticism of the war, abroad (which had been very mild) and at home, mounted. During the second and third weeks of June an important aspect and difficulty of the Israeli operation in Lebanon surfaced. Israel's war aims could not be accomplished without capturing the whole of Beirut; but capturing West Beirut had not been part of the Israeli war plan. That was a task left to the Lebanese forces, whose leader was to dominate the liberated and reconstructed Lebanese state. When it became obvious that the Lebanese forces had no intention of storming West Beirut, the Israeli leadership was in a quandary. Failure to evict the PLO from West Beirut would mean a strategic victory for the PLO, but the human and political costs of storming it were prohibitive. Following a few days of confusion an alternative strategy was devised, a siege of Beirut. For the two months of its duration the alternative strategy seemed hardly more attractive than the one it replaced. Israel beseiged an Arab capital and when it appeared that the PLO was, quite natural-ly, reluctant to leave, Israeli forces increased their pressure in order to support the efforts of the American mediator, Ambassador Philip Habib, to induce the PLO to evacuate the city peacefully. The pressure consisted of air raids, shell-ing, occasional interference with power and other supplies, and other such measures. Finally the PLO agreed to leave and completed its departure by the end of August.

Fourth, the PLOs departure and Bashir Jumayyil's earlier election to the presidency seemed to suggest that a significant part of Israel's ambitious war aims had been achieved. But the publication on September 1 of President Reagan's plan signified a divergence in the American and Israeli outlooks. Until then, the Israeli operation had been given an unprecedented degree of direct and indirect American backing. The Reagan administration, however, did not share the Begin government's views on the future of the West Bank, nor was it interested in an overtly pro-Israeli Lebanese government at odds with its Arab neighbors and their Lebanese supporters.

But the assumptions underlying both Washington's and Israel's policies in Lebanon were undermined in mid-September by the assassination of Bashir Jumayyil.

And fifth, one of the weaknesses of the original Israeli plan was that it had been predicated on the person and outlook of one leader. When Bashir Jumayyil was assassinated, Israel could not find another candidate who would be both effective and pro-Israel. Bashir's own brother, Amin, who was then elected, represented a very different political orientation. In the atmosphere that pre-vailed after the assassination, Israel dispatched her forces into West Beirut in an effort to consolidate the situation. By assuming the overall responsibility and by encouraging the Phalanges to seek out PLO "combatants" who presumably stayed behind in Palestinian neighborhoods, Israel became implicated in the massacre perpetrated by Christian Maronite militiamen. This resulted in its immediate loss of position in Beirut and in a domestic shock in Israel. A com-mission of inquiry was formed, which until February 1983 cast a shadow over the Begin government and then resulted in Ariel Sharon's ouster from the Ministry of Defense.

During the year following the war in Lebanon all efforts to put an end to the immediate problems and to set a process in motion for resolving the larger Lebanese crisis were to no avail. For one thing Syria recovered from the partial defeat of June 1982 and regained a decisive position in Lebanon. In so doing she was given considerable aid by the Soviet Union, which in the winter of 1982/83 saw an opportunity to regain some of the ground lost in the Middle East. Washington's policy was paralyzed by the contradiction between the desire to implement the president's own plan and the realization that this was interfering with the efforts to promote a settlement in Lebanon. Israel's policy was crippled by a growing public disenchantment with the Lebanese affair and by the loss of direction in Lebanon. Until September 1982 Israel's policy was based on cooperation with the major Maronite force; but after that the new leader of the Maronites, who was also the elected head of state, pursued a different policy. What was Israel to do?

In May 1983, after arduous negotiations, an agreement was signed between Israel and Lebanon. It arranged for Israel's withdrawal from Lebanon in return for an element of normalization and for security arrangements in the south. But during the following months the agreement remained a dead letter. The key was clearly in Syria's hands. For one thing Israel (and less explicitly the United States) declared that *all* foreign forces should leave Lebanon. By refusing to evacuate her own forces Syria was keeping Israel's forces in Lebanon as well. More ominously, Syria was exerting direct pressure on Amin Jumayyil's administration, demanding that it repudiate the agreement. Syria objected both to the text of the agreement and to its significance—Lebanese dependence on the United States and independence from Syria.

Thus, the first Israeli effort to conduct a war that would achieve more than the elimination of an immediate threat to the state's existence and security met with ambiguous results. The war's impact on the course of the Arab-Israel conflict and the Arab-Israeli settlement process is equally uncertain.

NOTES

1. For two general surveys of the military history of the Arab-Israeli conflict see T. Dupuy, *Elusive Victory; The Arab-Israeli Wars 1947-1974* (New York: Harper Row, 1978), and H. Herzog, *The Arab-Israeli Wars* (New York and London: 1982).
2. For assessment of the new relationship between Egypt and Israel, see H. Sachar,

Egypt and Israel (New York: M. Marek, 1981); and M. Kramer, ed. *The Peace Treaty with Egypt: Achievements and Setbacks* (a colloquium) (Tel-Aviv: Tel-Aviv University, The Shiloah Center for Middle Eastern and African Studies, 1981).

3. On the history of the first Arab-Israeli war, see N. Lorch, *The Edge of the Sword; Israel's War of Independence, 1947-1949* (2d. rev. ed.) (Jerusalem: Massada Press, 1968).

4. On the Arab States decision to intervene in the war, see E. Kedourie, "Panarabism and British Policy" *Political Quarterly* 28 (April-June 1957): 137-48.

5. S. Segev, ed. and trans., *Behind the Curtain* (Tel-Aviv: 1954) (in Hebrew). This is the Hebrew version of the report prepared by an Iraqi parliamentary committee charged with investigating the Iraqi army's failure in the 1948 War. For the general pattern of inter-Arab rivalries in the late 1940s, see Patrick Seale, *The Struggle for Syria* (London: Oxford University Press, 1965).

6. N. Bar-Yaacov, *The Israel-Syrian Armistice: Problems of Implementation, 1949-1966* (Jerusalem: Magnes Press, 1967).

7. A former high-ranking Jordanian officer published his memoirs of this period in an effort to discredit King Abdullah. *The Memoirs of Abdullah al-Tal* (Tel-Aviv: Maarachot, 1960). (in Hebrew).

8. Abdel-Nasser, who was besieged for several months in southern Israel, described in the *Philosophy of the Revolution* the importance of this experience in his political development.

9. For Soviet and American policies during this period, see Y. Ro'i, *Soviet Decision Making in Practice; the USSR and Israel 1947-1954* (New Brunswick, N.J.: Transaction Books, 1980), and Z. Ganin, *Truman, American Jewry, and Israel, 1945-1948* (New York: Holmes and Meier Publishers, 1979).

10. N. Safran, *From War to War; the Arab-Israeli Confrontation, 1948-1967* (New York: Pegasus, 1969); and F. Khouri, *The Arab-Israeli Dilemma* (Syracuse, N.Y.: Syracuse University Press, 1968).

11. Israel's outlook on this issue and the debate within the Israeli government on the correct response to the perceived threat are reflected in the eight volumes of the personal diary kept by M. Sharett in the early and mid 1950s and in M. Bar-Zohar's biography of Ben-Gurion (abridged version in Hebrew) (Jerusalem, 1980), 397-446.

12. For a general survey and critique of the literature on the Suez-Sinai affair see E. Kedourie, "Suez Revisited," in his *Islam in the Modern World* (New York: 1981), pp. 171-91. On the formation of the French-Israeli alliance, see M. Bar Zohar, *Bridge Over the Mediterranean; French-Israeli Relations 1947-1963* (in Hebrew) (Tel-Aviv: Am Hassefer, 1964); and S. Peres, *David's Sling* (London: Weidenfeld and Nicolson, 1970).

13. N. Safran, *From War to War*; and P. J. Vatikiotis, *Nasser and his Generation* (London: Croom Helm, 1978).

14. S. Shamir, "The Middle East Crisis: On the Brink of War," in *Middle East Record 1967*, ed. D. Dishon (Tel-Aviv: 1971), pp. 183-204; T. Draper, *Israel and World Politics; Roots of the Third Arab-Israeli War* (New York: Viking Press, 1968); W. Z. Laqueur, *The Road to War, 1967* (London: Weidenfeld and Nicolson, 1968); and M. Rodinson, *Israel and the Arabs* (New York: Pantheon Books, 1968).

15. This process is described in the memoirs of one of Nasser's associates. Abdul Latif al-Bagdadi, *The Memoirs of Abdul Latif al-Bagdadi*, vol. 2, (in Arabic) (Cairo; n.d.).

16. A. Hottinger, "Syria: War Psychosis as an Instrument of Government," *Swiss Review of World Affairs* (August 1966):3-5.

17. W. Quandt, "Political and Military Dimensions of Contemporary Palestinian Nationalism," in W. Quandt, F. Jabber and A. Mosley Lesch, *The Politics of Palestinian Nationalism* (Berkeley: University of California Press, 1973), pp. 43-153; G. Ben-Dor, "The Institutionalization of Palestinian Nationalism, 1967-1973," in *From June to October; The Middle East Between 1967 and 1973*, ed. I. Rabinovich and H. Shaked (New Brunswick, N.J.: Transaction Books, 1978), pp. 245-67.

18. For the Jordanian perspective on these developments, see E. Kam, ed., *Hussein Goes to War* (in Hebrew) (Tel-Aviv, 1974). This is a collection of four Jordanian accounts—by King Hussein, P.M. Sa'd Jum'a, and General Abu Nawwar—of Jordan's role in the Six Day War and the events leading to it.

19. Fouad Ajami, *The Arab Predicament* (Cambridge: Cambridge Univesity Press, 1981).

20. For an analysis of an American policy in the aftermath of the Six Day War, see William Quandt, *Decade of Decisions* (Berkeley: University of California Press, 1977).

21. Y. Bar-Siman-Tov, *The Israeli-Egyptian War of Attrition, 1969-1970* (New York: Columbia University Press, 1980).

22. J. Cooley, *Green March, Black September; the Story of the Palestinian Arabs* (London: F. Cass, 1973).

23. For a criticism of Israel's strategy during this phase, see E. Weizman, *Lecha Shamaim Lecha Eretz (Yours the Sky, Yours the Country)* (Tel-Aviv: Sifrait Maariv, 1975). The international political background of the War of Attrition is covered in the memoirs of H. Kissinger, *White House Years* (Boston: Little Brown, 1979), pp. 213-315.

24. Egypt's preparations for the war were described by Sadat himself in his book *In Search of Identity* (New York: Harper & Row, 1977/78), and by his bitter critic, Saad al-Din Shazly, in his own account, *The Crossing of Suez; The October War, 1973* (1980).

25. For three Israeli accounts of the debacle of early October, see H. Bartov, *Dado, 48 Years and 20 Days* (Tel-Aviv: 1981), A. Adan, *On the Banks of the Suez* (1980); and Z. Schiff, *October Earthquake* (Tel-Aviv: University of Publishing Projects, 1974).

26. For the international background, see Henry Kissinger, *Years of Upheaval* (Boston: Little Brown, 1982), pp. 450-544.

27. See the various essays in Malcolm Kerr and Sayed Yassin, eds., *Rich and Poor States in the Middle East* (Boulder, Colo.: Westview Press, 1982); and Fouad Ajami, "The Arab Road," *Foreign Policy* 47 (Summer 1982):3-25.

28. See the various accounts of the Egyptian-Israeli negotiations and the Camp David accords in Sachar, *Egypt and Israel*; and Shmuel Katz, *The Hollow Peace* (Jerusalem: Dvir, 1981).

29. See I. Rabinovich, *The War for Lebanon 1979-1982* (Ithaca: Cornell University Press, 1984).

3

Transformation:
External Determinants

Alvin Z. Rubinstein

The Arab-Israeli conflict is the world's oldest regional conflict. It is constantly fed by a series of unanticipated developments whose consequences profoundly transform its character and whose net effect is to exacerbate the underlying tensions, making them even less susceptible to resolution. As the succession of Arab-Israeli wars shows, the causes of the conflict are multiple, complex, and rooted in very different perceptions of security. To an extraordinary degree, the turbulence is due to external factors, which the key protagonists seek to exploit but over which they have little control.

For analytical purposes, these external factors may be identified as follows: technology (the effect of increasingly sophisticated and destructive weapons on strategic thinking and on the growing salience of real estate in security planning); U.S.-Soviet rivalry and involvement in the Arab world; the United Nations; oil; intra-Arab politics and rivalry; anti-Semitism; and international terrorism. Over time, inexorably, each of these factors has intensified the Arab-Israeli confict. As with a chain reaction, there is no longer any way of controlling one independent of the others; all interact, heightening the explosiveness of the critical mass.

TECHNOLOGY

Technology has telescoped geography and placed a premium on real estate in calculations of security. Each generation of weapons reinforces the enduring importance of strategic depth to absorb the initial shock of invasion, permit a rapid and orderly mobilization of reserves, and deploy for an effective counterattack. The technological revolution in weaponry and the study of its effect on military strategy are particularly important to Israel, because of the country's small size and conviction that its first defeat will also be its last. Israeli analysts are quick to note that had the Arab armies in October 1973 attacked an Israel confined to its pre-June 1967 borders, the outcome might have been very different.

No country is less favorably endowed with defensible borders or more vulnerable to attack than Israel. Since biblical times this narrow land bridge in the eastern Mediterranean linking Asia Minor and Africa, has seen dozens of invaders. As technology has shrunk distances, it has made even more difficult the defense of this tiny parcel of land. The statistics convey some of the enormity of the challenge faced by Israeli planners.

Under the U.N. partition plan, the Jews were allotted approximately 5,500 square miles (most of which was the Negev Desert) of the mandate and the Palestinian Arabs 4,600 square miles. When the first Arab-Israeli war (the costliest to date for Israel, with more than 6,000 killed) failed to destroy the infant Jewish state, Israel emerged in early 1949 in possession of 7,993 square miles (about the size of New Jersey) and two Arab countries had the remainder: Jordan controlled the West Bank, a kidney-shaped area of 2,270 square miles west of the Jordan River, stretching about 80 miles on a north-south axis and bulging from about 34 miles to within 9 miles of the Mediterranean in places; and Egypt held the Gaza Strip, a 25-mile-long and 4-9-mile-wide tongue of land that extends to within 40 miles of Tel-Aviv. The distance between Jerusalem and Amman is about 60 miles. From the Jordan River, it would take a tank column less than six hours to reach Tel-Aviv; from bases on the West Bank, a fraction of that time. Over 85 percent of Israel's population and industrial centers are within range of hostile artillery from almost any place on the West Bank. Such are the speeds of supersonic aircraft that Israel's warning time of planes coming from Jordanian or Syrian airfields is less than five minutes, depending on the point of origin. In such circumstances, air defense must always be on full alert.

From 1967 to 1982, before returning the Sinai Peninsula to Egypt as part of the Egyptian-Israeli peace treaty of March 26, 1979, Israel enjoyed optimally short and defensible borders. It is now less apt to return the Golan Heights to Syria or the West Bank to Jordan, since to do so would deprive it of strategic depth on any of its main fronts.

As Arab military power becomes more formidable, Israel insists on the need for secure and recognized borders. The flow into Arab arsenals of massive amounts of the most advanced weaponry that oil money can buy and the Soviet Union can provide to anti-American clients has made the Arab-Israel arena the most heavily militarized in the world. Talk of

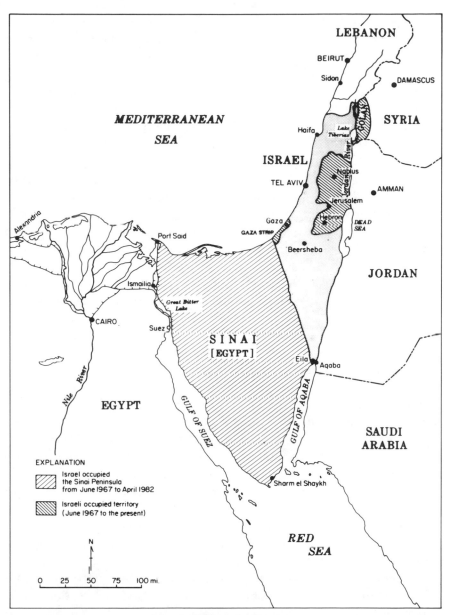

Map 3: 1967 to the Present.

71

trust and accommodation, and scenarios of compromise, stimulated by Egyptian President Anwar Sadat's dramatic decision to make peace with Israel, are belied by the extensive military buildup since the October War. According to *The Military Balance* for 1982-1983, published by the International Institute for Strategic Studies in London, the frontline Arab states (Egypt, Syria, Jordan, and Saudi Arabia) possess about 7,500 heavy battle tanks to Israel's 3,600; 1,200 combat aircraft to its 630; and four times Israel's artillery. Even allowing for the exclusion of Iraq, which will likely be preoccupied by its conflict with Iran for years to come, the military capacity of the other Arab states could provide an additional 50 percent to Arab forces, in the event of another Arab-Israeli war. In terms of equipment, combat-ready troops, and firepower, these figures are comparable to those of NATO forces in Europe. (France has only 1,100 tanks; Britain less than 1,000). What makes the military buildup especially dangerous is the confined area within which the weapons are deployed— the combined area of Israel, Jordan, Lebanon, and Syria being little more than one-half the size of France—and the political hairtrigger on which they are cocked.

Arab analysts would argue that the overall effect of the arms buildup and race has been to decrease, not increase, the interdependence between possession of territory and increments of security; that technology has rendered bits of real estate anachronistic; and that the range and destructiveness of modern weapons such as supersonic aircraft, missiles, and precision-guided munitions make virtually meaningless the possession of topographical obstacles such as hills or the rocky, boulder-strewn Golan Heights.[1] According to John Edwin Mroz, they believe Israel's "preoccupation with *secure and defensible borders* is a 'cover-up for real Israeli intentions to continue Israeli expansion and annexation of Arab lands in accordance with long-stated Zionist goals'."[2] These arguments are logical outgrowths of the position of key Arab actors, who not only possess much more territory for strategic defense and maneuvers, but also are not faced with the threat of extinction as nation-states. Moreover, downgrading the importance of real estate is a useful position in their efforts to persuade the United States to pressure Israel to pull back to the June 1967 borders.

Israeli planners, on the other hand, have become more—not less— convinced of the importance of real estate in an era of mobile, supersonic, and electronic warfare. In this respect, the October War, even more than the June War, was a doctrinal watershed. Whereas prior to 1967, Israeli military doctrine was rooted in "an offensive military strategy to compensate for its numerical disadvantage, lack of strategic depth, and absence of acceptable borders with it neighbors," with preemption and retaliation essential ingredients of military policy,[3] after October 1973 security became linked to territory. A month after the war, as the shock slowly wore off, Defense Minister Moshe Dayan in a major assessment of the tribulations ahead warned against returning to the "shrunken and twisted" boundaries of before June 1967 and against coming down from the Golan Heights or abandoning the River Jordan as a security frontier or removing radar installations from the Nablus hills.[4] Acknowledging that there were differing views within Israel and major differences with the United States over borders, he noted that boundaries would be the key issue at any peace conference and that "we must make it clear to ourselves, and to others what we will not give up under any circumstances—whether in return for guarantees, or under pressure, or whatever." Several years later, Israel's former Chief-of-Staff, Lt.-General Mordecai Gur, who is regarded as a relative dove on the issue of relinquishing territory for peace, made the same point:

> The question of the importance of territory in modern warfare is raised only by ignoramuses. The more sophisticated and deadly weapons systems become, not only does territory not lose its value at times it has no substitute. Since the Yom Kippur War and the introduction of sophisticated weapons systems and enlargement of the armed forces, the need for maneuverability has greatly increased. The deadliness of the sophisticated weapons systems obligates the bringing-up of large reserves, (and) their speedy concentration and dispersal. All this requires much territory.[5]

The modernization of Arab armies, and their ability to replace losses quickly and grow even stronger (for example, in 1967, Syria deployed 450 tanks of which 100 were destroyed—in 1973, 2,700 tanks, of which 1,000 were knocked out), has forged a consensus on the need for a territorial cushion. Judging by the findings of an independent study group organized by Israeli universities to the effect that "by 1986 five Arab countries— Syria, Iraq, Jordan, Saudi Arabia, and Libya—will be able to deploy 12,300 tanks, 11,100 armed personnel carriers, 8,050 artillery pieces, 230 surface-to-surface missile launchers, 2,370 combat planes, 1,045 helicopters, 520 surface-to-air missile batteries and 101 combat ships," no government in Israel, regardless of its political complexion, is likely to accept a major withdrawal from present security positions.[6]

Israel believes that within its present borders it can defend itself. Entrenched along the western slope of the Jordan River Valley, a wide rift that stretches from the Sea of Galilee to the Dead Sea, it can detect hostile activity, and has the depth essential for mobilization, deployment, and defense. By contrast, an Arab army operating from the West Bank with both the speed of advance and firepower that come with modern weapons is seen as a military planner's nightmare. Nor would a demilitarized Palestinian state diminish the potential threat:

> Even if such a state had no significant regular forces of its own (how would anyone keep it to that promise?), it could enable a regular Arab army to move from east of the Jordan to within 10 to 15 miles of the Mediterranean in three hours or less—far less time than it would take Israel to mobilize. An Arab armoured column could then cut Israel in no less than an hour, on any one of 50 available roads.[7]

The perennial shadow cast by proximate Arab military forces means that any territorial concessions made by Israel concerning Golan and the West Bank would eventuate in far less favorable lines of defense, established nearer to its centers of population and industry, and in circumstances that would complicate defensive dispositions in the event of a simultaneous attack from several directions. Precisely because modern weapons technology initially gives an aggressor a lethal edge, Israel's diminutive size, small population, reliance on a civilian rather than a standing army, and limited resources make real estate a valuable asset in any planning for survival.

Suggestions that early-warning stations and demilitarized zones could be a suitable alternative for defensible borders and strategic depth, allowing sufficient time to absorb an initial assault and mobilize a counterattack, lose their persuasiveness as they seek to specify the terms of the trade-off—"how much distance is it possible to exchange for how many early-warning stations, or how much distance is it possible to exchange for such and such a number of demilitarized kilometers."[8] The calculation loses cogency because the problem is trying to square security needs with so small a circle of land. According to Moshe Arens, demilitarized zones introduce the doubtful "trigger" concept, "according to which entry into demilitarized zones would constitute the 'trigger,' the red line that would provoke a parallel preventive action. We point to a considerable number of areas in which the 'trigger' did not in fact operate, and we can also foresee situations in the future, based on political motives and considerations connected with the decision-making process of various bodies, which cast doubt upon the efficiency of the 'trigger'."⁹

Whereas the issues raised by Israel's occupation of the West Bank (Judea and Samaria) are primarily political, involving as they do the future of the Palestinians, those pertaining to the Golan Heights are strategic and military, enormously complicated by the capability of modern weapons. In December 1981 the government of Menachem Begin annexed the 500 square miles of occupied land on the Golan Heights, but no Syrian government is apt to accept the loss as permanent. Just as Syrian forces on the Golan constituted a threat to Israel, so now, as seen from Syria, do Israeli troops there threaten Damascus, 40 miles away. No immediate solution is in prospect, since neither side has been willing to accept a demilitarization acceptable to the other.

The problem is to find a balance between potential risk and palpable gain, as Egypt and Israel did in 1979, when diplomatic recognition and a peace treaty led to Israel's return of Sinai. That treaty is intended to preclude another armed conflict between the two countries, and it reduces the likelihood of war occurring in other Arab-Israeli sectors. But it is not a promising model for the Syrian-Israeli (or Jordanian-Israeli) fronts. Whereas Sinai serves as a sizable buffer zone separating the heartland of Egypt from the heartland of Israel and makes a surprise buildup and attack virtually impossible, the Golan Heights (and West Bank) are so situated that whoever controls them retains a major military advantage. One need not be a geographical determinist to appreciate the advantage that control gives to the possessor.

Unlike the Arab states, Israel has a small regular army. It relies on its ability to mobilize and deploy its reserves quickly. Also, it cannot afford to fight a long war. Given its vulnerability and limited resources, Israel needs to deter wars, not wage and win them. Though deterrence failed in 1967, 1970, and 1973, still it is at the heart of Israel's defense policy, and the conviction is strong that the present borders with Syria and Jordan best serve the security needs of the country for the foreseeable future. Because of the buildup of powerful Arab arsenals, Israel's propensity is to hold on to the terrain it controls, thereby reinforcing Arab beliefs in its inherently expansionist impulse and fueling new tensions and a costly, dangerous arms race.

U.S.-SOVIET RIVALRY AND INVOLVEMENT
IN THE ARAB WORLD

The involvement of the Soviet Union and the United States has significantly affected the evolution of the Arab-Israeli conflict. Each for its own different reasons favored the partition of Palestine and made the creation of the state of Israel possible. Indeed, without the votes of the Soviet Union and its East European satellites, the required two-thirds majority in the U.N. General Assenbly would not have been mustered. During the crucial period between the U.N. vote for partition on November 29, 1947 and the end of the British mandate at midnight on May 14, 1948, the Soviet Union provided vital assistance to the Jewish underground. Disregarding the U.N. arms embargo on the Middle East, it arranged for Czechoslovakia's sale of arms and their transit through Hungary, Romania, and Yugoslavia to Palestine through the British blockade; permitted Jewish immigrants to leave Soviet-controlled Eastern Europe for Palestine; made military facilities available to teach them how to use small arms; and trained Jewish pilots and other officers (mainly in Czechoslovakia).[10] These cadres played a critical role in the 1948 war.

Much has been made of President Harry S Truman's de facto recognition of the new state of Israel minutes after the British mandate ended. But it was the Soviet Union that on May 17 was the first country to extend de jure recognition, and that gave the most significant assistance to Israel during its war of independence. Without the flow of arms, immigrants, and support from the Soviet bloc, Israel would not have survived beyond infancy. Thus, out of his desire to weaken the British position in the Middle East and possibly his expectation that given the disproportionate number of Russians and East Europeans in key posts the leadership would be pro-Soviet, it was Stalin who was instrumental in the creation of the Jewish state. However, after the General Armistice Agreements of 1949 ending the First Arab-Israeli War, Moscow abandoned its partisanship toward Israel and gradually reversed its policy, by the mid-1950s embracing the Arab side of the conflict. The reasons for this turnaround were a combination of Stalin's anti-Semitic campaign at home, attacks on Zionism and "cosmopolitanism" as facades for his purges of allegedly independent-minded and nationalist Communists in Eastern Europe, disillusionment with Israel's pro-Western orientation, and realization that a pro-Arab tilt offered more possibilities for weakening the West's control of the Middle East.

After Stalin died in March 1953, exploitation of divisions in the Arab world and courtship of anti-Western Arab governments became a prominent feature of Soviet diplomacy. The arms deal with Nasser in August 1955, brokered through Czechoslovakia, signified the advent of the USSR's forward policy in the Arab world. Moscow's aims were unmistakably strategic: to undermine the U.S. policy of containment, establish a Soviet presence, and encourage the anti-Western components of Arab nationalism. The prime targets were Egypt and Syria, both of which opposed Western military pacts in the area and welcomed alternative sources of arms to counter their Western-supplied regional rivals.

Moscow concentrated on Nasser, whose nationalization of the Suez Canal Company, help to the Algerians rebelling against France, and military buildup stung Britain, France, and Israel, respectively, and prompted their attack on him in October 1956. Though it was President Eisenhower's opposition that forced the aggressors to withdraw and saved Nasser, it was the Soviet Union whose prestige rose spectacularly in the Arab world as it replaced lost Egyptian arms, extended economic assistance, and championed Nasser in the United Nations.

The decade that followed saw important changes in the Arab world: Nasser's emergence as the dominant figure on the Arab scene; the destruction of the pro-Western monarchy in Iraq in July 1958, leading to the dissolution of the Baghdad Pact and Iraq's embrace of nonalignment with a pro-Soviet tilt; and the rise of radical nationalist, antimonarchical, anti-Western Arab regimes and movements. In this setting, Moscow exploited the Arab-Israeli conflict to penetrate the Arab world and polarize Arab-Western relationships. It extended increasing amounts of economic aid, including assistance for the construction of the Aswan High Dam. But its stake was still modest; and it did not have the military capability to challenge the United States directly.

Despite occasional tiffs with Nasser, whose anti-Communist outbursts and on-again, off-again efforts to improve relations with the Western countries annoyed Moscow, the Soviet leadership gave pride of place to its Cairo connection. After May 1961, with Albania's eviction of the Soviets from the naval base they had enjoyed at Valona since 1945 and the U.S. deployment of Polaris submarines in the Mediterranean, it pressed efforts to obtain naval facilities in Egyptian ports. This quest, buttressed by the Soviet high command's interest in a foothold on the Yemeni coast, prompted Moscow to subsidize Nasser's Vietnam-like intervention in the Yemeni civil war in late 1962. While help to Egypt did not bring privileged access until after the 1967 war, it did encourage Nasser to follow a policy in Yemen that narrowed his options, made him increasingly dependent on the USSR, and foreclosed any possibility of a rapprochement with the United States, which acceded to Saudi Arabia's policy of opposing the Nasserist side in the Yemeni fighting.

While Moscow from the very beginning discerned some advantage in partisanship on Arab-Israeli issues, Washington was more embarrassed than engaged, and tried to keep its distance from them. From 1949 to 1967 it saw the conflict as detrimental to the fashioning of an anti-Soviet containment policy and to the forging of close links with Arab nationalists and the oil-rich Arab countries. Until the June War, U.S. decision making on the Middle East was dominated by a pro-Arab and antiimperial outlook that considered Israel an irritation and Britain and France colonial anachronisms, all to be avoided lest they embarrass Washington's courtship of the Arab world. But even Eisenhower's rescue of Nasser failed to secure his friendship or that of any other Arab nationalist.

U.S.-Egyptian relations deteriorated, primarily because Nasser's aims were antithetical to Washington's. The Kennedy administration soon discovered that labeling protagonists according to some predesignated formula was a prescription for political disaster. Thus, notwithstanding his intent to demonstrate that the United States would not automatically support conservative regimes against progressive ones, but would extend economic aid without regard to an Arab government's political system or foreign policy and would steer clear of regional disputes, Kennedy could not ignore Nasser's Soviet-backed intervention in Yemen. The importance of a special relationship with Saudi Arabia and access to Saudi oil led him to oppose Nasser's Yemeni adventure. When Lyndon Johnson succeeded to the presidency, he tried to maintain a correct relationship with Cairo, but the Yemeni War and Nasser's testiness soured the effort. In general, throughout this period of unrequited courtship of Arab radical nationalist regimes (Egypt, Iraq, Algeria, Syria), Washington gingerly steered clear of Arab-Israeli issues. With the exception in 1962 of Kennedy's sale to Israel of some batteries of Hawk surface-to-air missiles for air defense, the United States refused to sell arms to Israel, whose principal suppliers prior to the 1967 war were France and Britain.

The superpowers' response to the June War transformed the Arab-Israeli conflict from a troublesome regional conflict into a dangerous one with global implications, though this was not immediately apparent. Both superpowers watched as the local antagonists fought. Even if Moscow had contemplated intervention, which was unlikely, the battle was decided too quickly for its aid to have been effective. Militarily, in June 1967, Moscow lacked, as it no longer did in October 1973, a major airlift capability and a Mediterranean fleet that could neutralize the U.S. Sixth Fleet. The Soviet decision to reequip Egyptian and Syrian forces after Nasser's stunning defeat surprised Washington, but was not considered a cause for immediate alarm. Preoccupied in Vietnam, the United States was content to watch the dust settle. Unlike Eisenhower, Johnson did not pressure the Israelis to withdraw unilaterally. Different circumstances, he believed, entitled them to hold on to bargaining chips for negotiations leading to an eventual settlement. Johnson, and later Nixon, consigned the Arab-Israeli problem to the State Department, an indication of low priority, where it remained mired in bureaucratic infighting, isolated from the White House's priorities until the spring of 1970.

The Soviet Union, too, proceeded cautiously. Worried over deteriorating relations with China and interested in detente in Europe, it concentrated on rebuilding Egyptian and Syrian armies and supporting the Arabs diplomatically in the United Nations. In August 1968 it intervened in Czechoslovakia; and in early 1969 its China problem took an ominous turn, as fighting broke out along the Ussuri River. Moreover, with the start of strategic arms limitations talks (SALT) and the coming to office in West Germany in the fall of 1969 of Willy Brandt, who favored improved relations with East Germany and the Soviet Union, Moscow had reason to prefer the status quo: Nasser was dependent, the Soviet military had acquired coveted military privileges (the use of air bases and ready access to Egyptian port facilities), and U.S. standing in the Arab world was at an all-time low. (Many Arab governments had broken off diplomatic relations, blaming Washington for the Arab's defeat, even though it had not aided Israel.) As the superpowers edged toward negotiations that looked to detente in Europe and agreement on strategic delivery systems, they shared a desire to keep the lid on the Middle East pot.

Nasser had other ideas. To lend credibility to Egypt's diplomatic efforts and his public pronouncements, which were designed to create a crisis atmosphere that would impel the United Nations and especially the superpowers to intervene and force an Israeli withdrawal from occupied Arab lands, he started his War of Attrition in September 1968. Desultory Egyptian bombardments along the Suez Canal and occasional commando forays into Israeli-occupied Sinai intensified in the spring of 1969 and in the summer assumed the character of a new war. The fighting jeopardized the superpowers' tacit understanding to maintain the status quo and exposed the ineluctable implications of their deepening involvement, which was to be even more dangerously manifested in October 1973.

But Nasser's military pressure on Israel backfired, resulting in heavy

Egyptian losses along the canal from the relentless pounding by the Israeli air force and in Israeli deep penetration raids, which by mid-January 1970 had extended to the outskirts of Cairo itself. Fearful of defeat, Nasser made a secret visit to Moscow, where he persuaded Soviet leaders to raise the ante of aid sharply—to commit missile crews, pilots, and air defense teams for the protection of Egypt's heartland. Washington watched anxiously, wondering how far Moscow was prepared to go on behalf of Egypt, as Soviet combat forces blunted Israeli attacks and moved Egypt's missile umbrella back to the canal. The cease-fire of August 7, 1970 ended the fighting until 1973, when the involvement of the superpowers begat near confrontation.

Over the years, expanding Soviet and American commitments have added a number of dimensions to the Arab-Israeli conflict, whose very character has been altered significantly as a consequence. These dimensions may be viewed in terms of their local, regional, and global aspects.

At a local level, Soviet arms gave Arab leadership a military option. In 1967, 1969-70, and 1973, they made war possible. Without them, the Arab-Israeli conflict could not have become the world's costliest and most dangerous. The availability of increasing quantities of highly sophisticated and diverse weaponry to the region's most militant and anti-American regimes has stiffened their opposition to compromise settlements that fall short of maximalist demands. The effect is to keep the region's armed camps on tenterhooks, planning and waiting for the next outbreak of fighting.

For its part, the Soviet Union fuels the arms race because it realizes that its principal attraction for anti-Western Arab states is its open weapons tap and its readiness to shield them from possible defeat at the hands of Israel or their Western-armed regional rivals (as for example, in protecting Libya against Egypt). Arms and protection do not directly bring influence, but they do enable Moscow to foster opposition to U.S. policy. As the world's largest producer of conventional weapons, the Soviet Union has ample stockpiles to draw from. Its willingness to replenish, unhesitatingly, Arab losses in battle has political effects; for example, replacing Syrian losses in Lebanon, as in the summer of 1982, eases the pressure on hardline Arabs to consider negotiations as a possibile way out of the impasse with Israel. In striking fashion, with each resupply of a client who is thereafter made stronger than before, Moscow has signalled its political determination to stay the course and deny the United States a free hand in the Arab East.

At a regional level, the Soviet Union uses the Arab-Israeli conflict to assure itself at any given time of a welcome in some parts of the Arab world, notably where there is undiminished opposition to accommodation and a political settlement with Israel, and an anti-American policy bias. Through the consequent polarization, Moscow hopes to frustrate U.S. efforts to organize a Western-oriented coalition and foster cooperation in the region. The Soviet Union has gone very far in protecting clients who oppose Israel from defeat at the hands of their pro-U.S. rivals. Since 1967, there has not been one instance in which it whittled away or reneged on a basic commitment. At times this required that Moscow defer to a client's preferences and even risk confrontation with the United States. But each time Moscow paid the price—in 1969-70, during Nasser's War of Attrition; in October 1973; in 1976 during Syrian President Hafez Assad's intervention in Lebanon; and again in 1982 after the Israeli-Syrian fighting in Lebanon's Bekka Valley.

A global implication that has emerged from the superpowers' involvement and affected the character of the Arab-Israeli conflict is their seemingly shared aim of denying Israel—or severely limiting—political benefits from any military victory. The reasons are quite simple: the Arabs are 40 times more numerous; they possess strategically valuable real estate and vast reserves of oil; and they enjoy widespread diplomatic support in the rest of the Muslim world and elsewhere among the Afro-Asian and Latin American members of the international system. And each superpower considers it useful, in the context of their ongoing rivalry, to attract as many adherents as possible to its side.

The United States is firmly committed to the survival and security of the state of Israel, but its national interest requires decent relations with the Arab world. To this end, since 1973, it has mounted impressive diplomatic efforts to negotiate piecemeal settlements of the Arab-Israeli conflict. Its initiatives and pressures are felt most acutely by Israel. Without them, however, Sadat would not have embarked on his historic journey to Jerusalem and Camp David, nor would there have been an Egyptian-Israeli peace treaty. Finding ways of advancing the peace process is integral to U.S. policy toward the Arab world. This will from time to time inevitably result in serious disputes with Israel. But all the countries of the region have come to accept the centrality of the United States in any attempt to promote a political settlement.

With the exception of Jimmy Carter's abortive diplomatic initiative in September-October 1977, successive U.S. presidents have sought to keep the Soviets out of serious negotiations between Arabs and Israelis. For example, shortly after the October War, Secretary of State Henry

Kissinger arranged disengagement agreements between Egypt and Israel and between Syria and Israel without Soviet participation; and Carter's monumental effort that led to Camp David was made without the Soviet Union. Though none of this was to Moscow's liking, the Soviet Union has never undertaken a major diplomatic initiative of its own to foster an Arab-Israeli settlement: its hostility toward Israel, with which it has yet to restore diplomatic relations broken in June 1967, is so pronounced as to call into question its ability to serve as an honest broker; and, in the case of Egypt at least, Moscow was viewed with great suspicion by Sadat, who preferred that it not be brought into the negotiations. In the Middle East, Moscow is known as an arms supplier, not a peacemaker.

When looking to the future, it is important to keep the past clearly in mind. The October War was a watershed in U.S.-Soviet rivalry in the Arab world. For the first time both superpowers were equally involved in a crisis each viewed with the utmost seriousness, not only with regard to their respective client states but with regard to each other; for the first time they were locked in direct confrontation in the Arab-Israeli arena; for the first time they found themselves on a collision course there, even though elsewhere they were diligently trying to stabilize their global relationship; and this was the first crisis in a period when the Soviet Union enjoyed nuclear equivalence. They invested the specific local stakes at issue with an importance that affected basic perceptions of the global balance of power.

THE UNITED NATIONS

The United Nations bears much responsibility for the globalization of the Arab-Israeli conflict. On this issue, more than on any other of our age, it became a cockpit of contentiousness, an arena for a struggle that seeks advantage, not accommodation, where sleight-of-hand maneuvering is regularly on public display.

For approximately the first decade after the establishment of the United Nations in 1945, the five permanent members of the Security Council (Britain, China, France, the United States, and the USSR), each with a veto power over substantive questions affecting international peace and security, dominated the deliberations of the organization. With decolonization and the more than tripling of the United Nations's membership in the second and third decades of its existence, the great powers, especially the superpowers, had to adjust their policy to the changing character of the U.N. system, a development they had not fore-seen or encouraged, yet one they dared not ignore. For political and psychological reasons, the Soviet Union and the United States want the backing of Third World countries, even though the latter do not possess the wherewithal to alter significantly the relationship between the super-powers themselves.

With near universality of membership, the General Assembly, as well as the many regional economic commissions, specialized agencies, and ancillary functional organizations, all of which lay outside the purview of the veto power, fell under the sway of the Third World countries. To maximize their bargaining power, these nations formed miniblocs along geographic lines, for example, the Arab bloc, the Latin American, and the sub-Saharan African. All of this placed a premium on bloc voting and on the unquestioning support of one bloc for another on whatever issue it deemed to be of critical importance. Bloc voting tended to become groupthink, and groupthink determined the outcome of votes on Arab-Israeli issues.

The United Nations slowly acquired an anti-Israeli character. After voting for partition, the General Assembly looked on abjectly as Arab armies attacked its creation. (Heavy responsibility for the failure to fore-stall the attack devolves on the U.S. government, then at the height of its influence in the United Nations. Had Truman acted decisively—extended de jure recognition and used U.S. power to uphold partition—the costly cycle of Arab-Israeli wars might have been avoided.) The Arab governments took "great pains to show that no state of war existed, because if it did then they were liable to formal charges of aggression under the Charter, with the possibility of sanctions being applied against them. Also, it would have implied recognition of Israel: a state can declare war only on another state, not on groups of territories and bandits."[11] Not until 1950, a year after the armistice agreements were signed, did Arab representatives, in offhand remarks on the existence of war, "declare war" on Israel. The occasional Security Council resolution critical of the Arabs, such as the one of September 1, 1951, calling on Egypt to permit ships bound for Israel to transit the Suez Canal, was ignored or violated.

The United Nations did have one achievement to its credit in the Arab-Israeli sector in the decade prior to the June War: the establishment of UNEF (United Nations Emergency Force) by the General Assembly on November 5, 1956, to separate Israeli and Egyptian forces and act as a buffer in Sinai and the Gaza Strip. Its usefulness ended abruptly in May 1967, when Secretary-General U Thant acceded with undue haste to

Nasser's request for its removal. By his ineptness U Thant brought on the June War. He also made Israel leery of ever again relying on U.N. peacekeeping forces for its security.

As the body responsible for preserving international peace and security, the U.N. Security Council has adopted two resolutions that are generally accepted as the cornerstones on which an eventual settlement can be built. Resolution 242 of November 22, 1967 remains the key document setting forth the basis for a "just and lasting peace in the Middle East." The result of intensive diplomatic negotiations after the June War, it calls for "withdrawal of Israeli armed forces from territories" (not from *all* the territories) occupied in the war; for "termination of all claims or states of belligerency and respect for and acknowledgment of the sovereignty, territorial integrity and political independence of every State in the area and their right to live in peace with *secure and recognized* boundaries free from threats or acts of force"; and for "a just settlement of the *refugee* problem" (no mention is made of the Palestinians or a Palestinian state) (italics added). Resolution 338 of October 22, 1973, adopted at the end of the October War, calls for implementation of Resolution 242 in all of its parts.

These operative resolutions have been consistently undermined by a succession of extravagantly worded General Assembly resolutions, which, though having only a declaratory and recommendatory character, actually so poison the atmosphere as to preclude negotiation between Arabs and Israelis. For example, General Assembly Resolution 3236 Concerning the Question of Palestine, adopted on November 22, 1974, recognized "the inalienable rights of the Palestinian people in Palestine" to self-determination and the right to national independence and sovereignty; reaffirmed "the inalienable right of the Palestinians to return to their homes and property from which they had been displaced and uprooted"; and "further recognizes the right of the Palestinian people to regain its rights by all means in accordance with the purposes and principles of the Charter of the United Nations." It requested the Secretary-General "to establish contacts with the Palestine Liberation Organization on all matters concerning the question of Palestine." The date of the resolution was a deliberate symbolic attempt to supersede Security Council Resolution 242 and place the PLO in the forefront of attempts to settle the Arab-Israeli conflict. The immediate aims of such resolutions are to isolate Israel and to bring unbearable pressure on it in order to exact unilateral concessions.

As a result, since 1973, all progress toward a settlement and toward ensuring that another war will not occur has been made outside the framework of the United Nations—the series of limited disengagement agreements concluded after the October War; Sadat's historic initiative in November 1977; the Camp David agreements in September 1978; the Egyptian-Israeli peace treaty of March 26, 1979; the deployment of the Sinai Multinational Force and Observers on April 26, 1982, the day after Israel completed its withdrawal from Sinai, in accordance with the Egyptian-Israeli treaty.

In the United Nations attempts have been made to isolate Israel internationally, to make it a pariah among nations. The process that began in the 1950s gathered momentum with the sudden coming of age of Arab oil and money.

Nothing has epitomized the institutionalization of the Arab-Israeli conflict by the United Nations more than UNRWA (United Nations Relief and Works Agency). Established in early 1950 to provide emergency assistance to the 700,000 Palestinian refugees who had lost homes and livelihood as a result of the 1948 war, it became a sinecure for bureaucrats and a breeding ground for hatred and irredentism.

The Arab governments originally refused to cooperate, on the grounds that resettlement of the Palestinians would signify surrender of rights to repatriation in Israel. This alleged concern for a principle veiled indifference to the suffering of fellow Arabs and provided a convenient issue that could be used for a variety of domestic, intra-Arab, and international needs. Only Jordan permitted the Palestinians to become citizens. (Note: The policy of the Arab governments elicits historical comparison with the experience of France, West Germany, India, and Pakistan, all of which acted differently. By way of illustration, in the generation after 1945 more than four million Europeans were expelled from Arab countries—from Libya, Egypt, Algeria, Tunisia, and Morocco; and 800,000 Jews were forced to leave Arab lands, of whom 600,000 went to Israel. They had no U.N. programs established for them, but were promptly absorbed in their new homelands.)

By 1980 a new generation of Palestinians had been born, and UNRWA was keeping two million Palestinians on welfare, their shanty-towns having burgeoned throughout the West Bank, Gaza, Jordan, Lebanon, and Syria. In the process of administering aid programs, it lost its international and eleemosynary character, and was taken over by the PLO. Under UNRWA's imprimatur, the PLO allocated housing and operated schools, health clinics, food-distribution centers, and training camps for guerillas. Over this 30-year period, the United States contributed more than one billion dollars, the Soviet Union nothing, the wealthy Arab governments less than 50 million dollars. The defeat of the PLO forces in Lebanon and Beirut in the summer of 1982 brought to light the full extent to which UNRWA camps had been organized into fronts for caches of arms, centers that "could operate under the cover of a civilian population and cry 'foul' in the event of reprisal," and training grounds for international terrorists.[12]

UNRWA is but one of the many instances that illustrate how the Arab states have utilized the United Nations in the fight against Israel. Israel has been refused membership in any regional economic organization or broadly based political grouping. Because of Arab pressure it is the only Middle East country that is not a member of the U.N. Economic Commission for Western Asia; nor is it part of the Group of 77, the non-aligned grouping, first formed in 1968 by 77 less-developed countries (LDCs) to pursue a common economic strategy (membership exceeds 100, but the original name was retained). Israel has often been accused of "aggression," whereas at no time during the 1948-67 period was Jordan ever even criticized for its seizure and annexation of East Jerusalem and the West Bank, in contravention of the 1947 partition decision; nor was Iraq ever labeled an aggressor for its attack on Iran in September 1980. Even the cultural and educational arena has become politicized: thus, in November 1974, UNESCO's General Conference voted to withhold a trifling amount of money for archeological digs in old Jerusalem and to reject Israel's request to be a member of one of UNESCO's regional groupings. Likewise affected was the World Health Organization (WHO): on May 12, 1983, one day after its director-general reported that an investigation had dismissed as unfounded the charges that Israel poisoned West Bank school girls in March, the WHO's annual Assembly voted 65 to 17 with 25 abstentions to condemn Israel for the outbreaks of illness.

The Arabs' greatest success on the U.N. battlefield was the General Assembly resolution that declared, "Zionism is a form of racism and racial discrimination." The anti-Zionist resolution of November 10, 1975 marked the apogee of Arab influence in the United Nations (and, not coincidentally, of OPEC's strength). Tactically it was possible because of skillful Arab exploitation "of an originally African issue (the U.N. Third Committee's Decade for Action against Apartheid) by the introduction of seven amendments to the resolutions then debated, naming Zionism as an example of racial discrimination the Decade was to combat."

Ultimately, some African states persisted in their opposition to the resolutions as amended; others compromised for the wider "good" of passing out anti-apartheid resolutions, while a third group of countries went along fullheartedly with the *de facto* anti-semitic resolution.

Moreover, a number of African (and especially Latin American) states that were originally opposed to the by-then consolidated single anti-Zionist resolution, voted in its favor out of anger at either U.S. pressure or U.S. Ambassador Moynihan's October 3rd San Francisco speech in which he stated that Idi Amin ('this racist murderer') was by 'no accident' also President of the O.A.U.[13]

The resolution produced a cascade of pro-Palestinian sentiments and the "PLO-ization of the U.N.," which intensified invective against Israel and efforts to isolate it.[14] On various occasions, of which the emergency special session of the General Assembly on July 29, 1980 is typical, resolutions were adopted calling for Palestinian "self-determination," for opposition to "all policies and plans aimed at the resettlement of the Palestinians outside their homeland," and for the right of the Palestinian people "to establish its own independent sovereign state."[15] The aim of these parliamentary exercises is, the PLO's chief representative at the United Nations acknowledged, to demonstrate the "irrelevance of [Resolution] 242 to the question of Palestine."[16] Resolutions tailored to PLO specifications are routinely adopted at the United Nations, but they are not the stuff of which diplomatic achievement is made, as Secretary-General Kurt Waldheim discovered when he dropped the facade of the honest broker and openly advocated statehood for the Palestinians in a blatant bid for Arab-bloc support of his candidacy for reelection.[17]

If there is any truth in the observation that the United Nations has become an arena "in which the Arabs are allowed to relate to Israel as if there was a war, while Israel must relate to the Arabs as if there were peace,"[18] no explanation for how this situation came to pass is complete without attention to the power of oil.

OIL

When the Organization of Arab Petroleum Exporting Countries (OAPEC) imposed an oil embargo against the United States and other countries during the October War, it was the first time that Arab oil producers had unsheathed the oil weapon in an effort to affect the outcome of an Arab-Israeli war and prod the United States to bring pressure on Israel; it signified that henceforth political considerations would influence the determination of who obtained Arab oil. It also conveniently dovetailed with the efforts of OPEC (Organization of Petroleum Exporting Countries) to gain monopolistic price control over the world market, a process that had shown signs of strength even before the war.[19]

The effect of Arab petropower was immediately apparent. Twenty African countries, many of them recipients of assistance from Israel, broke off diplomatic relations, though only five had done so after the June War. During the next few years in the highly charged U.N. atmosphere, the string of anti-Israel and pro-Palestinian resolutions attracted near-unanimous support among the Afro-Asian and Latin American countries. Third World countries with little interest in the Arab-Israeli conflict dutifully conformed to bloc dictates, mindful that to get along, one had to go along. As one Nigerian delegate said, "Arab friends insist on our support for their formula. Whether it is accurate or not, it might produce the desired results. That's politics, isn't it?"[20] As importers of oil, most Third World countries hoped Arab oil producers would extend concessionary prices, long-term loans, and grants—petro-balm for their political support.

The West European countries, for the most part traditionally firm supporters of Israel, were also heavily affected by OPEC's price hikes and the Arabs' sudden accumulation of enormous wealth. They, however, were better able than the LDCs to adjust to the quadrupling of oil prices in the year after the war, when oil rose from about $1.77 a barrel to about $9 a barrel (and $34 by 1982).

After the 1973 war, the European Community (EC) quickly signaled a desire for better relations. On November 6, EC foreign ministers noted that "in the establishment of a just and lasting peace, account must be taken of the legitimate rights of the Palestinians." Shortly thereafter, a series of working committees and a political dialogue were established between the EC and the Arab League. Each party perceived this Euro-Arab dialogue quite differently: the Europeans saw it as "another avenue of approach toward stabilizing the price of oil, and ensuring its supply, by placing EC-Arab economic relations on a long-term footing";[21] the Arabs viewed it as preliminary to EC's recognition of the PLO and condemnation of Israel. The Europeans sold sophisticated weapons, courted Arab investment capital, criticized Israel, and in a statement of June 29, 1977, called for the establishment of a "homeland for the Palestinian people." Though disagreeing on the question of recognition of the PLO, in their Venice Declaration of June 13, 1980, they recognized that the PLO enjoys widespread support among Palestinians and "will have to be associated with negotiations"; by not mentioning Security Council Resolution 242, they opened the way for full acceptance of all Arab demands for a return to pre-June 5, 1967 borders and establishment of a Palestinian state. Golda Meir's rebuke of West European socialists after the October War for their lack of support echoed in some ears: "Their throats are choked with oil."[22]

The EC tilt heightened Israel's sense of isolation and dependence on the United States, and complicated its trading and economic relationships with European firms, most of which preferred not to jeopardize access to lucrative Arab markets by doing business with Israel. An Arab blacklist of firms dealing with Israel is drawn up by the Central Boycott Office, based in Damascus since 1951, but each Arab government determines whom it will penalize. Judging by the available data, fear of being blacklisted effectively deters trade with Israel; for example, Britain's share of Israel's imports dropped from 16 percent in 1980 to 8 percent in 1982.

Though Arab petrodollars created serious difficulties for Israel, their effect was limited, because they are not readily transformed into the political influence that can produce desired changes on key substantive issues. Thus, the oil-rich Arab governments finance massive arms purchases; hire the votes of oil-poor LDCs at the United Nations and at meetings of the nonaligned countries; engage able lobbyists from among the ranks of former government officials; and let contracts for billions of dollars for construction and industrial development. Their wealth assures them of electoral support, but not the leverage to move Israel.

By the late 1970s and early 1980s, the Arab oil weapon had lost, for the foreseeable future, much of its frightening aspect, namely, the ability to cripple the economies of major Western importers. As a result of the global recession and unexpected success of energy conservation measures, the demand for oil declined, reversing the cycle of price rises and sharply reducing OPEC's income. Production outstripped demand, notwithstanding the withdrawal from the world market of more than five million barrels of Iranian crude oil a day after the Iranian Revolution. The earnings of the 13-member OPEC group, which had soared to $91 billion in 1974 and peaked at $272 billion in 1980, dropped to $191 billion (estimate) in 1982.[23] This contraction could eat into Arab financial reserves—primarily Saudi Arabia's and Kuwait's—and "have a startling psychological impact, particularly when accompanied by sharp budget cuts, cancellation of major industrial projects, eviction of foreign workers, and cuts in foreign aid, including the war subsidy to Iraq."[24]

There were other reasons as well for the limited effectiveness of the oil weapon. For one, the United States, though hurt, was not hobbled by the rising oil prices on the international market. Indeed, because of its own productive capacity and the increased output of non-OPEC producers, it rode out the crisis better than the West European countries. One analyst believes that the "Oil Arabs" now realize that for the oil weapon to perform effectively on the Arab-Israeli front it has to be directed at the United States in a way that can "cause pain but not excessive damage" and that they are working on such a strategy.[25] At present, however, the oil glut attentuates Arab leverage.

Another reason has been the disappointment of the oil-poor LDCs in the disparity between Arab professions of goodwill and concessions, between rising oil prices and OPEC aid, and between OPEC's revenues and their own foreign payments deficits. Despite the rhetoric of Third World solidarity, they see the Arabs placing most of their bets for movement on the Palestinian issue on the European Community and the United States, and not on anti-Israeli votes in the United Nations.[26] The Africans, to mention one group, value Arab-bloc support on resolutions relating to southern Africa and the New International Economic Order (NIEO), but they are upset at the Arab investment of petrodollar surpluses in Europe and America rather than in Africa; moreover, "Arab aid commitments to non-Arab Africa never exceeded 15 percent of all Arab concessional assistance . . . ; Arab aid disbursements often lagged behind commitments by as much as 35 to 45%; Arab oil appeared all too frequently to be distributed on the basis of political and religious considerations rather than need; and . . . when Arab and African interests become directly opposed, the Arabs—in African eyes—appear willing to forget the fraternal aspects of the relationship."[27]

Finally, rivalries within the Arab world prevent optimum use of the oil weapon. They are also a major factor in an assessment of the past, present, and future of the Arab-Israeli conflict.

INTRA-ARAB POLITICS AND RIVALRIES

The divisions, rivalries, and internal upheavals in the Arab world have profoundly affected the Arab-Israeli conflict in ways that are continually changing and that are as far-reaching as they are unpredictable.

Though deeply rooted in Arab history, they have been indelibly marked by the Ottoman and Western periods of rule. The present-day system of 22 Arab nation-states is the product of post–World War I British and French imperialism and the process of decolonization after World War II. It has endured, despite erratic and emotional efforts at fostering a greater "Arab unity," at giving the term *Qawmiyya*, the sense of loyalty to the larger community, modern forms.

Intra-Arab relations have been justly characterized as a kind of cold war, in which incessant conflict is generated by the clash between those impelled by different visions of authority, society, and organization—whether Islamic, pan-Arab, radical secular, or socialist.[28] Whatever the reasons, basically, differences come down to a struggle for political power. Competing conceptions of who is to rule in what name is the line that divides cliques, factions, movements. They predate the Arab-Israeli conflict and are generated by developments having little or nothing to do with it. For example, it clarifies the vision to realize that the rivalry between Egypt and contemporary Iraq (which was created after World War I out of the Ottoman provinces of Baghdad, Basra, and Mosul) is a hoary, recurrent one, dating from the clash between the Nile civilization of Pharaonic Egypt and the Tigris-Euphrates civilization of Mesopotamia. Thus, when the Arab League was established by the British in March 1945, each considered itself the natural legatee of pan-Arabism.

Another intense, more modern rivalry, between Iraq and Saudi Arabia, dates back to the mid-1920s, when the Saudi family seized power by driving the ruling Hashemites out of Mecca, created the Kingdom of Saudi Arabia, and viewed with suspicion the Hashemite kings (sons of the ousted sherif of Mecca) whom Britain had installed in Iraq and Transjordan (Jordan). Even after Hashemite rule was ended in Iraq as a result of the bloody coup in July 1958, relations remained poor, because of the hostility of Iraq's radical Baath (Resurrection) party to the traditionalist Saudi monarchy and because of Baathist ambitions in the Gulf and opposition to strong Saudi ties to the United States. After the beginning of the Iran-Iraq War in September 1980, however, Iraq's need for Saudi financial assistance and an end to its threat to Saudi preeminence on the Arabian Peninsula led to better relations—for the time being.

There are comparable rivalries, for example, between Libya and Egypt, Egypt and Saudi Arabia, Syria and Iraq, Algeria and Morocco, Libya and the Sudan, and Syria and Jordan. The extensive literature in the social sciences has periodically attempted to categorize them as struggles between those who advocate the nation-state and those who espouse confederation of a unitary state; between monarchist and republican, radical and reformist, revolutionary and traditionalist; Baathist and Nasserite, Islamic fundamentalist and pragmatic relativist, city dweller and Bedouin. Or it may be that no elaborate formulations have quite the explanatory power of the observation on factionalism among the Arabs made by Ibn Khaldun, the great Arab historian of the fourteenth century:

> Every Arab is eager to be the leader. Scarcely a one of them would cede his power to another . . . the Arabs are the least willing of nations to subordinate themselves to each other, as they are rude, proud, ambitious, and eager to be the leader. Their individual aspirations rarely coincide. But when there is religion (among them) through prophecy or sainthood, then they have some restraining influence in themselves. The qualities of haughtiness and jealousy leave them. It is, then, easy for them to subordinate themselves and to unite (as a social organization).[29]

Explanations change like wadis after a desert storm.

The intra-Arab rivalries that directly but in different ways affect the Arab-Israeli conflict involve countries (and movements) that are contiguous to Israel. Egypt, Syria, Jordan, Lebanon, and the PLO are the principals. It is they who have borne the brunt of the Arab wars with Israel, they who have the most at stake, and they who most affect the course and character of the conflict. (Perhaps Saudi Arabia, situated just across the narrow Gulf of Aqaba from Israel, should now be included, because of its enormously enhanced military capability since the mid-1970s.)

The impact of these rivalries has varied. The first Arab-Israeli War was an outgrowth of the mutual suspicions of the members of the Arab League and "their anxiety to deny their rivals the opportunity to annex parts of Palestine or establish a dominant influence there."[30] The establishment of the Arab League had been an expression of Britain's attempt to preserve its influence in the Arab east and of pan-Arab sentiment and unhappiness over Palestine. The organization was immediately split, with Egypt and Saudi Arabia aligning against the Hashemite kingdoms of Iraq and Jordan. With respect to Palestine, writes the distinguished historian, Elie Kedourie, "the problem was two-fold: first, how to defeat Zionist ambitions . . . ; second, —and just as important—how to ensure advantage for oneself in the struggle for Palestine and how to ensure that one's rivals within the League did not in any way make the Palestine-Arab cause a vehicle for their own territorial and power-political ambitions."[31]

They could agree only on the need to frustrate the General Assembly's partition decision. Soon after the U.N. vote, Arab troops entered Palestine, while Britain was still the mandatory power. Fighting spread, and on May 15, 1948 the Arab League informed the Security Council of its military intervention. There was no unified Arab command: Egypt, Syria, Iraq, and Jordan all sent in troops for reasons of their own, without any overall plan. Jordan, supported by Iraq, sought to place Palestine under Hashemite rule and move toward the pan-Arab realization of a "Greater Syria," that is, a merger of Jordan, Palestine, Syria, and Iraq into a unitary Arab state; Egypt and Saudi Arabia, on the other hand, wanted an independent Palestine under Haj Amin al-Husseini, the grand mufti of Jerusalem, who had instigated the terrorism and anti-Jewish violence in Palestine in the 1930s, spent the war years in Berlin working for the Nazis, and turned up in Cairo in 1946 to spark anti-Zionist agitation.[32]

No one inquired what the Arabs of Palestine thought or wanted.

Egypt's King Farouk sought to deny Palestine to Jordan and restore the monarchy's sagging prestige at home with a speedy victory on the battlefield. Israel's resistance turned his anticipated triumph into a bewildering defeat and caused antiregime riots in Cairo (and in July 1952, his peaceful deposal by a group of army officers, led by Gamal Abdel Nasser, angered by the government's humiliating performance in the Palestine war). Jordanian successes in seizing the West Bank and East Jerusalem prompted the Egyptian press to denounce as a "stab in the back for Islam" the call of the Jordanian-created Palestine Congress for "the union of Arab Palestine under Transjordan under the title of 'South Syria'."[33]

By their intervention the Arab governments inadvertently contributed to Israel's territorial enlargement, internal cohesiveness, and international support. Their actions also played a crucial role in the formation of Israel's emphasis on military preparedness and quest for defensible borders.

A combination of domestic pressures and another intra-Arab rivalry —this time between Egypt and Iraq—also set in motion the chain of events that culminated in the 1956 war. Iraq's accession to the Western-sponsored Baghdad Pact in 1955 was interpreted by Nasser as a ploy to pry arms from the communism-obsessed West and thereby to strengthen Baghdad's claim to leadership in the Arab world. In reaction, and to satisfy the army's desire for modern arms to deal with Israel, he turned to Moscow. The subsequent influx of Soviet arms led Ben-Gurion to launch a preemptive attack a year later.

Intra-Arab rivalry was the catalyst for the chain reaction in May-June

1967. The Arab-Israeli sector had been relatively quite for almost a decade. The Arab world was absorbed with pan-Arabism, radical nationalism, and anti-Westernism. In Nasser, whose resistance in 1956 had made him into a charismatic figure in the Arab world, pan-Arabism found a champion. The union with Syria, short-lived though it was (1958 to 1961), the overthrow of the Iraqi monarchy in July 1958, the growing prominence of the unity-spouting Baath movement, and the seeming precariousness of the monarchy's hold on Jordan all seemed to augur further strides toward the illusive goal of Arab unity. But as Ibn Khaldun had observed centuries earlier, every Arab saw himself as the leader. Though deified by the masses, Nasser found bitter rivals in the Baath party leaderships brought to power by coups in Iraq and Syria (1963). The Baathists, conspiratorial and usually at odds with each other, vied with Nasser in denouncing the West, preaching the destruction of Israel, and calling for the toppling of the monarchies in Jordan and Saudi Arabia. The more they consolidated personal power in the hands of a narrow range of sectarian supporters (the Takritis in Iraq and the Alawites in Syria), the more they gave lip service to unity and indulged in demagoguery and vilification.

In May 1967 tension suddenly escalated between Syria and Israel. To Syrian taunts that he was hiding behind the blue flag of the United Nations, Nasser reacted by sending his army into Sinai, demanding the withdrawal of UNEF, and closing the Straits of Tiran. There was no reason for his excessive display and deployment of strength, no plan for liquidating Israel, no calculation of consequences, and no Israeli threat—only an impulsive set of responses and a hastily formed coalition with heretofore hostile Syria and Jordan. Overnight the embittered exchanges of previous years were muted in a moment of high excitation. The stunning Arab defeat, as momentous as the one in 1948, was testament to the moral bankruptcy and irresponsibility of Arab leaders, and it irrevocably altered the pre-1967 status quo.

Six years later, Egypt and Syria, intent on regaining their lands, mounted a coordinated attack, but gave little thought to how to end the battle and secure their gains. Within weeks their cooperation vanished in a welter of recrimination. Sadat responded to Washington's intercession, discarded the Soviets, and looked to the Americans to complete at the negotiating table what he had begun on the battlefield. By leaving Syria to fend for itself, he reaffirmed the hostility between Cairo and Damascus. What divides them now are antithetical policies epitomized by Egypt's pro-U.S. orientation under Sadat and Hosni Mubarak, treaty with Israel, and eschewal of force to settle the Palestinian issue. By his dramatic turnabout, Sadat transformed and defused the Arab-Israel conflict. As regards confrontation with Israel, observed Fouad Ajami, "it being a military task, there simply is no way that another war could be waged without Egypt. In one metaphor, recent Egyptian policies are a 'gladiator's revolt': the Arab state that did most of the fighting decided to change its profession."[34]

Events in Lebanon since the Israeli invasion of June 1982 confirm Ajami's assessment. Neither Syria nor any other member of the anti-Egypt Arab coalition (known as the Steadfastness Front) came to the help of the Palestine Liberation Organization, Libya's Qaddafi suggesting that Arafat commit suicide. The PLO was mauled, perhaps beyond recovery, by Israeli forces and driven from its strongholds in southern Lebanon and Beirut, where vast caches of arms and equipment from East and West had been accumulated.[35] By being deprived of an independent territorial base whence to organize a mini-state-in-exile and strike at will against Israel, it has suffered the most grievous defeat in its history, far more than its defeat in Jordan in September 1970 and its bloody expulsion a year later.

Jordan's role in intra-Arab rivalries has also influenced the course of the Arab-Israeli conflict. The part of Palestine that King Abdallah seized in 1948, his grandson, King Hussein, lost in 1967 when, in a moment of uncharacteristic recklessness, he succumbed to the mixture of Syrian and Egyptian pressure and euphoria. The resulting emergence of Palestinian nationalism as a force in its own right; Israel's reunification of Jerusalem, settlement of the West Bank, and greatly improved military advantage vis-à-vis Jordan; and reputed reminders from Arab leaders that they prefer the PLO to stay uncoupled from Jordan in any negotiations concerning occupied territories west of the Jordan River, have all made Hussein wary of proposals that seek to enmesh him in talks with Israel. He professes a willingness to explore a possible solution of the Palestinian issue with Israel but hedges these statements to Western officials and media with conditions that enable him conveniently and safely to keep aloof.

King Hussein may occasionally nibble at Washington's bait to enter into talks with Israel about the future of the West Bank, Gaza, and Eastern Jerusalem, but he is unlikely to be hooked. For reasons that have to do with history, demography, and politics, he knows that a revival of the PLO's fortunes can only weaken his position; on the other hand, continued stalemate, with Israel bearing the burden of coping with Palestinian aspirations, greatly enhances his chances of survival.

Palestinian nationalism is the main threat to Hussein's rule. Hussein and the Bedouin tribes on whom he depends find themselves a minority in their own country. When the emirate of Transjordan was created by the British in 1922 from the original Palestine mandate, the population east of the Jordan River was overwhelmingly Bedouin. But after 1948 the better-educated and politically restless Palestinians threatened to wrest political control from the monarchy, prompting a ban on all political parties as far back as 1957. Today, Jordan proper has a population of about 2.5 million, of whom less than 40 percent are of Bedouin stock. A return of territories occupied by Israel in 1967 with its more than one million Palestinians and strong PLO constituency could trigger new tensions between them and those of Bedouin stock and jeopardize Hussein's dearly-paid-for stability.

Palestinian nationalist fervor has been Hussein's *bête noire* since a fanatic assassinated his grandfather in September 1951. After Arafat's forces had behaved as if the country were theirs and Hussein an interloper, he forced them to flee to Lebanon and Syria in 1970. During the PLO's decade of domination in parts of Lebanon, its arrogance and ruthlessness aroused the same hostility among the Lebanese as it had among the non-Palestinian Jordanians. This explains Hussein's high-wire diplomatic balancing act: he can not say anything against the Palestinians and their "just rights," but he does not want them as part of his domain. Too much should not be attributed to the public reconciliation that took place after the Israelis drove the PLO out of Beirut in August 1982. The last thing Hussein wants is to become a point man for Palestinian aspirations.

Hussein also has reason to avoid peace with Israel because of the vestigial threat from Syria, which is wedded to a vision of Arab unity that entails absorption of Jordan. Several times since 1970, Syria had threatened invasion. The periods of tension are far longer, and come more frequently, than those of accommodation.

These manifold intra-Arab rivalries are aggravated by domestic uncertainties caused by the erratic lurch toward modernity and the still problematic ability to develop strong states capable of promoting security, stability, change, and social justice. Oil has not proved the lubricant for political transformation. Nor has the rhetoric of revolution. As long as Arab regimes lack legitimacy, rule over schismatic societies mired in incessant strife between the tug of the past and the pull of the future, and see the Palestinian issue as both a threat and a convenience, as the "wild card" in the deadly game of Arab politics, a major breakthrough on ending the Arab-Israel conflict is difficult to imagine.

ANTI-SEMITISM

The Arab-Israeli conflict is also fueled by enduring religious and cultural antagonisms at whose center lie very difficult historical experiences and memories. Reconstructions and embellishments of the past serve purposes as varied as legitimizing and undermining authority, and fostering nationbuilding or political mythology.[36] For certain Israelis, what looms large is the Holocaust; for others, the expulsion from Arab lands; for still others, the double standard of the international community. For some Arabs, what looms large is the justness of Palestinian claims to their land; for others, the alien and threatening pro-Western implant of Jews who came in the late nineteenth century and wrested the land from the Arabs; for still others, the Koran's portrayal of the Jews as an iniquitous people, destined for suffering and humiliation.[37]

Religion, though not a primary cause of the Arab-Israeli conflict, is an intrinsic element. It is an important component of the fervor and force that drives the Arabs and Israelis and leads both to have frequent recourse to, and be influenced by, religious symbols.

Though the Arab world is often referred to as if it were a functioning entity, it is, as we have seen, rent by political, ideological, ethnic and religious cleavages. Egypt is very different from Saudi Arabia, Lebanon from Libya, and Syria from Morocco—but certain generalizations must be hazarded.

In the early 1970s, Malcolm Kerr examined the parallels in Arab and Israeli attitudes that "have both arisen in an especially direct way out of their respective religious traditions and are perhaps as much unbroken extensions as surrogates of religious sentiment":

> These are: (1) a sense of one's own special historic destiny in the face of challenge by the adversary; (2) a caricaturized image of the adversary; (3) a belief in the necessity of awaiting or forcing a fundamental transformation in the adversary's character and outlook; (4) the accretion of vested political and psychological interest in the continuation of the conflict; and (5) the prominence of a religious mentality and of quasi-religious symbolism coloring political attitudes.[38]

He noted, among other things, the romanticization of Palestine by the Arabs "as a land of milk, honey, and orange groves, stolen from its rightful owners by the unbelievers" and the frequent parallel to the Crusader episode in which the Arabs would wait and fight for 100 years to regain their patrimony; and on the Israeli side, the intensification of biblical analogies, "sharpened by the unremitting hostility of the Arab enemy" in a pervasive atmosphere "of Armageddon-like totality and finality," which encouraged "in Israelis and their sympathizers a sense of the specially ordained righteousness of their cause, of being charged with a sacred mission to see the conflict through to its successful end steadfastly and determinedly refusing to yield to the temptations of half-solutions by means of compromise and modus vivendi."[39] The hard-line strategies that Kerr discerned on both sides of the Arab-Israeli divide seem solidly entrenched and likely to dominate decision-making perceptions and elites for the foreseeable future, despite the diplomatic breakthrough between Egypt and Israel, and possibly between Lebanon and Israel. In Israel, for example, the word *pe⁰shara* (compromise) has become a political shibboleth, avoided like the plague by spokesmen for the Likud government.

The misuse of religion in the political arena and the hardening of political attitudes that it both reflects and creates may be exemplified in a few frequently heard propositions.

One such statement—that Arabs, being Semites, cannot be anti-Semitic—is a semantic confusion in which Semitic is used, first, to indicate a language group and, second, the Jewish people. By "Semitic," European philologists in the late eighteenth and nineteenth centuries designated a language category. Thus, whereas the term "Aryan" was "first applied to a group of languages spoken in south Asia, to which Sanskrit and its derivatives belonged, and then extended to a larger group of languages in Europe and Asia, more commonly known as Indo-European," the term "Semitic" was "applied at about the same time to another family of languages including Hebrew, Arabic, Aramaic, and, later, some other languages of the Middle East and North Africa":[40]

> One may call the Arabs and Israelis fellow-Semites in the sense that both speak Semitic languages, and that is all. To assume or imply any further content would be rather as if one were to describe the English and say, the Bengalis as fellow-Aryans, and to suggest that they have some common identity because of that.[41]

The erroneous categorization of Jews as a race was an outgrowth of the nineteenth-century European nationalism and its absorption with nationality, ethnicity, and the nation. When filtered through successive subterranean layers of European xenophobia, distorted Darwinism, and Christian animus toward Jews, it spawned modern anti-Semitism, which from the very beginning was specifically an anti-Jewish phenomenon.

It is difficult to say whether the increase in Arab anti-Jewish feeling is due to Arab defeats at the hands of Israel, intensifying sectarian and ethnic tensions within Arab societies, or officially fostered hostility toward a formerly subject people of second-class status. Arab spokesmen maintain they have no hostility toward Jews, only toward "Zionists." But the appellation Zionist is used for virtually all Jews, and even non-Jews who adopt pro-Israeli positions on specific political issues. The belief that all Jews place the interests of Israel above the interests of their own countries is evident in the comments of even so urbane a diplomat with extensive experience in the West as Ismail Fahmy, who was Egypt's foreign minister from late 1973 to November 1977 and who dealt closely with Secretary of State Henry Kissinger during most of that period. According to Fahmy, Kissinger showed "his true colors" during the October War, when, "pretending to be the peace-maker and the go-between, he was in fact always acting on behalf of Israel; this is not surprising considering that he is a Jew himself." And "for all the fanfare, Kissinger in the Middle East was basically Israel's envoy. He never brought us a genuine American proposal."[42] Fahmy implies that successive U.S. presidents, the Congress, and public opinion were all manipulated by Kissinger the Jew. Such insularity is reminiscent of the time not terribly long ago when analogous thinking concluded that Roman Catholics the world over felt a primary loyalty to Rome, irrespective of their nationality.

The anti-Jewish Arab attitude seldom distinguishes between religion and nationality: Jews (whether Zionist or not) were expelled from most Arab countries, those still in Syria are confined to ghettos, treated as second-class citizens, and forbidden to leave the country; Westerners of Jewish origin are frequently barred from many Arab countries. Religion, not nationality or political affiliation, is the cutting edge for discriminatory treatment.

Another often-advanced thesis is that Muslims, Jews, and Christians are all people of the Book, and as such are respected by the Arabs: "The Arabs have a deep and natural respect for Judaism as a universal religious faith and as spiritual values."[43] This statement, issued by the Arab League four days after the anti-Zionist resolution was passed in the U.N. General Assembly, was intended to reject charges that the condemnation of Zionism was in any way related to anti-Jewish prejudice. Regrettably, the record tells a conflicting story.

The persecution of Arab Jews, irrespective of their political outlook, that accelerated after the creation of the state of Israel, is part of a process of Arabization and Islamization that narrowed the spectrum of opportunities for other ethnic and religious minorities as well, and that prompted many Christian Arabs, who tend as a group to be better educated, to emigrate to the West from Jordan, Iraq, and Lebanon.

When Jordan ruled East Jerusalem, which includes the Wailing Wall—Judaism's holiest site—it forbade Jews to worship there or at other religious sites on the West Bank, and desecrated Jewish cemeteries. The Saudis, heirs to the stern, puritanical Wahhabi strain of Sunni Islam and guardians of Mecca, rest their hostility toward Jews on the Koran's descriptions of them as opponents of the Prophet. This hostility was strongly felt by Ibn Saud, the founder of Saudi Arabia, and his son and successor, King Faisal, who told an American Middle East specialist, "only Moslems and Christians have holy places and rights in Jerusalem. The Jews have no shrines in Jerusalem . . . the Jews have no rights in Jerusalem. Another wall can be built for them, and they can wail against that."[44] Diplomats of Jewish origin have been barred from serving in Saudi Arabia and other Arab countries.

In the Arab media, especially radio, which plays a central role in the promulgation of official attitudes, and in contemporary Arab literature, no differentiation is made between Jew and Zionist or between Jew and Israeli:

> The Jews' characteristics have remained constant since they were described in the Koran. The Jew is unrepentant in his war against Muhammad, and whether cooperating with infidels against the Prophet's mission, or whether clothed in the rags of a miser engaged in usury, or whether in an Israeli officer's uniform, he has not changed and will not change. He will always be a swindler, a miser, despicable and arrogant, a person who subverts justice, morality and humanity. Israel's existence is an affront, a fact contrary to Allah's word in the Koran, a negation of eternal and universal laws. Therefore the State of Israel— as Arab nationalists believe—is destined to be destroyed, and the task of every Arab is to restore the Jew to the position of scorn laid down by the Koran.[45]

A third proposition states that if the Jews who came to Palestine after 1917 returned to their countries of origin, peace in the Middle East would be possible. This statement implies that Jewish immigrants from the West are responsible for triggering the clash of cultures and wrenching Palestine from the Arab world. But 53 percent of Israel's present Jewish population are from Arab countries, and it is this emerging bloc of Sephardim that is far more suspicious and severe in its attitude toward compromise with the Arabs than the Ashkenazim of European origin.[46]

This disturbing interplay between religion and politics is a factor of growing intensity in the Arab-Israeli conflict. The religious element is difficult to disentangle from the political and military issues that usually command attention, but to sidestep it would be shortsighted.

INTERNATIONAL TERRORISM

The last external determinant to be examined is international terrorism, which has been defined as "the deliberate, systematic murder, maiming or menacing of the innocent to inspire fear in order to gain political ends."[47] Ideologically and politically, terrorism takes many forms. Its roots are to be found in the anarchic and episodic attacks on authority by the angry young men of nineteenth-century Europe, and the violence it perpetrates is justified by idealism and ultimate ends.[48]

In the context of the Arab-Israeli conflict, terrorism acquired prominence after the June War, when Palestinian guerilla groups hijacked planes, attacked Israeli civilians, and established links with such terrorist groups as the Bader Meinhof, the Japanese Red Army, the Italian Red Brigades, and New Left groups in the United States, where opposition to U.S. "imperialism" and policy in Vietnam became associated with anti-Israeli positions. In the summer of 1982, when Israeli forces drove the PLO from West Beirut, they exposed the elaborate and well-financed connections between the PLO and the most nefarious terrorist groups operating on the international scene. The destruction of the PLO's base in Beirut was a serious blow to international terrorism, which was deprived of a major stronghold, perhaps its most important in the non-Communist world. According to one Israeli analyst, "the PLO had provided installations for 40 international terrorist organizations, half of them European and the other Latin American, Africa, and Asian. . . the Japanese Red Army had more men in Lebanon than in Japan."[49]

In the West, the terrorist activities of the Palestinian and other Arab groups and the services (in return for arms, money, and sanctuary) performed for them by their diverse political allies of the Left and the

Right are frequently anti-Jewish in character. Whether in Rome, Brussels, Paris, or Athens, the targets are not only Israeli but Jewish: synagogues, schools, shops, and so on. Under the banner of justice for the Palestinians, its partisans commit injustices that bear the stamp of anti-Semitism. The net effect has been to heighten Israel's sense of beleaguerment and to harden stereotypical attitudes among those Israelis who do not believe that the Arabs would ever willingly accept the existence of the state of Israel as a natural phenomenon in the Middle East.

When Arab terrorism is abetted and financed by anti-Zionist intrigues from the corridors of the Kremlin to fashionable salons in the West, the result is an unholy alliance of communism, anti-Semitism, and anti-Zionism. The consequences are a growing rigidity of political positions and reluctance on the part of key protagonists to take some risks for peace; a trend in all camps toward deprecating advocates of reason, negotiation, and accommodation; and an internationalization of a regional conflict.

* * * * * *

The foregoing essay has explored some of the ways in which important external determinants have affected the evolution and dynamics of the contentious issues lying at the heart of the continuing Arab-Israeli conflict. An appreciation of their implications is essential for understanding Israel's policies and options, the parameters and pressures shaping the Palestinian problem, and the long-term prospects for a comprehensive settlement.

NOTES

1. John Edwin Mroz, *Beyond Security: Private Perceptions Among Arabs and Israelis* (New York: International Peace Academy, 1980), pp. 111-112.

2. Ibid., p. 113.

3. Ibid., p. 114.

4. Mark Segal and David Landau, "Dayan Says War May Only Be Beginning," *Jerusalem Post Weekly* (November 27, 1973). Another Israeli official noted: "In mountainous terrain, such as that of Judea and Samaria, even a formidable tank force can be blocked by smaller forces that control the critical passes. Invading tank forces, however large, must resolve themselves into single files to negotiate the narrow stretches, nullifying much of their firepower. This allows defending forces to stop the offense, sometimes simply by knocking out the lead tanks. As the number of Arab tanks facing Israel's eastern front increases—from under 3,000 in 1967 to 7,300 in 1982—the importance for Israel of controlling the Judean and Samarian mountains increases." *Washington Post*, January 8,

1983. A recently declassified 1967 memorandum by the U.S. Joint Chiefs of Staff concluded that "from a strictly military point of view, Israel would require retention of some captured territories in order to provide militarily defensible borders." It specified the Gaza Strip, the Golan Heights, the southern and western parts of the West Bank, and portions of Sinai near Eilat and the Strait of Tiran. Richard Brody, "What the Joint Chiefs Saw as 'Defensible Borders'," *Wall Street Journal*, March 9, 1983.

5. Quoted in Zeev Schiff, "Territory and Security," *Midstream* 24, No. 7 (August/September 1978): 14. See also Yigal Allon, "Israel: The Case for Defensible Borders," *Foreign Affairs* 55 (October 1976): 42-43.

6. Drew Middleton, *New York Times*, October 26, 1982.

7. Alan Dowty, "A PLO State on the West Bank Won't Solve the Problem," *Jerusalem Post International Edition* (September 6, 1977), p. 10.

8. A point made by Dr. Moshe Arens, formerly a member of the Knesset, and Israel's defense minister, in Center for Strategic Studies, *Proceedings of Panel Discussion on Secure Borders* (March 2, 1978) (Tel-Aviv University: CSS Paper No. 2, October 1978), p. 13.

9. Ibid.

10. Yaacov Ro'i, *Soviet Decision Making in Practice: The USSR and Israel 1947-1954* (New Brunswick: Transaction Books, 1980), pp. 141-161; see also, Arnold Krammer, *The Forgotten Friendship: Israel and the Soviet Bloc. 1947-53* (Urbana: University of Illinois Press, 1974), pp. 54-106.

11. Earl Berger, *The Covenant and the Sword: Arab-Israeli Relations 1948-56* (London: Routledge & Kegan Paul Ltd, 1965), p. 74.

12. Marie Syrkin, "How Long the PLO Camps?," *Midstream* 28, (August/September 1982): 56.

13. Samuel Decalo, "Africa and the U.N. Anti-Zionism Resolution: Roots and Causes," *Cultures et développement: Revue internationale des Sciences du Développement* 8, No. 1 (1976): 114.

14. William Korey, "The PLO's Conquest of the U.N.," *Midstream* 25 (November 1979): 10.

15. *New York Times*, July 30, 1980.

16. *New York Times*, December 16, 1980.

17. *New York Times*, July 30, 1980.

18. Gil Carl Alroy, "Dynamics of Violence in the Middle East," *The Reporter* (May 15, 1968), p. 25.

19. For example, James E. Akins, "The Oil Crisis: This Time the Wolf is Here," *Foreign Affairs* 51 (April 1973): 462-90; Dr. Uzi Arad, *The Short-Term Effectiveness of the Arab Oil Embargo* (Tel-Aviv: Tel-Aviv University, Center for Strategic Studies, CSS Paper No. 1, August 1978), p. 5.

20. *New York Times*, January 21, 1980.

21. Adam M. Garfinkle, *Western Europe's Middle East Diplomacy and the United States* (Philadelphia: Foreign Policy Research Institute, 1983), p. 5.

22. Golda Meir, *My Life* (London: Weidenfeld and Nicolson, 1975), p. 376.

23. OPEC members are Algeria, Ecuador, Gabon, Indonesia, Iran, Iraq, Kuwait, Libya, Nigeria, Qatar, Saudi Arabia, the United Arab Emirates, and Venezuela. Accounting for less than 40 percent of total world crude production in recent years, its potential power derives from the ability to withhold supplies under tight market conditions.

24. S. Fred Singer, "What Do the Saudis Do Now?" *Wall Street Journal*, March 18, 1983, p. 26.

25. By establishing greater control over the marketing of their petroleum, "the Arabs would not threaten a true limitation of supply so much as chaos. The United States would be susceptible to this suggestion insofar as the popular image of the Arabs in our country identifies them with unruliness. The mere knowledge that the Arabs were reducing shipments, and had extended their control over the trade through their own refineries, ships, and marketing channels would create anxieties. The purpose of an oil strategy would be to make supply sufficiently tight for the American public to become aware of the dangers that were involved. Herein lies the one source of pressure to which American leaders respond—the American public. Thereafter, the Arabs might conclude, the scene would be set for serious negotiations,. . . The Arab purpose would be to get the United States to put the full force of its diplomacy behind a Palestinian settlement." William R. Brown, "The Oil Weapon," *Middle East Journal* 36 (Summer 1982): 310, 315.

26. Paul Hallwood and Stuart Sinclair, "OPEC's Developing Relationships with the Third World," *International Affairs* (Spring 1982): 274, 283.

27. Victor T. LeVine, "The Arabs and Africa: A Balance to 1982," *Middle East Review* 14 (Spring-Summer 1982): 59.

28. See Malcolm Kerr, *The Arab Cold War* (New York: Oxford University Press, 1971).

29. Ibn Khaldun, *The Muqaddimah: An Introduction to History*, vol. 1. Translated from the Arabic by Franz Rosenthal (New York: Pantheon Books, 1958), pp. 304-5.

30. Elie Kedourie, *Islam in the Modern World* (New York: Holt, Rinehart and Winston, 1980), p. 79.

31. Ibid.

32. B.Y. Boutros-Ghali, "The Arab League 1945-1955," *International Conciliation*, No. 498 (May 1954), p. 412.

33. Esmond Wright, "Abdallah's Jordan: 1947-1951," *Middle East Journal* 15 (Autumn 1951): 439-60.

34. Fouad Ajami, "Geopolitical Illusions," in *The Middle East and the Western Alliance*, ed. Steven L. Spiegel (Boston: George Allen & Unwin, 1982), p. 156.

35. *New York Times*, October 9, 1982. The dollar value exceeded one billion dollars; the quantity was enough to equip several combat divisions.

36. Bernard Lewis, *History: Remembered, Recovered, Invented* (Princeton: Princeton University Press, 1975), pp. 55-69.

37. S. Abraham, "The Jew and the Israeli in Modern Arabic Literature," *Jerusalem Quarterly*, No. 2 (Winter 1977): 119.

38. Malcolm H. Kerr, "The Arabs and Israelis: Perceptual Dimensions to their Dilemma," in *The Middle East: Quest for an American Policy*, ed. Williard A. Beling (Albany: State University of New York Press, 1973), p. 4.

39. Ibid., pp. 30-31.

40. Bernard Lewis, "Semites and Anti-Semites; Race in the Arab-Israel Conflict," *Survey* 17 (Spring 1971): 169.

41. Ibid., p. 170.

42. Ismail Fahmy, *Negotiating for Peace in the Middle East* (Baltimore, Md.: The Johns Hopkins University Press, 1983), pp. 31, 168.

43. Paul Hoffman, *New York Times*, November 15, 1975.

44. Edward R.F. Sheehan, *The Arabs, Israelis, and Kissinger* (New York: Reader's Digest Press, 1976), pp. 74-75. See also, David Holden and Richard Johns, *The House of Saud* (London: Pan Books, 1982), pp. 132-33, 290, 309; and Bernard Gwertzman on Henry Kissinger's meeting with King Faisal, *New York Times*, March 24, 1974.

45. Abraham, *op. cit.*, 135-136.

46. For an analysis that links religious components and political outlook to Begin's hard-line policies, see Ofira Seliktar, "Israel: The New Zionism," *Foreign Policy*, No. 51 (Summer 1983): 118-38. See also Nissim Rejwan, "Israel's EthnoPolitical Cleavage," *Midstream* 29 (June/July 1983): 18-22. Rejwan's sense of the watershed in Israeli politics gives more attention to the cultural aspects of religious outlook.

47. Address by Lord Chalfont, a retired British diplomat, to the European-Atlantic Group in Longon on July 13, 1981.

48. For example, Mordecai S. Chertoff, ed., *The New Left and the Jews* (New York: Pitman, 1971).

49. *New York Times*, November 11, 1982.

4

Israel: From Ideology to Reality

Alan Dowty

THE DOMINANCE OF IDEOLOGY

Israel, like the United States and a handful of other countries in the modern world, is the result of an idea imposed on reality rather than the simple outgrowth of geographic and ethnic circumstances. In the American case, the idea was representative government and freedom from arbitrary rule; for Israel, the idea was the achievement of Jewish self-determination by establishment of a Jewish state in the historic homeland.

Just as the ideas of the American Revolution can be understood only in the context of the liberalism and rationalism of the late eighteenth-century Enlightenment, so political Zionism—the drive for Jewish political sovereignty—reflected late nineteenth-century European nationalism, with its stress on ethnic identity, self-determination, and the idea of the nation-state. Of course the aim of a return to Zion has always been central to Jewish thought and ritual, affirmed in daily prayer and by the continuing presence in Palestine of a small Jewish community. But it was the ideological ferment of nineteenth-century Europe that transformed what had been a vague religious aspiration into a largely secularized political movement with an active program for Jewish settlement and sovereignty in Palestine.

The center of the Jewish world at the time was Tsarist Russia, including the Baltic states and Poland, in which some five million Jews—close to 75 percent of world Jewry—resided. From the time of the assassination of Tsar Alexander II in 1881, this population was subjected to a wave of officially-inspired persecution that was part of the regime's response to the impact of revolutionary and nationalistic ideas within Russia.

The historic Jewish response to such repression was flight to more hospitable locales, and there was little difference this time. Between 1881 and 1914 nearly three million Jews left Russia, most of them for the United States and other Western countries. But a small number, roughly 1 percent, were motivated by Zionist ideals to return to historic Palestine (then a part of the Ottoman Empire).

Why did this tiny proportion choose such a novel response to such an age-old problem? Anti-Semitism was a major thread of Jewish history, but it had never sparked any major movement for a return to Eretz-Israel (the Land of Israel, as geographic Palestine was known in Hebrew). Zion had always appeared much more bleak and inhospitable than the alternatives, and this was certainly no less true in the declining years of Turkish rule there. Furthermore, the previous century had been the century of emancipation: ghetto walls had been torn down across Europe, as the secularization of politics and society had removed ancient barriers to Jewish participation in public life. Why, in such an improving climate, should a part of the Jewish community suddenly reject patterns of minority existence that had persisted for two millennia?

As Adam Garfinkle has pointed out in Chapter 1, part of the answer to this question was that, for Jews, emancipation itself posed new dilemmas to which traditional solutions were irrelevant.[1] In a society sharply divided along religious lines, Jews suffered many disabilities—but the very sharpness of the division left them with a clear sense of their own identity and relationship to the larger society. When nationality replaced religion as the main point of reference, Jews were in a more problematic position. The relationship of Judaism to Christianity was clear, but the position of Jews as Frenchmen, Germans, or Russians was ambivalent. Presumably the path to integration was open, but there was serious question whether it could ever be totally successful, and whether such success would require the complete loss of any meaningful identity as Jews.

One possible response was, indeed, total assimilation. And in fact a large part of the Jewish community chose this path. Another answer was to seek out an ideology that skirted the dilemma by "transcending" the whole problem of nationalism. Thus the appeal to large numbers of Jews—especially in Eastern Europe—of socialist doctrines that proclaimed the priority of class interests over national and ethnic divisions.

Others responded, however, by embracing the idea of nationality and extending it to include the Jewish people. In an age when Greeks, Italians, Serbs, Romanians, and even Albanians were discovering their own national identity, it was no surprise that Jews would react with a reaffirmation of their identity. By virtue of their 3,500-year history as a people, with distinctive cultural patterns, languages, religion, and a strong self-identity enforced by external hostility—by any test, in fact, but that of geographic concentration—most Jews felt their claim to recognition as a nation no less valid than that of the other emerging nationalities of the period.

Jewish nationalism was not only an emulation of other nationalisms, however. It was also a defense against their excesses, which became more obvious with the passage of time. The "liberal" nationalism of the earlier period, tied to concepts of democracy and freedom, had indeed improved the situation of Jews throughout Europe. But in its later manifestations, nationalism came to put more stress on race and on cultural and ethnic homogeneity. The position of minority groups within the new nationalist states became increasingly precarious, and in some cases even worse than in prenationalist days. In particular, a new and more vicious "ethnic" anti-Semitism developed during the late nineteenth and early twentieth centuries, culminating in the genocidal obsessions of Nazi Germany.

For many, this destroyed the credibility of assimilation as a solution. When religious divisions were foremost, Jews at least had the option of conversion. But one could not "convert" to a new ancestry; consequently even the most thoroughly assimilated Jews were not totally accepted in the new postnationalist European societies. This was driven home by events like the Dreyfus trial—in liberal France yet!—where a Jewish army officer, totally French in culture and loyalty, became a natural target for unfounded suspicions of treasonous behavior. A piece of final evidence, some decades later, was the fate of the Jews of Germany, who were perhaps the most assimilated community in Europe.

If nationality were to be the basis of society and politics, religious tolerance would not be enough. Jews would not only remain outsiders in the new nation-states, but their situation would be more untenable than ever. Many early Zionists, including Theodore Herzl himself, began as assimilationists, but became convinced by events that integration would not end the persecution of Jews as a minority.

The conclusion that some drew from this was that the position of the Jewish people should be regularized through the achievement of political sovereignty. This was seen not only as an inherent right, for Jews no less than for Serbs or Albanians, but also as a necessary response to the position of Jews as an exposed minority in Europe and elsewhere. A Jewish state would give Jews the necessary framework for their own national self-expression. It would also serve as a refuge to those in distress, and by its very existence would normalize the position of Jews who chose to remain outside its borders.

These were ideas shared by all Zionists. But the dominant mode of Zionism that developed in eastern Europe—Labor Zionism—added to this some particular beliefs about the shape of the new society to be built. Like the basic Zionist thrust, these ideas were shaped by the ideological currents of late nineteenth-century eastern Europe.

Labor Zionism added a social dimension to Jewish nationalist thought. It adopted socialist ideals of the public ownership of the means of production, equality, and a classless society (reflecting the same spectrum as socialism itself, from dogmatic Marxism to the most gradualist approaches). Labor Zionism also focused attention on the "unnatural" economic role that had been forced on Jews by conditions in the Diaspora (dispersion), and on the consequent need to change the traditional Jewish occupational structure. It urged Jews to move out of such accustomed trades as commerce, finance, and the professions, and to create a Jewish proletariat based on manual labor, a return to the soil, and self-reliance in all spheres of production. The establishment of the *kibbutz*, or rural communal settlement, was a perfect expression of these ideals.[2]

In contrast to most other nationalisms, therefore, Labor Zionism put a strong stress on self-transformation as well as the achievement of external political aims. In the words of one Zionist slogan, Jewish pioneers came to Eretz-Israel "in order to build and to be built in it." It was, in some ways, a revolt against traditional Jewish life, a "revolution against Jewish history."[3] Not surprisingly, Labor Zionists found themselves under considerable tension with existing Jewish institutions and leadership, and especially with the religious establishment.

Labor Zionist ideology dominated among the settlers in the Second *Aliya*, or wave of immigration, who reached Palestine in the years between 1905 and 1914.[4] Those who came in the First Aliya, between 1881 and 1904, had settled on the land, but remained dependent in most cases on continuing financial support from abroad and on hired Arab labor locally. The Second Aliya, impelled by the Russian Revolution of 1905, was strongly imbued with the socialist ethos that had by that time swept through Russia. Its members founded the kibbutz movement and the first labor organizations, as well as a number of political movements. Most of the non-Marxist movements merged in 1929 to form *Mapai* (Hebrew acronym for Workers' Party of Eretz-Israel).

There were of course nonsocialist strands in the Zionist movement. Religious Zionism accepted the aim of rebuilding a Jewish state in Palestine, but sought to do so in strict accordance with traditional Jewish law. Religious Zionists formally organized in 1902 as the *Mizrahi* (acronym for

Spiritual Center) faction within the Zionist movement. But given the character of Zionism as a product of secular nationalism, religious Zionists remained a small minority both within the Zionist movement and within the Jewish religious community.

The Revisionists, organized under the leadership of Vladimir Ze'ev Jabotinsky in the 1920s, were inspired by twentieth-century European nationalism in the same way that Zionism itself had initially been influenced by nineteenth-century nationalism. Revisionism rejected the stress on practical settlement activity and the willingness of Labor Zionists, focused on such activity, to forego wider territorial claims. Revisionists objected when the British separated the East Bank (Transjordan, later the state of Jordan) from the original Palestine mandate. They also rejected proposals, in the 1930s, to partition what remained of the mandate (Western Palestine) into Arab and Jewish states.

Revisionists stressed an exclusive Jewish claim to all of Palestine, on both banks of the Jordan River. They sought to realize this claim through a political-military strategy, rather than by the slow buildup of a Jewish presence through grass-roots settlement activity. This was Zionism from the top, rather than the Zionism from the bottom that Labor Zionists preached. In particular, Revisionists hoped to achieve Jewish sovereignty over all of Palestine by aligning themselves with the interests of the British Empire and otherwise playing the game of world politics skillfully (backed up, of course, by whatever military power could be mobilized).

While Labor Zionists hoped that common class interests would enable Arabs and Jews to cooperate, and that a Jewish socialist commonwealth could thus be built without encroaching on Arab rights, Revisionists put nation above class. Within Palestine they were ready to recognize the rights of Arabs as individuals, but they denied the validity of Arab national claims there.

The General Zionists, originally, were simply those Zionists who were not socialists, religious, or revisionist. They occupied a centrist position by virtue of their opposition to both Left and Right. In the early years of the movement, General Zionists were a de facto majority, and as late as the 1921 Zionist Congress, 73 percent of the delegates were so identified. But they were not organized as a formal movement until the 1930s, by which time Labor Zionists were in control.

By the late 1920s, in fact, Labor Zionism was dominant both in the international movement and in the Yishuv. Its ascendancy was due in part to its focus on concrete settlement activity within Palestine, which gave it a more solid base of support, and to the increasing importance of the Yishuv within Zionism as a whole. This Labor dominance was to last for half a century, until the Israeli elections of 1977. Yet behind this long period of dominance lay an anomaly that is central to an understanding of recent Israeli political history.

As noted, the First and Second Aliyot represented only a tiny part of the mass exodus of Jews from Eastern Europe in the pre-World War I period. Consequently, those who chose Palestine over America usually did so on the basis of strong personal motivation and attachment to Zionist goals. Most of those coming after the establishment of the British mandate (in 1920) lacked this ideological commitment, at least to Labor Zionism specifically. With the closing of easy access to the United States and elsewhere during this period, entire communities arrived in Palestine as refugees whose options had been foreclosed or drastically limited. Many of these were middle-class or professional Jews who fled Poland and Germany during the 1920s and 1930s. Later came the refugees from the Holocaust (the Nazi destruction of European Jewry) and the "displaced persons" from World War II. After the establishment of the state of Israel in 1948, there was a mass influx of entire Jewish communities from the Arab world.

Altogether, about two million Jewish refugees reached Palestine or Israel during these years. With their descendants, these groups constitute a vast majority of the present population of Israel. Any explanation of Israeli political attitudes that does not begin with this reality—that Israel is a nation of refugees—is inadequate.

The puzzle, then, is not the eventual decline of Labor Zionism, but rather its long hold on power. During most of that time, the bulk of the population held no strong prior commitment to socialism, the dignity of manual labor, a return to the soil, a change in the traditional Jewish occupational structure, the secularization of Jewish life, a pragmatic approach to territorial issues, or other features of an ideology rooted in the ferment of late nineteenth-century Eastern European revolutionary movements. They did not come to Eretz-Israel in order to wage a "revolution against Jewish history."

What we have seen in the last decade or so is a reassertion of traditional Jewish occupational and social patterns, religious beliefs, and non-European influences that has finally ended the dominance of Labor Zionism. Like other "new societies," Israel has moved from ideology to patterns more reflective of its human and material realities.[5] As the leading study of Israeli society has put it, there has been a weakening of the "movement style of life," and an accentuation of occupational, economic, and ethnic differences.[6] While politics created society in the Yishuv, the more common pattern is now emerging: social realities are creating policy.

This fact, together with the weakening of some of the external pressures on Israeli policy, has broadened the range of choice in Israeli politics—at the cost of adding considerably to its confusion and unpredictability.

THE EMERGENCE OF THE ESTABLISHMENT

The fact that they were building a "new society" made it easier for the Zionist pioneers to apply their ideological precepts in a wholesale fashion. They began with a clean slate, freed of the need to deal with established institutions. In the early days of the Yishuv, they also constituted a fairly homogeneous society: the major splits were ideological, and there existed among all Zionists, whatever their particular ideology, a strong sense of common purpose and unity.

But building from scratch also had its problems. Resources were scarce (necessitating continued dependence on the Diaspora), and there was no infrastructure upon which to build. Every step involved important new decisions and precedents, and was therefore a potential source of division on ideological and practical grounds. And, unlike most other national movements, Zionism faced the problem of geographic dispersion of its people and competing national claims on its homeland, from a population already established on its soil. Zionists did not ignore this problem—from the very outset they debated it endlessly—but they were far from agreement on how to solve it.

The mandate period was therefore critical in molding Israeli society. The Yishuv organized itself as a "quasi-state" within the mandatory framework, and established the institutions that were to dominate Israeli life.[7] The Histadrut, or Labor Federation, grew to play a role in the economy far beyond that of an ordinary labor union. The Jewish Agency, an organ of the World Zionist Organization, handled relations with Jewish communities abroad, represented the interests of the Yishuv diplomatically, and coordinated immigration and settlement within Palestine. The Yishuv also had an elected assembly (Knesset Israel), with an executive body (Va'ad Leumi, or National Council) attached to it. Most importantly, a political elite based in Palestine, and dominated by Labor Zionists, had emerged and taken charge of the destinies of the Yishuv.

At least one party or movement represented each of the four major Zionist camps. Apart from Mapai, Labor Zionism included the more doctrinaire Hashomer Hatsa'ir (The Young Guard), later the basis of Mapam (acronym for United Workers Party). The General Zionists tended to divide into two parties, later known as General Zionists and Progressives, which eventually (1961) merged to form the Liberal Party. The Revisionists split with the World Zionist Organization in 1935 and organized the New Zionist Organization; they also established the paramilitary National Military Organization (Irgun Tsva'i Leumi), which was reconstituted as the Herut movement, under the leadership of Menachem Begin, in 1948. In the religious Zionist camp there were two parties—Mizrahi and its labor counterpart Hapoel Hamizrahi—which later merged to form the National Religious party.

During the mandate the Jewish population of Palestine grew from about 60,000 to over 650,000. The Third Aliya, immediately after World War I, like the Second Aliya, consisted largely of committed Labor Zionists from Poland and Russia. But the succeeding waves of immigrants, as noted, were largely refugees whose Zionism was more a matter of necessity than choice. The Fourth Aliya, in the mid-1920s, brought in a number of middle-class Polish Jews fleeing anti-Semitic economic measures. The Fifth Aliya, in the 1930s, was triggered by persecution in Germany, Austria, Poland, and Romania, which forced many urbanized, professional Jews to seek refuge in Palestine. Another 100,000 refugees from the Holocaust arrived, legally or illegally, during the 1940-47 period. Of the 483,000 Jewish immigrants officially admitted during the mandate period, 88 percent were from Europe.

The Yishuv consequently developed as a Western society with a strong Eastern European flavor. Political institutions followed Western models, with a significant British influence on the structure of the parliamentary system. But there was also a strong element of Jewish political culture, based on the experience and precedents of Jewish communal life over the centuries.

Since Jewish communal institutions had lacked governmental authority, they operated by bargaining and consensus among different groups and interests, with unclear lines of authority and jurisdiction. Such a system of self-governance was of necessity voluntaristic and pluralistic, with power shared among groups in rough proportion to their importance and strength. These "contractual" traditions of government within the Jewish community were thus republican and even democratic, being reminiscent of modern theories of "consociational democracy" that describe systems in which power is shared by consent among different groups.[8] In any event, this experience was immediately relevant to the circumstances of the mandate, and enabled the Jewish community of Palestine to make a fast start in building functioning governmental institutions.

Another tradition of importance was the *millet* system of the Ottoman Empire, under which the various religious communities of the Middle East governed themselves in matters of religious law, including personal status, marriage, divorce, and certain property matters. Since this practice was established long before the mandate, Jewish rabbinical courts already exercised wide authority in these spheres and continued to do so. (In fact, this also resembled the traditions of Jewish community life, as described above.) Consequently, Israel developed the anomaly of an entrenched religious establishment in a largely secularized society.

Given the key role of ideology, the style of politics that developed was principled and passionate.[9] It amounted to the assertion of ideals over reality, without which there would be no Zionism. At the center were the political parties, which were actually ideological movements. Together with the Histadrut, the parties provided a set of institutions and services substituting for the governmental and societal infrastructure that did not exist: schools, newspapers, banks and loan funds, health-care plans, youth movements, sport clubs, housing companies, and various welfare services. Most of the new settlements were also established by particular movements. The strength of Israeli parties is not just a result, in other words, of the electoral system later adopted; rather, it was the dominance of parties that shaped the electoral system.

Other legacies of the mandate included a disillusioned cynicism on Arab-Jewish issues. At the outset Labor Zionists had believed that their goals could be achieved without displacing the Arab population in Palestine or injuring its basic interests. This was perhaps somewhat utopian, but Arab-Jewish cooperation in building the Jewish national home was actively sought. Chaim Weizmann, representing Zionist interests, negotiated in 1919 with Emir Faisal of the Hashemite dynasty, the most prominent spokesman for the Arab world at the time. Similar efforts were made in following years, down to the London Round Table Conference of 1939.

But the net result of all these negotiations was an unremitting Arab opposition to Jewish immigration into Palestine, and to any form of Jewish self-rule there beyond that of minority status as customarily recognized in the Moslem world. This opposition was also expressed in demonstrations, riots, and armed attacks on Jewish settlements. The clash may have been inevitable, since the minimal Zionist aim—a Jewish state in at least part of Palestine—was never likely to be acceptable, in an age of rising Arab nationalism, to an Arab population that regarded its claims to Palestine as exclusive (in mirror image to the Revisionists, who claimed an exclusive Jewish right to all of Palestine).

In any event, each new wave of Jewish immigration evoked a new round of violence; there were widespread Arab assaults on Jews in 1920-21 and in 1929, while in 1936-39 there was a general uprising that approached the dimensions of a civil war. In addition, leadership of Palestine Arabs passed into the hands of the more fanatical elements, and in particular those of Haj Amin El-Husseini, the mufti of Jerusalem. The mufti, whose forces liquidated many of the more moderate Arab leaders during the 1936-39 period, preached the destruction of the Jewish community in Palestine, and later fled to Nazi Germany, where he gained further notoriety by endorsing that regime's "solution" to the Jewish problem.

The impact of all this on the Yishuv was to discredit efforts to achieve a negotiated settlement of Arab-Jewish issues. Those who promoted such an effort—in particular, Chaim Weizmann, president of the World Zionist Organization during much of this time—were gradually pushed aside by those within the Labor Zionist movement who stressed the need of self-defense and of creating facts on the ground. Foremost among the latter was David Ben-Gurion, who by the early 1930s had become the most prominent leader in the Yishuv. His outlook was reinforced by the many refugees who reached Palestine during these years, and by the devastating impact of the Holocaust soon thereafter.

But while Ben-Gurion represented a "realist" perspective on the question of diplomacy versus practical measures, he also represented a pragmatic approach to territorial issues, in contrast to the Revisionists. The leadership of the Yishuv had reluctantly come to terms with the British partition of the Palestine mandate, in 1922, by which 80 percent of the territory—everything east of the Jordan River—was established as the Emirate of Transjordan under the rule of Abdallah, Faisal's brother, and closed to Jewish settlement. Under Ben-Gurion's leadership, they also accepted in principle British proposals, in the late 1930s, to partition what remained into Jewish and Arab states (though there was considerable criticism of the specific borders proposed). Finally, a majority under Ben-Gurion also accepted the U.N. partition plan of 1947, which from a Jewish perspective was an improvement on the 1930s proposals, but which still left Jerusalem outside the proposed Jewish state.

The Revisionists opposed all of these measures, beginning with the creation of Transjordan, and split with the existing leadership over its acceptance of the principle of partition. As noted, they continued to insist on the priority of Jewish national rights in *all* historic Palestine (including Transjordan).

By the end of World War II, the Jewish community of Palestine had achieved tremendous cohesion, a sense of unity, and determination in the face of adversity. The Yishuv was able to maintain a level of organization and self-defense extraordinary for a community without formal governmental powers: it levied and collected taxes, established an army, represented its own interests internationally, administered welfare and educational services, and set its own economic and social policies—all entirely on a voluntary basis. The strength of this social cohesion was apparent in the 1948 war.

THE CLASSIC CONSENSUS

During the period from independence to the Six-Day War (1948-67), a combination of external and internal circumstances shaped a national consensus on most political issues that helped maintain Labor Zionist dominance, while disguising the developments that were slowly eroding it.

The overwhelming reality was that the state of Israel was closed off by a wall of hostile Arab states that remained committed to reversing the results of the 1948 war. The six neighboring Arab states enjoyed a population advantage over Israel that varied, during this period, between 50/1 and 20/1.[10] The imbalance in resources, weapons, finances, and other measures of power seemed almost equally formidable.

Nor could Israel rely on international support to redress this imbalance. The circumstances that led to a convergence of American and Soviet support for Israeli statehood in 1948 changed, and from the early 1950s the Soviet Union was increasingly the ally and armorer of Israel's enemies. Most Western countries would not sell arms to Israel, though many sold arms to Arab states. The international climate became yet more hostile with the rise of the Third World, which for ideological and political reasons chose to regard Israel as part of the colonial West and the Palestinian Arabs as victims of Western imperialism.

Against this, Israel did have some offsetting strengths. It held the advantage in mobilization capacity, training and morale, technological skills, and some intangibles such as social unity and the determination that comes from knowing that survival is at stake. (Israelis referred to this as the weapon of *ein breira*, or "no alternative.")[11]

Most choices seemed to be dictated, indeed, by security considerations. Israel was often cited as the classic case of a foreign policy so constrained by threats that there was no choice at all; in the words of one leading expert, "the external pressures on Israel were so severe, and the country was forced into so tight a corner, that the basic principles of its foreign policy became hardly an exercise of sovereignty at all, but rather an acceptance of necessities to which there was no alternative."[12]

Economic pressures reinforced this sense of constraint. Not only did Israel bear a crushing defense burden by any standard, but in the first years of statehood it also faced economic warfare (the Arab boycott) and a massive influx of new immigrants on top of the usual problems of new nationhood. In the first three and a half years after independence, the population doubled, mostly by refugees ill-equipped to integrate rapidly into the Israeli economy. Consequently, despite the Zionist ideal of self-reliance, Israel was forced into an unusual degree of dependence on a continuing import surplus—a dependence that became a permanent fixture.

The economic pressures meant that policies would be determined less by ideological predilection than by basic needs. Socialists could take comfort in the fact that a large measure of centralized economic planning would be required. On the other hand, however, they could not afford to be doctrinaire in this planning; everything had to be done on a pragmatic basis, with a focus on what would work most quickly rather than what was most ideal by abstract standards. Socioeconomic policies did not, therefore, become an intense political issue, despite the serious ideological cleavages that existed on paper. They also exercised only a marginal influence on foreign policy decisions during this period.[13]

To these pressures were added the experiences and perceptions of a Jewish generation that had passed through the successive waves of twentieth-century anti-Semitism, culminating in the Holocaust. The Jewish worldview is, in any event, the product of 20 centuries of religious and ethnic persecution; no minority in history has been so unremittingly conditioned to regard the world as an essentially vicious place. The Holocaust was merely the latest and most brutal chapter in a long history.

Nevertheless, Jews throughout the world were stunned by what they saw as the world's indifference to Nazi genocide. They noted the lack of any international effort to save Jewish lives in Europe, to the extent of refusing to accept refugees. Even after the war, the Palestinian Jewish community, most of whom lost family and friends in the Holocaust, were not allowed to receive the survivors.

A mood of despair and outrage, born of the mandate experience and the Holocaust, intensified during the period of the Israeli War of Independence. Though the United Nations recommended establishment of a Jewish and an Arab state in Palestine, no effort was made to enforce this decision against armed Arab opposition. The Jewish community was left to its own devices against the regular armies of five Arab states, some of which were armed by Western states, while Israel faced a general arms embargo (broken only, to some extent, by Soviet-bloc countries). Despite the widespread perception that another Holocaust was in the making, the world seemed as indifferent, or as passive, as it had the first time.

This sense of isolation in a hostile world was yet further strengthened by the events of 1956-57 and 1967. In the first case, Israel faced universal condemnation for what most Israelis regarded as a necessary act of self-defense, and was then forced to withdraw from Sinai in return for assurances that turned out to be valueless when tested ten years later. But when these guarantees did collapse, in 1967, Israel again stood unprotected by any but its own devices. Once more, as Israelis saw it, only the strength of their own armed forces turned aside a renewed genocide.

These pressures and perceptions created a remarkable consensus that overrode many of the splits in Israeli society.[14] This consensus was based on a pessimistic view of human nature and of world politics, and on a belief that justice could never be guaranteed without the backing of force. Words and opinions were belittled; the stress was on deeds. ("It doesn't matter what the world says, but what the Jews do.")

A second element of the consensus was a belief that Arab threats should be taken seriously—that they were not just words—and that the security of Israel was always in jeopardy, since a single defeat would mean the end of the state. Demonstrations of Arab moderation were regarded with suspicion, as they were likely to be tactical maneuvers rather than alterations in the basic design of destroying Israel.

There was, therefore, no choice but self-reliance. International support or guarantees could not be trusted and were not a reliable basis for national security. The only reliable outside allies were the Jewish communities of the world. Apart from other forms of support, the Diaspora was also important as a source of immigration, the raison d'etre of the state. Israel was concerned, too, with the well-being of Jewish communities abroad, apart from considerations of national interest, and its relations with other nations have often been affected by the position and interests of Jewish communities within those countries.

Given their perceived vulnerability and the reality of self-reliance,

Israelis became believers in an active defense. They stressed the need to anticipate, to seize the initiative, and to take the war to the other's territory. The preemptive attacks of 1956 and 1967 are cases in point. In terms of concrete defense doctrines, this was expressed in the focus of mobility, forward deployment, and threats of punitive counterblows that in some ways anticipated strategies of nuclear deterrence.[15]

But if Israel tends to active defense on a military level, it also showed an aversion to risk taking in politics or diplomacy. Israeli diplomacy tends to be reactive, responding to events and shunning bold initiatives.[16] Costs and risks are assessed in an extremely conservative fashion.

Another element in the consensus was a pro-Western orientation. There were, in the beginning, neutralist tendencies in the Israeli leadership, given their East European ties, socialist sympathies, and hopes of continuing support from both sides of the cold war. But the behavior of the Soviet Union from the early 1950s, toward both Jews within its borders and Zionism generally, soon led to a revision of this attitude. Even before the Soviet Union had for tactical reasons adopted a pro-Arab stance and moved to arm Israel's enemies, it had for ideological reasons tried to discredit the ideal of Israel as a homeland for all Jews, including those of the Soviet Union. In the Soviet version of socialism, there was little room for recognition of Jewish nationality.

Israel thus found itself pushed into closer cooperation with those who opposed the Soviets. This was reinforced by a natural affinity of values with democratic Western countries, as well as the importance of Jewish communities in the West and especially in the United States. Economic realities also played a role, as the Israeli economy quickly developed close linkages with the West. Pro-Soviet views, which had once been frequently heard in Labor Zionist circles (especially in Mapam), practically disappeared from Israeli public debate within a decade.

On specific issues, there was a consensus that the Arab refugees from the 1948 war should be dealt with only in the framework of final peace treaties with the Arab states, and that most of them would have to be resettled in Arab countries (just as the Jewish refugees from Arab countries had been resettled in Israel). As time passed, there was also general agreement on the 1949 armistice lines as a basis for final borders. Talk of settling for less—the 1949 lines were more favorable to Israel than the 1947 partition plan—faded away, while those who still sought the whole of Palestine were stymied by the seeming impossibility of the goal. By 1967 even Herut, in adopting a common electoral platform with the Liberals, had dropped specific territorial claims beyond the existing lines.

The dominant view was that the key to an Israeli-Arab peace was negotiation with Jordan, which had annexed most of what was to have been the Arab state in Palestine (that is, the West Bank). In fact, negotiations with Jordan's King Abdallah were carried out immediately after the 1948 war, and ended only when the king was assassinated.

There was, therefore, general acceptance of the traditional Labor attitude that a compact but clearly Jewish state in part of Palestine was preferable to the assertion of sovereignty over all of Palestine, which would always have a large Arab population even if Jews did, by some miracle, come to constitute a majority. Already in the 1930s, Ben-Gurion had distinguished between the aspiration of rebuilding the entire homeland and more realistic goals; one should not surrender the ultimate dream, but in the meantime it was necessary to focus on the achievable.[17]

In the context of the 1950s and 1960s Ben-Gurion was the key representative, then, of a "low territorial profile," which sought to combine minimal rule over Arabs with an active defense.[18] The molding of a consensus was furthered by Ben-Gurion's strong personality and by the fact that many Israelis, especially new immigrants, tended to identify him with the state itself because of his historic role in Israel's founding. In addition, there was from the beginning a marked tendency for Israeli public opinion to defer to the official leadership on matters of foreign policy. The Israeli public is highly politicized and well informed on the issues; in fact, the universality of radio news listening is such as to give political discussion the atmosphere of an ongoing town meeting. Opinion is noted for its rapid shifts in response to recent events. Yet, at the same time, there is clear deference to authority on these issues, expressing perhaps the primacy of basic security requirements in the minds of most Israelis.[19]

The political system also contributed to the molding of consensus. As before, Israel's leadership had to rely on intense bargaining and coalition building in order to govern effectively. Unable to adopt a written constitution because of unbridgeable gaps of principle, the political elite devised a system whose stability rested on the sharing of power, both within the government and between the government and other institutions. The other institutions included the Jewish Agency (which continued to deal with world Jewish ties, immigration, and settlement), the Histadrut (which continued to fulfill quasi-governmental functions in the economy), and the religious establishment with its autonomous powers.

Within the government, power is shared through a parliamentary system. Formally, all authority flows from the Knesset, or assembly, of 120 elected members. But the key role is played, as before, by the parties. Representation in the Knesset is by party, with one of the most uncompromising systems of proportional representation in the world. Essentially the entire country is one electoral district, and each party presents a list of up to 120 candidates, carefully numbered in order. Voters then choose a single party list, and each party is awarded a number of seats proportionate to its percentage of the total vote. If 25 percent of the voters choose a particular party, it would receive 25 percent of the Knesset seats (or 30 seats), which would go to the first 30 candidates named on its list.

The key to this process is, of course, the party list, since position on the list determines a candidate's chances of success. This has normally been centralized in the hands of the party leadership, though the process has become more open in recent years.[20] In any event, the entire electoral system reflects and reinforces the centrality of parties in Israeli politics. (It has also assured their proliferation, since any party able to muster 1 percent of the vote is guaranteed representation in the Knesset.)

During the first two decades, the system also guaranteed that Mapai was the center of every government, but that it had to share power with other parties. Mapai was the largest single party and was located in the middle of the political spectrum; it was inconceivable that any combination of parties on the two ends of the spectrum could organize a majority without it. On the other hand, since Mapai never controlled a majority by itself, it was forced to seek coalition partners both from the Left and from the Right. The strength of the prevailing consensus is shown by the fact that only the Communists on the far left, and (until 1967) Herut on the far right, were ruled out as potential coalition partners. All other parties could conceivably become part of the government, and nearly all of them did at one time or another.

The fact that the system was not polarized made cooperation easier. Different issues cut in different ways; Mapai and the National Religious Party might disagree on religious issues, but find common ground on economic policy, while the relationship between Mapai and Mapam might be the other way around. In this situation of cross-cutting alliances, no party would be in total opposition to any other party; all would find some grounds for cooperation on at least one set of issues. Observers have identified at least three axes, or sets of issues, that cut in different ways in Israeli politics during this period.

First, there was the normal socioeconomic dimension of left-right that is the basis of most party classification. On this axis, Labor Zionist parties were leftist and General Zionists (the chief ideological supporters of a free market) were rightist. Second, there was the axis of Israeli-Arab relations, which overlapped but was not identical to the first dimension.[21] There was, for example, a party to the left of Mapai on economic issues—Ahdut Ha'avoda—that took a more hardline position on defense and territories. Conversely, the Progressives, a nonsocialist party, took a fairly dovish position in foreign policy.

The third axis, religious issues, was yet more independent of alignments on the other two axes. The religious parties were not deeply involved in economic or foreign policy, beyond the prevailing consensus, but focused on religious matters. As late as 1968, a leading analyst could note that "religious issues in Israel are largely independent of the left-right split."[22]

This meant that the religious parties enjoyed a key position in the bargaining to establish a governing coalition. Though controlling only 10-15 percent of the seats, their malleability on most economic and foreign policy issues—in fact, on anything but religious issues—made a bargain with them nearly irresistible to Mapai. In return for certain consessions on issues on interest mainly to the religious community, the government would gain the consistent support of 10-15 percent of the Knesset on all other issues (and often this was enough for a majority.) The alternative was hard bargaining with parties that would make serious demands on mainstream issues. Consequently, the religious parties—the National Religious Party in particular—became the "balancers" of the system; the NRP has been a member of every governing coalition since the state was founded.

The remarkable political stability during this period is expressed in the consistency of voting behavior. As Table 1 shows, in the seven elections between 1949 and 1969, Labor Zionist parties as a bloc consistently gained about 50 percent (49-54 percent, to be precise) of the vote. The Center/Right parties (a category that combines General Zionists and Revisionists) consistently received a little less than 30 percent (26-29 percent). Religious parties varied between 12.5 and 15 percent.

This striking regularity took place during a period of mass immigration and enormous social and political upheaval. A number of explanations are usually offered:[23]

Given the consensus produced by the concern for survival, there was a tendency to stick to existing leadership.

In the circumstances of mass immigration, parties were able to recruit new members in rough proportion to their existing strength.

TABLE 1. Knesset Seats by Bloc and Party, 1949-69

	Year of Election						
	1949	1951	1955	1959	1961	1965	1969
Labor Zionists	65	60	59	63	59	63	60
Mapai, Labor[a]	46	45	40	47	42	45	56
Others	19	15	19	16	17	18	4
Center-Right	33	35	33	31	34	32	34
Herut	14	8	15	17	17		
General Zionists,						26	26
Liberals[b]	7	20	13	8	17		
Others	12	7	5	6.	—	6	8
Religious	16	15	17	18	18	17	18
NRP		10	11	12	12	11	12
	16						
Others		5	6	6	6	6	6
Others	6	10	11	8	9	8	8
Communists	4	5	6	3	5	4	4
Arab lists	2	5	5	5	4	4	4

[a]In 1968, Mapai merged with two smaller parties to form the Israel Labor party. Since 1969, the Labor Party and Mapam have appeared in elections on a joint list (the Alignment).

[b]The General Zionists and the Progressive Party merged into the Liberal Party in 1961, and the Liberals (without most of the former Progressives) formed an electoral bloc with Herut from 1965.

Source: Compiled by the author.

Newcomers were more interested in concrete benefits than in ideology, and this instrumental dependence again worked in favor of the existing establishment, which had control of the benefits.

Ben Gurion and Mapai were identified with the state, as the aura of the founding period had not yet faded.

The tendency to defer to official leadership in certain policy areas carried over into "lethargic" voting behavior at the polls.[24]

As a result of this continuity, Israel in the late 1960s was guided by a traditional political elite noted for its stability, longevity, and homogeneity, despite the growing pluralism of Israeli society. A typical member of this elite was a veteran of the Second or Third Aliya, of eastern European origin, committed to Labor Zionism, ideological in basic outlook but pragmatic in execution. (Some would say that "improvisation" best describes this style.) Ben-Gurion, again, would serve as the classic prototype.[25]

The longevity of this elite's tenure in power delayed the process of generation change, to an Israel-born leadership, that might have been expected sooner. The *sabra* or native-born generation of Labor Zionist leaders was generally thought to be less ideological and more down-to-earth than its forebears.[26] But this group—Moshe Dayan, Yigal Allon, Shimon Peres, Yitzhak Rabin—did not reach the top rungs of power until the 1970s. As a result, the change never fully took place, since it was soon superseded by a more fundamental revolution in Israeli politics.

Most of the younger generation of leaders made their initial mark through the defense establishment, rising to high command positions before leaving the army (as is the practice in Israel) while still in their 40s. As army officers as well as sabras, they were usually associated with hardheaded views on defense and security.

Available evidence indicates, however, that there has been limited military influence on high-level decisions, and that, in fact, the spectrum of views in the military command does not differ significantly from that of the general public.[27] This is due in part to the universal military service and the absence of any clearly defined military caste in Israel; society and army are so closely interwined at all points that the army is "civilianized" to the same extent that the society is militarized.

In any event, the important decisions on Israeli policy are made by the party leaders who sit in the cabinet. So long as they can hold the governing coalition in line, they enjoy wide latitude in foreign policy. During the first two decades, only two Israeli governments fell over foreign policy issues—both over questions relating to Germany, which, as an intensely emotional issue in Israel, was one of the few areas outside the prevailing consensus.

The picture up to the Six-Day War, therefore, was one of unusual continuity, despite (because of?) the extreme pressure under which the government operated. Israel had one of the few regimes—practically the only one in the region—that could claim such stability in leadership and policy over such a long period. But appearances were deceptive. Underneath the surface were forces for change (some of them already identified) that would eventually shatter the hold of the traditional establishment.

THE END OF LABOR DOMINANCE

The 1967 war marked the visible beginning of the process that undermined the traditional consensus in Israel. This seems paradoxical, since the war appeared to be a triumphant vindication for the existing leadership, and since it appeared to relieve some of the pressures under which it operated. But the long-term impact of the war was to accelerate some of the basic trends that had been quietly developing for two decades: decline of traditional ideology, the replacement of the "movement style of life" with TV-age mass politics, and the growing assertiveness of non-European and religious groups.[28]

Moreover, precisely by removing some of the pressures and dangers that Israel had faced, the Six-Day War opened up new choices in foreign policy. There was more freedom of maneuver than in the past, and options long considered unrealistic—on both left and right—could be put on the agenda again. There was, in the words of one scholar, an "unfamiliar freedom to formulate policy."[29] And as the area of debate enlarged, there was a greater tendency to challenge the official line.

The leadership had emerged from the war with an apparent consensus on postwar policy. They envisioned limited changes in the 1949 armistice lines: Jerusalem would be reunited under Israeli sovereignty, and there would be minor rectifications in Israel's favor on the West Bank. The Straits of Tiran, for which Israel had fought twice, and the Golan Heights, from which the Syrians had habitually bombarded Israeli settlements, would also remain under Israeli control. Jordan was still seen as the key to future negotiations, based on the return of the bulk of the West Bank (particularly the Arab population centers) to King Hussein.

But given the experience with the assurances of 1957, there would be no withdrawal except as part of a final peace treaty. With the West Bank and Sinai as leverage, and given her convincing military superiority, Israel could afford to wait for the Arab states to come to the negotiating table.

The biggest worry in this scenario, as the leadership saw it, was that the superpowers might interfere, as they had in 1957. The leverage could not operate on the Arabs if the United States joined the Soviet Union in pressing for an immediate and unconditional Israeli withdrawal. In this connection, Israel had to be concerned about its increased dependence on outside support, in the economic and military spheres, that was demonstrated by the war. Relations with the United States became a major source of anxiety.

As a consequence of its general approach to the occupied territories, the Israeli government adopted an "open bridges" policy on the Jordan and discouraged the emergence of independent Arab leadership on the West Bank. Both of these measures served to protect the Jordanian presence in the territory, in anticipation of a peace treaty with Hussein that would trade the West Bank for recognition and normalization. The government established settlements in those areas where border changes were anticipated, largely on security grounds. Policy in this area was guided by what was called the "oral law," since Israel's claims could not be presented formally at this stage. In accordance with the oral law (a concept borrowed from Jewish tradition), settlements were concentrated in the Jordan Valley, on the Golan Heights, and on the border between Egypt and the Gaza Strip.

The settlements in the Jordan Valley were also connected to what became known as the Allon Plan. In this conception, Israel would establish a security frontier, distinct from a political boundary, on the Jordan River. Most of the West Bank and nearly all its Arab population would be demilitarized and returned to Jordan, to which it would be connected by a corridor through the Israeli security belt on the Jordan.

This, then, was the general framework of ideas within which Israel's Labor governments worked. But the Labor approach was challenged from the outset. Herut, and others, opposed any return of the West Bank, a part of the historic Land of Israel, to "alien" rule. On the other end of the spectrum, there was a challenge to the Jordanian approach: the detachment of the West Bank from Jordan opened up the possibility of establishing a Palestinian entity there, as envisioned in the U.N. partition plan. Finally, within parties as well as among them, there were endless nuances on what was to be returned, to whom, and under what conditions. The issue of the occupied territories, and the establishment of Israeli settlements within them, became the litmus test of Israeli politics. Increasingly, everything else came to be measured against this overriding issue.

As noted, party loyalties and cohesion were already being undercut by general changes in society and in the style of life. Israel was becoming more urbanized, with a growing middle-class crystallization.[30] The hold of old ties and of old institutions was being broken. Especially notable was the decline in "kibbutz ideology," in the agrarian values and the socialist dimension of classic Labor Zionism.[31]

This was expressed in a new kind of "mass politics," with a large floating vote influenced more by the issues of the moment, personalities, and general public mood than by ideological loyalties. It was reflected in the changing role of the media. Since late 1968 television had come to play a large role in election campaigns and in shaping public images of candidates and issues, in place of the classic party-sponsored political rallies of the past. The party press, which had once dominated the newspaper scene, was pushed aside by the popular independent papers that were more closely tuned to the general public mood.

This was not exactly the "end of ideology," in the words of one theory. Ideology in Israel has shown great staying power, and some of the changes taking place were in fact merely from one ideology to another (as in a shift from the Labor Zionist view on territory to the no less ideological Revisionist view).[32] There can be little doubt, however, that the intensity of ideological commitments lessened in Israel, as it has elsewhere, and that ideology became less important as an explanation of political behavior. Even the new territorial maximalism was not always the old ideological nationalism of Herut; there was little heard of the claim to the East Bank, and in many ways the new nationalism was much more a "gut reaction" to such things as PLO terrorism, the distrust of outside guarantees, and continuing feelings of insecurity and defiance in a hostile world.

The Labor Party had contributed to its own undermining by developing state institutions that replaced many of the services provided in the past by the party. Much of its ability to recruit new immigrants had been tied to its ability to deliver benefits. Now this dependence—often the only bond to the Labor Party—was broken by the growth of government services outside the party system.

The ideological loosening was seen in the growing tendency of parties to coalesce into larger blocs for electoral purposes, presenting a common list to the electorate. Mapai, Ahdut Ha'avoda, and Rafi (a splinter party established by Ben-Gurion toward the end of his career) merged to form the Israel Labor party in 1968. From 1969, the Labor Party and Mapam presented a single list (the Alignment) in all Israeli elections. The Liberals and Herut formed an electoral list (Gahal) in 1965, and in 1973 this was expanded, with the addition of some smaller parties, to establish the Likud (Unity). In all of this, the cooperating parties overcame ideological differences that in an earlier period would have been considered insuperable.

As the two major blocs grew, the system became more polarized. The Alignment and Likud, between them, captured 82 of the 120 Knesset seats in 1969, but 95 seats in 1981. Tied to this was a decline in the cross-cutting issues that had prevented a clear polarization of Israeli politics, and a convergence of the three separate axes that had characterized political divisions in the past.

With socialism on the decline, the socioeconomic dimension became less distinguishable from divisions on foreign policy. Ahdut Ha'avoda followed the lead of its Labor partners on both issues, while the Liberals and Herut overcame their differences on foreign policy. (Those Liberals who followed the dovish Progressive position split to form the Independent Liberal Party.) At the same time, the NRP and other religious groups became increasingly hawkish, reducing the independence of the religious dimension. In the words of one analyst, there was a "gradual reduction of the multi-dimensional character of the political scene."[33]

The polarization of Israeli politics was accompanied by a shift of opinion to the right, as the dominance of Labor Zionist ideology slipped. The inconsistency of largely leftist leaders and largely centrist followers has already been noted; there was a significant gap between the traditional ideology of Knesset members and the opinions of the electorate as a whole (especially the younger generation). To observers in the 1960s it was clear that the electorate was voting to the left of its opinions on the issues.[34]

The gap was closing, however, as the party vote came to resemble issue positions more closely. Throughout the 1970s, opinions in the Knesset moved to the right.[35] This reflected both the increased number of Likud members (from 26 in 1969 to 43 in 1977) and the increased hawkishness of the NRP members of parliament.

Already in the period immediately after the 1967 war it was noted that most of the public (up to 95 percent in some polls) were unwilling to return most of the West Bank to Arab rule. This stood in stark contrast to a government policy based precisely on leaving such a possibility open. Yet, rather paradoxically, 80 percent of the public (on the average) also said they were satisfied with the government's general performance.[36]

Some of the seeming contradiction is explained by the general disbelief in the possibility of a peace treaty, which was regarded as a necessary condition for return of the West Bank. Responses on questions about the occupied territories were very sensitive to their wording: if the return of territory were posited as part of a settlement, a much higher percentage of the public expressed willingness to return to the 1967 borders with minor changes (according to one poll from the same period, up to 50 percent.)[37] But since most of the public did not believe that a treaty was possible, they remained opposed to the return of territories under prevailing circumstances.

The persistence of a basic pessimism in Israeli opinion is striking. The Continuing Survey of the Israel Institute of Applied Social Research has been tracking most facets of Israeli opinion in depth since 1967.[38] According to Continuing Survey data, during the 1973-77 period around 80 percent (and never less than 72 percent) felt that the aim of Arab states was not just the return of occupied territories, but included the destruction of Israel. After Sadat's initiative in late 1977 this percentage dropped to about 50 percent, but then rebounded to the 60-70 percent range shortly afterward.

Moreover, during the same period between 80 and 90 percent believed there would be another war with Arab countries in the near future, with the median guess being between two and six years. Again, this percentage dropped to about 50 percent with Sadat's visit to Jerusalem, but by early 1980 was again above 80 percent.

But the basic conclusion drawn from the Continuing Survey data is the fluidity of Israeli opinion and its responsiveness to events, despite this background pessimism. The impact of Sadat's visit has already been seen; on other questions the sensitivity to events is even more striking. On the question of whether Arab countries are ready to make real peace, the yes responses were less than 50 percent after the 1967 war, declined to less than 10 percent in late 1970 (during the War of Attrition), rose to the 40-50 percent range after the 1973 war, ranged between 20 to 40 percent in the 1974-77 period, climbed to 80 percent with Sadat's move, and fell to 50 percent after the euphoria dissipated. There was also a sharp differentiation by country, with a much higher percentage believing Egypt was ready for peace (even before 1977), and a much lower percentage believing the same of Syria.

There was a similar pattern on the basic question of surrendering territory in return for peace. When asked to what extent they were willing to surrender territory in order to reach a peace agreement, those willing to return all the occupied territories ranged between 5 and 15 percent, those willing to return some of the territories varied from 50 to 70 percent, and those willing to return none of the territories were recorded from 10 to 40 percent. There was again great sensitivity to specific events and the mood of the moment; the 1973 war produced a sharp drop in the percentage responding "none," as did the Sadat visit. Answers also differed sharply according to the territory in question, with the greatest flexibility on Sinai (apart from control of the Straits of Tiran), and the least on the Golan Heights and Jerusalem.

In short, Israeli attitudes are subject to rapid change in response to new developments. In the words of the leading study (based on Continuing Survey data), "the relationship between public events and Israelis' attitudes is strong, immediate, and consistent in direction and magnitude with those events' potential for affecting the well-being of society."[39]

In considering the role of public opinion, it is also important to recall the tendency of the public to defer to the government's lead. To take one example, despite the trend to the Right, on the eve of the 1977 elections 61 percent of one sample still claimed to be closest to the Alignment (Labor) position on foreign policy, against only 30 percent for Likud. But immediately after the election, and before any other changes had taken place, the same question drew only a 38 percent support for the Alignment's foreign policy, while identification with the Likud rose to 53 percent.[40]

To take another significant case, the Continuing Survey data had never shown a percentage less than 71 percent opposed to returning Sharm El-Sheikh, which controls the Straits of Tiran, to Egypt. Yet after the Sadat initiative in 1977, the government quickly decided on precisely such a move, and outside opposition evaporated, except for a vocal but small minority.

Foreign policy issues, then, played at best a secondary role in the shift to the right and the rise of the Likud. The basic societal, economic, ideological, and political trends already delineated were clearly more important. Furthermore, these trends were reinforced by some important demographic changes. As noted, the younger generation were less tied to traditional ideology, and thus greater supporters of the Likud. The same was true of the *Sephardi* voters—those of Asian or African background, mostly from Arab countries, and their children. Given the numerical edge of the Sephardim among the youth (they comprise two-thirds of all schoolchildren), these two categories overlapped to some extent.

It was only in the 1970s that the ethnic differences between Sephardim and Ashkenazim (Jews of European or American origin) became a factor in Israeli politics. Before then, for the reasons outlined, the large influx of Sephardim had not changed the voting patterns, and had not influenced foreign policy.[41] By the mid-1970s, however, the basic difference in outlook broke through the mold, and a distinctive Sephardi influence on the direction of Israeli politics emerged.

In part, the Sephardi outlook was a matter of accumulated resentments against the system. As relative latecomers, the immigrants from Middle East countries had started at the bottom of the ladder, and had often been exposed to an attitude of superiority on the part of the "Europeans." That the Establishment espoused an ideology of equality that favored the downtrodden did not seem to help; the fact was that, whatever its theories, the Left was the establishment. Furthermore, the Sephardim tended to take a Middle Eastern view of society, which was not class-based but saw deprivation chiefly in relation to established authority. In any event, after a period of incubation, there was a growing alienation from the Labor establishment that was especially marked among the younger Sephardi generation that had grown up in Israel.

Integration of the Sephardim into the power structure had, indeed, proceeded slowly. To use Knesset membership as an index, only 3.3 percent in the First Knesset were from the Sephardi community, and in the Eighth Knesset (1973) this had risen to only 10 percent—at a time when Sephardim already constituted a majority of the population.[42]

The Likud was attractive to Sephardi voters because it, too, was "outside" the system. In addition, because of their personal hardships in Arab countries and their general approach to politics, Sephardi voters tend to be more hawkish on Arab-Israel issues.[43] They responded to Begin's appeal on traditional historic and religious grounds, as opposed to the cold rationalism of Western liberalism and socialism represented by the Labor party. Having endured as a minority in the Arab world, they saw no injustice in West Bank Arabs continuing to live under Israeli rule.[44]

The Sephardi influence was first felt in local politics. From the early 1960s, Sephardi mayors and councils came to power in the development towns where they constituted a majority. The breakthrough on the national level came in 1977, when Sephardi voters supported the Likud by an estimated two-to-one margin.

The absence of a consensus on foreign policy was also illustrated by the growth of extraparliamentary groups on both ends of the spectrum. On the left, such groups as Peace and Security, and later, Peace Now, charged both Labor and Likud with lack of diplomatic flexibility. On the right, the Land of Israel movement (in Hebrew, Movement for the Entire Land of Israel) emerged soon after the 1967 war to oppose return of any occupied territories; later, in the 1970s, Gush Emunim (Bloc of Faithful) came into being to push Jewish settlement in the West Bank.

If the wait and see government posture on the territories had produced results, subsequent history might have been different. As time passed, however, and the anticipated Arab response did not come, doubts about the official strategy grew and other options became more attractive.

One obvious alternative was not to withdraw from the territories occupied in 1967 and to perpetuate the Israeli presence in all parts of the historic homeland—especially in Judea and Samaria, as the West Bank was known in Jewish tradition. This could be seen as the revival of a traditional perspective, rather than as a new idea. It was, in one interpretation, not only the viewpoint of the Revisionists but also an expression of a traditional religio-historic aspiration predating Zionism. One could point to deep-seated feelings against the partition of Eretz-Israel, even among those (such as Ben-Gurion) who reluctantly accepted it on pragmatic grounds. There had been, it was said, no ideological commitment to the 1949 armistice lines by the government of Israel; the government had merely recognized reality. They were therefore free now to respond to new realities.[45]

There were, of course, variants to this viewpoint. The Land of Israel movement, for example, did not originally associate itself with Begin's Herut because Begin was a partner in the government during the 1967-70 period, and because Herut tended to focus on the West Bank rather than on the other territories occupied in 1967 (such as Sinai), while the Land of Israel movement stressed the importance of keeping all the occupied territories.

Another clear option was to make a more active search for peace, rather than waiting for the Arab states (especially Jordan) to respond to the implicit deal Israel was offering. This was also in a sense the continuation of an earlier tradition, frozen over the preceding 20 years, but going back to the diplomatic efforts of Chaim Weizmann. Proponents of this approach felt that the control of Arab lands and population made it possible for Israel to demonstrate its goodwill and the limited scope of its territorial ambitions.

There was also a new external reality: the appearance of Palestinian Arabs as an independent actor in the conflict, after their eclipse for two decades. The Palestinian claim was now being presented forcefully as a national claim, rather than as a refugee problem. This cast some doubt on the viability of the traditional Labor position, which posited a solution through negotiation with Jordan. Instead, the possibility of a Palestinian state or entity, centered on the West Bank, seemed to fit the new realities better. This presented a challenge to the old consensus within the Labor party itself.[46]

Labor was in fact pulled in many directions. In addition to the dovish critics, there were those, centered around Defense Minister Moshe Dayan, who favored the development of a permanent Israeli presence on the West

Bank. As a split between Dayan and the old guard developed, government policy became increasingly inconsistent. The enthusiasm for U.N. Resolution 242 (based on withdrawal in exchange for peace) varied from one period to the next, and the official position on establishing new settlements became increasingly murky.[47]

As Rael Jean Isaac points out, in the end the government adopted elements of both new options: it sought out new diplomatic openings, both with Jordan and elsewhere (with West Bank leaders, for example), while allowing a slow growth in the Israeli presence in the territories. But while the success of peace options depended on the response of the other side, the establishment of new settlements was a cumulative process that could be accomplished unilaterally. Thus, the success of the second option rested in Israeli hands, and as time passed was likely to move closer to realization.[48] Furthermore, the government's hand was being forced, increasingly, by groups such as Gush Emunim, which sought to establish new settlements, without government authorization, precisely in the Arab population centers of the West Bank rather than in the relatively uninhabited security belt upon which official settlement efforts had focused, in accord with the Allon Plan and the oral law. Though confidence in the government was already declining, the Yom Kippur War of 1973 dealt it a punishing blow. It seemed to confirm a growing image of complacency, deterioration, and lack of clear direction. On the eve of the 1973 war, according to the polls of the Israel Institute of Applied Social Research, around 60 percent of the Israeli public still perceived the general situation in Israel as positive. After the war, and throughout the 1974-77 period, this dropped to 10-20 percent.[49]

The changing climate finally triggered the long-expected "changing of the guard" to a new generation of Labor leadership (Rabin, Peres, Allon). But the Rabin government, in the 1974-77 period, was unable to reverse the trends already set in motion. Labor continued to suffer from the lack of a sense of direction, which was aggravated by bitter personal rivalries among the new leaders (especially Rabin and Peres).

The issues were not limited to foreign policy. Economic problems mounted in the wake of the Yom Kippur War, and polls showed that economic worries had become more prominent than ever among Israelis. The general malaise was compounded by scandals in the ruling party as the 1977 elections approached, further strengthening the image of a leadership corrupted by its lengthy tenure in office. The evaluation of government performance, which had been 90 percent positive in 1967, had plummeted to 15 percent by mid-1977.[50]

The unsettled state of affairs was underlined by the appearance of the first serious new political movement in Israel's political history. The Democratic Movement for Change (DMC), under the leadership of archeologist Yigal Yadin (a former army chief of staff and prominent public figure), brought together a number of centrist and reformist elements aroused by the war and its aftermath. It threatened to draw votes from Labor, in particular.

Nevertheless, there was little expectation that the governing party would be cast into the wilderness. It might very well be weakened by the elections, as an angry electorate punished it for its sins, but it was still inconceivable that it would not continue as the core of the Israeli government.

But the visible and not so visible developments that converged in May 1977 changed the face of Israeli politics irrevocably. After half a century on the outside, the Revisionist Zionists, under Menachem Begin, came to power.

THE NEW ERA

It was clear that Labor dominance was fading, but no one had expected the final fall so soon. As Table 2 shows, there was a steady upward trend in Likud strength, from 32 seats in 1969 (counting the parties that later joined the Likud), to 39 in 1973, and 43 in 1977 (plus two for Ariel Sharon's party, Shlomzion, which joined the Likud im-

TABLE 2. Knesset Seats by Party, 1969-1981

	Year of Election			
	1969	*1973*	*1977*	*1981*
Alignment (Labor)	56	51	32	47
DMC	—	—	15	—
Likud*	26	39	43	48
NRP	12	10	12	6
Other religious	6	5	5	7
Others	20	15	13	12

*In 1969, electoral bloc of Herut and Liberals (Gahal). In 1973, Gahal joined with smaller parties to form the Likud (Unity) electoral bloc.

Sources: Compiled by the author.

mediately after the election). But this in itself would not have been enough for a change of government.

The rest of the explanation lies in the other factors weakening Labor, which lost 19 seats between 1973 and 1977. Foremost among these was the appearance of the DMC, which won 15 seats. Most of the DMC votes—two-thirds is the usual estimate—came from former Alignment supporters.

Clearly the election was not simply a referendum on foreign policy, but involved many other factors. As noted, however, it served to legitimate the Likud position on foreign policy in the public mind, and there was a significant swing of opinion to the Likud on these issues after the election. This was not just a change in parties, but a watershed in Israeli politics. It brought to power a new orientation, with new values and political symbols.

The Likud was still a loose alliance of parties, containing Herut, the Liberals, the Land of Israel movement, and four smaller rightist or centrist parties. Increasingly, however, the Likud came to be dominated by Herut, given Begin's central position and the general feeling that it was Herut (and Begin) that accounted for the coalition's electoral success. And Herut itself had always been dominated by Menachem Begin.

Begin had led the Revisionists in Palestine since the early 1940s, and his approach had changed little during that period. He remained committed to the same principles espoused by Jabotinsky in the 1920s and 1930s, which had now finally been vindicated by electoral victory after five decades of defeats (and were soon to be vindicated again by his success in achieving Israel's first peace treaty, something that had always eluded the "appeasers" of Labor). Begin was also very definitely a product of the Holocaust, having lost most of his family to the Nazis. His entire approach was premised on uncompromising defense of Jewish interests, disbelief in the benevolence of any actor in world politics, and a maximalist interpretation of Jewish rights and claims on the basis of history, injustices suffered by Jews, and practical necessity.[51]

Begin's consistent opposition to "the return of Judea and Samaria to alien rule" added an entirely new dimension to the conflict over that area. Israel was now committed to remaining on the West Bank, though possibly with arrangements for Arab autonomy, and to preserving the right of Jews to live anywhere they chose in the historic homeland. The latter aim struck a deep chord in the general population, who recalled that Jews had lived in Hebron until 1929, and who objected to the idea that any part of Eretz-Israel should be kept, in the infamous Nazi phrase, "Judenrein" (free of Jews).

At the same time, the Likud government did not move to annex the West Bank, given the problem of an Arab population that, together with Arabs already in Israel, would within a generation or two constitute a majority within the country (not to mention the price to be paid in world reaction and American support). But the new government could and did lend support to the establishment of new settlements in the heart of the West Bank. In this regard the natural inclinations of the Likud leadership were reinforced by the political leverage of Gush Emunim, which exercised considerable influence on the National Religious Party, upon which the government was dependent much of the time for a working majority. In addition, public opinion tended to be very permissive toward new settlements, which tapped the still-deep respect in which such pioneering enterprises had always been held. The irony was that this time it was the Revisionists and their allies who were engaged in building Zionism "from the bottom," through the very sort of settlement activity they had once denounced as inconsequential.

Toward Sinai, however, the Likud approach was more practical; Sinai did not have the historic-religious significance of Judea and Samaria. Begin was able, therefore, to respond to Satat's initiative with a rapid reversal of the Israeli position (affirmed by every government since 1967) that Sharm El-Sheikh would never be returned to Arab rule. Not only was every inch of the Sinai Peninsula surrendered to Egypt, but Begin even agreed to dismantle Israeli settlements (an action almost without precedent) in order to conclude a treaty.

The main sticking point in negotiations with Egypt was not Sinai, or any bilateral Egyptian-Israeli issue, but the connection between an Egyptian-Israeli treaty and basic Israeli-Palestinian issues. The solution, reached at Camp David, was to disconnect the two subjects to the extent possible. The Israeli government committed itself, at the same time, to autonomy for West Bank Arabs during a five-year transition period, but with certain important stated and unstated reservations. First, Israel still reserved the right to claim Israeli sovereignty in the negotiations at the end of the transition period. Second, Begin made clear that the autonomy envisioned was personal, applying to the Arab population but not the West Bank as a territory (which accorded perfectly with traditional Revisionist thinking). Finally, Israel made it clear that, following a temporary pause, settlement of the West Bank would continue.

There was a question is some minds over the extent to which these changes represented Israeli opinion, and whether the 1977 elections might not have been an aberration. This was settled by the 1981 elections. By this time the DMC had disappeared, with most of its votes presumably

returning to the Alignment. Furthermore, Likud popularity had dropped, despite the temporary boost given by the Sadat visit and the
Egyptian-Israeli treaty. Economic problems were monumental; efforts to
return to market mechanisms had the effect of pushing inflation from an
already-high 40 percent a year to an astronomical 120 percent. In any
event, the Likud hardly dared touch most aspects of the welfare state,
since much of its voting base was paradoxically in lower-income groups.

In addition, the governing coalition had suffered several embarrass-
ing defections. Foreign Minister Moshe Dayan, who had been invited by
Begin to join the government (their views on the West Bank being
compatible), had eventually resigned over other issues. Defense Minister
Ezer Weizmann left the government in anger over what he saw as Begin's
inflexibility. Some of Begin's former comrades on the right, in contrast,
split with the government over the peace treaty with Egypt and founded
a new, ultranationalist party (Tehiya). By early 1981, some polls showed
the Likud winning only 20 seats in the coming elections.

This, however, turned out to be misleading. As the election results
show (Table 2), Likud continued to demonstrate the slow but steady
accretion of strength that had been apparent since 1969, gaining an
additional five seats over 1977. Thus, while Labor regained the votes that
had been lost to the DMC, it failed to return to its historic level of
strength, and now appeared practically on a par with the Likud. Furthermore, although the Likud had only a one-vote edge, the remaining seats
were held by parties that, by and large, preferred Likud to Labor (religious
and nationalist parties accounting for 18 of the 25 seats).

Another trend that continued was the increasing polarization of the
system. Likud and Labor between them won 95 of the 120 Knesset seats;
only 20 years earlier, in 1961, the two largest parties controlled 59 seats.
The polarization was also beginning to make serious dents in the religious
vote, as the National Religious Party lost half its seats (some of them,
apparently, to the Likud, and some to a new Sephardi religious party).
Ironically, the election left the religious parties in a better bargaining position, despite their loss of votes, given the close balance between the two
major blocs.

Ethnic divisions appeared even more sharply in this campaign. An
estimated 60 percent of the Sephardi voters supported the Likud, against
roughly 30 percent for the Labor Alignment. The proportions were
exactly reversed among Ashkenazi voters (60 percent Alignment, 30 percent Likud). Labor obviously had not effectively bridged the ethnic gap.
New voters—predominantly Sephardi—were still choosing the Likud by

a wide margin. During the 1969-81 period, Labor succeeded in adding only 75,000 votes to its overall total, while the Likud total grew by 375,000 during the same years.[52]

The Likud's strongest support still came from lower-income groups, despite its identification with conservative economics. After four years in the opposition, Labor was still seen as the establishment.

The election results did not mean, however, the replacement of Labor dominance by Likud dominance. What was emerging was a basically competitive political system, polarized between two major blocs, either of which could serve as the core of a functioning government. Despite the continuation of demographic trends favoring the Likud, the margin was still close enough, loyalties still fluid enough, and the floating vote still large enough, that future elections could still go either way.

The Likud government that emerged from the elections was in some ways more narrowly based than its predecessor, given the departure of such figures as Dayan and Weizmann. By the same token, it was perhaps more decisive and more unified, since a single viewpoint tended to dominate more completely. The major personality, apart from Begin, was Ariel Sharon, a Patton-style military hero whose reputation for impulsiveness and extreme hawkishness had kept him out of a key position during the first Begin government. But Sharon could no longer be denied, and he became defense minister.

During the period that followed, new settlements on the West Bank were pursued vigorously. (The government adopted a strategy of establishing residential communities within commuting distance of Israeli cities, thus broadening the potential base of "pioneers" beyond those ready to live in primitive isolated encampments.) At the same time, talks with Egypt over the nature of the transitional autonomy regime reached an impasse; this had the effect of relieving immediate pressures on the Israeli government.

Interventions in Lebanon, in 1978 and 1982, came in response to the effort of the Palestine Liberation Organization to develop southern Lebanon into an effective base of operations against Israel. In a sense, the Israeli actions demonstrated again the broadened area of choice that it now enjoyed. With a reduction of the Soviet role in the region and the signing of the Egyptian peace treaty, Israel's security position was better than it had ever been. Thus the 1982 attack on the PLO in southern Lebanon, and the decision to pursue the PLO forces to Beirut and beyond, represented policy choices that, wise or unwise, would have been a luxury rather than a necessity in an earlier period. The Lebanon campaign was, in a sense, Israel's first "optional" war—one that policy makers could have chosen to fight at a different time, or in a different way, or possibly not at all.

Consequently, the war aroused serious internal opposition in a way that earlier campaigns had not. Much of this opposition, however, was focused on the extent of the campaign and the manner in which policy was made and announced, rather than on the basic decision to pacify the northern border (which was still regarded, by most, as necessary). Public reaction peaked, in any event, when widespread demonstrations (including a rally attended by almost 10 percent of the country's population) forced the government to establish an official body of inquiry into the massacre of Palestinian civilians at the Sabra and Shatila refugee camps in Beirut. The subsequent workings of the Kahan Commission— which publicly interrogated officials up to the prime minister himself and forced the resignation of Ariel Sharon as defense minister—were strong testimony to the continued vigor of Israel's domestic political institutions and pluralistic traditions.

Growing discontent with the prolonged Israeli presence in Lebanon, fed by continuing casualties in the more exposed positions, led in mid-1983 to a planned partial withdrawal to a more easily defended line. But the full pullout of Israeli forces remained problematic, as the government was committed to remaining in southern Lebanon until the Syrians and PLO withdrew from their positions in eastern Lebanon. Withdrawal without this achievement would, in the eyes of the government, open it up to serious attack from its many domestic critics. Consequently, the essential decision was in effect left to Syria, which displayed little initial inclination to cooperate.

There was again, by mid-1983, a wave of discontent with the Begin government. Evaluation of its performance in the Continuing Survey dropped from 66 percent approval in August 1982, to 44 percent in January 1983.[53] By mid-year, the Likud and Labor were again running neck-and-neck in the preference polls, after Likud had held an 18-seat margin at the beginning of the year.[54] Begin also suffered a loss of prestige when his candidate for president of Israel (the ceremonial head of state chosen by the Knesset) was defeated by the Labor candidate, Chaim Herzog.

Some of the discontent, again, could be traced to economic woes. Before the 1981 elections, Yigal Hurwitz, who had tried to institute a serious belt-tightening regime to bring the economy under control, was replaced as finance minister by Yoram Aridor. Aridor instituted a series of tax cuts, mainly on consumption items, that improved the Likud's popularity in the election but aggravated Israel's basic economic problems, in particular the negative trade balance.

The balance of payments deficit continued to worsen, and by early 1983 Israel had only three months of cash reserves. Foreign aid by this time was being used almost entirely to pay debts; the debt service now amounted to 32 percent of export earnings. Inflation, which had been reduced somewhat, was back over 140 percent a year. Labor productivity was not keeping up with wage increases.

To this uncertainty was added the question of what would come after Begin. Given his centrality in the government, and the highly personalized patterns of politics that had developed over the years, it seemed clear that Begin's departure in September 1983 would leave a large vacuum. The choice of Foreign Minister Yitzhak Shamir as Begin's immediate successor assured the temporary continuation of dominance by a traditional Revisionist viewpoint, but the strong challenge by Deputy Prime Minister David Levy—representing the Likud's Sephardic voting base—showed that the winds of change were blowing in the governing party.

But Labor was also in considerable disarray, with the continuing personal rivalry between Peres, the titular party leader, and Rabin, the former prime minister who had been forced to step aside for Peres in 1977. A new wild card in Labor circles was Yitzhak Navon, the former president, who as a popular public figure and a Sephardi was potentially Labor's strongest candidate for prime minister. Some polls showed Navon ousting the Likud from power as head of the labor ticket.

Underneath the partisan furors, however, there was still a great degree of consensus in Israel on basic approaches to foreign policy. Most Israelis could still be characterized as risk-averse, disbelieving in Arab moderation, preferring an active defense, reticent about bold political or diplomatic initiatives, and apprehensive about the degree of dependence on superpower support. (The United States is regarded as too eager to promote agreements, and not realistic enough about the hostile forces in the world.)

There has been a broadening of choices available to the Israeli government, as many constraints have loosened over time. There has been less ideological rigidity (despite Begin's image), and more real options available in any given situation. But the bottom line is that the political scene remains highly fluid, with rapid shifts of opinion and swings of mood. Views on such a fundamental issue as the return of occupied territories still shift as much as 10 percent from one month to the next.[55] Specific policies are still shaped, in other words, by events beyond Israel's control, and especially events in the Arab world. As has been seen in the response to Sadat's initiative in 1977, Arab leaders can, through dramatic moves of their own, rewrite the terms of Israeli politics. Despite the reassertion of realities in Israel's public life, the nation is still not master in its own house.

NOTES

1. This thesis is developed by Shlomo Avineri, *The Making of Modern Zionism: The Intellectual Origins of the Jewish State* (New York: Basic Books, 1981), pp. 5-13.

2. For a fuller elaboration of Labor Zionist ideology (labeled "kibbutz ideology") and its role in Israeli thinking through the 1960s, see Alan Arian, *Ideological Change in Israel* (Cleveland: Case Western Reserve University Press, 1968).

3. Avineri, pp. 226-27.

4. The Hebrew term *aliya* (pl. *aliyot*), meaning ascent, is used to denote immigration to Palestine or, after 1948, to Israel.

5. For discussion of this point, see Daniel Elazar, "Israel's Compound Polity," in *Israel at the Polls: The Knesset Elections of 1977*, ed., Howard R. Penniman (Washington, D.C.: American Enterprise Institute for Public Policy Research, 1979).

6. Shmuel N. Eisenstadt, *Israeli Society* (New York: Basic Books, 1967), pp. 211-14.

7. The origins of Israeli political institutions in the Mandate period are analyzed by Dan Horowitz and Moshe Lissak, *Origins of the Israeli Polity: Palestine under the Mandate* (Chicago and London: University of Chicago Press, 1978).

8. Jewish political culture is discussed in the writings of Daniel Elazar; see, for example, *Kinship and Consent: The Jewish Political Tradition and its Contemporary Uses* (Washington, D.C.: University Press of America, 1983); also, the article in Penniman (footnote 5), pp. 5-10, 29-33. On consociational democracy, see Horowitz and Lissak, pp. 10-13, 228-30; and Emanuel Gutmann and Jacob M. Landau, "The Political Elite and National Leadership in Israel," in *Political Elites in the Middle East*, ed., George Lenczowski, (Washington, D.C.: American Enterprise Institute for Public Policy Research, 1975), p. 171.

9. See elaboration in Arian, pp. 172-73.

10. Michael Brecher, *The Foreign Policy System of Israel: Settings, Images, Process* (New Haven: Yale University Press, 1972), p. 69.

11. See discussion in Brecher, pp. 89-93.

12. Ben Halpern, *The Idea of the Jewish State*, 2nd ed. (Cambridge, Mass.: Harvard University Press, 1969), p. 248.

13. Brecher, pp. 109-13.

14. For a fuller discussion of the forces molding consensus during this period, see Rael Jean Isaac, *Israel Divided: Ideological Politics in the Jewish State* (Baltimore, Md.: The Johns Hopkins University Press, 1976), Ch. 1; see also Yoram Peri, "The Rise and Fall of Israel's National Consensus," *New Outlook* 26 (May 1983): 28-31; and Ibid. 26 (June 1983):

15. Israel's defense doctrines as a function of geographic and military realities are analyzed lucidly by Avner Yaniv, "Deterrence without a Bomb: Israel's Security Policy in Perspective," *Orbis* (forthcoming, Fall 1983).

16. For example, Avi Shlaim and Avner Yaniv, "Domestic Politics and Foreign Policy

in Israel," *International Affairs* 56 (April 1980): 242-62, who emphasize the internal causes of a conservative, risk-averse diplomacy, and especially the lack of sufficient unity within governing parties for pursuit of a coherent strategy.

17. Isaac, pp. 33-35.

18. Shlomo Aronson, *Conflict and Bargaining in the Middle East* (Baltimore, Md.: The Johns Hopkins University Press, 1978), Ch. 1.

19. Asher Arian, "The Passing of Dominance," *Jerusalem Quarterly* 5 (Fall 1977): 25-26.

20. Efraim Torgovnik, "Israel: The Persistent Elite," in *Politican Elites and Political Development in the Middle East* ed., Frank Tachau (Cambridge; Schenkman Publishing Co., 1975), pp. 234-35.

21. Arian, 1968, pp. 48-49, presents the statistical backing for separate scales on economic and foreign policy issues. Elazar, pp. 10-11, also argues against a unidimensional view, presenting a picture of a triangular relationship among three major camps (Elazar puts Revisionists and General Zionists together in the "Civil Camp," and they have in fact appeared as a single electoral list since 1965).

22. Arian, 1968, p. 55

23. See Eisenstadt, pp. 332 ff.; Leonard Fein, *Politics in Israel* (Boston: Little, Brown, 1967), pp. 228-29.

24. Arian, *The Choosing People* (Cleveland: Case Western Reserve University Press, 1973).

25. For a fuller picture, see Gutmann and Landau; Brecher, Chs. 10-14; Yuval Elizur and Eliahu Salpeter, *Who Rules Israel?* (New York: Harper & Row, 1973); Torgovnik; R. Hrair Dekmejian, *Patterns of Political Leadership: Lebanon, Israel, Egypt* (Albany: State University of New York Press, 1969).

26. The classic portrait of the generation split is Amos Elon, *The Israelis: Founders and Sons* (New York: Holt, Rinehart and Winston, 1971).

27. Don Peretz, "Israeli Foreign Policymaking," in *Middle East Foreign Policy: Issues and Processes*, ed., R.D. McLaurin, Don Peretz, and Lewis W. Snider (New York: Praeger, 1982), pp. 157-58; see also Brecher, pp. 134-37.

28. For discussion of this point, see Nadav Safran, "The Effects of Isareli Politics on its Foreign Policy," in *Dynamics of a Conflict: A Re-examination of the Arab-Israeli Conflict*, ed., Gabriel Sheffer (Atlantic Highlands, N.J.: Humanities Press, 1975), pp. 201-11.

29. Isaac, p. 134.

30. Eisenstadt, esp. pp. 211 ff.

31. Arian, 1968, esp. pp. 133-35.

32. Ibid., p. 23. Isaac, p. 16, argues that in some ways the challenge to Labor ideas represented an renewal of traditional ideology.

33. Emanuel Gutmann, "Parliamentary Elites: Israel," in *Electoral Politics in the Middle East: Issues, Voters and Elites* ed., Jacob M. Landau, Ergun Ozbudun, and Frank Tachau (London: Croom Helm, 1980), p. 294. See also Avner Yaniv and Fabian Pascal, "Doves, Hawks and Other Birds of a Feather: The Distribution of Israeli Parliamentary Opinion on the Future of the Occupied Territories 1967-1977," *British Journal of Political Science* 10 (April 1980): 260-67.

34. Arian, 1968, pp. 36, 43, 52-53.

35. Yaniv and Pascal.

36. Isaac, p. 134.

37. Ibid., p. 150.

38. All Continuing Survey data are from Russell A. Stone, *Social Change in Israel: Attitudes and Events, 1967-1979* (New York: Praeger, 1982).

39. Ibid., pp. 300-1.

40. Arian, 1977, pp. 26-27.

41. Brecher, p. 96.

42. Gutmann and Landau, pp. 183-86.

43. See Mina Zemach, *Positions of the Jewish Majority in Israel Toward the Arab Minority* (Jerusalem: Van Leer Institute, 1980), cited in Peretz, pp. 174, 192.

44. On Sephardi political attitudes, see Nadav Safran, *Israel: The Embattled Ally* (Cambridge, Mass.: The Belknap Press of Harvard University Press, 1978), pp. 89-94; Dan Horowitz, "More than a Change in Government," *Jerusalem Quarterly* 5 (Fall 1977): 9-13; Asher Arian, "Elections 1981: Competitiveness and Polarization," *Jerusalem Quarterly* 21 (Fall 1981): 16-27; Daniel Elazar, "Israel's New Majority," *Commentary* 75 (March 1983): 33-39.

45. For a full exposition of this viewpoint, see Isaac, esp. pp. 18-44 and 61-63.

46. Ibid., p. 150; Peri.

47. For a full picture of governmental inconsistency on the settlement issue, see Avner Yaniv and Yael Yishai, "Israeli Settlements in the West Bank: The Politics of Intransigence," *Journal of Politics* 43 (1981): 1105-28.

48. Isaac, esp. pp. 101, 128, 136.

49. Stone, pp. 149-55.

50. Ibid., pp. 265, 268-71.

51. The best picture of Begin's thinking is still that in his own account of the prestatehood days: Menachem Begin, *The Revolt* (New York: Henry Schuman, 1951).

52. For a full analysis, see Arian, 1981.

53. *Jerusalem Post International Edition.* January 30-February 5, 1983.

54. Four different polls are reported in ibid., June 19-25, 1983.

55. Ibid., February 6-12, 1983, and April 17-23, 1983.

5

The Palestinian Dimension

Aaron David Miller**

After nearly four decades of confrontation between Arabs and Israelis, the problem of the Palestinians remains the greatest obstacle blocking further progress toward resolution of the Arab-Israeli conflict. It is, to be sure, not the only problem left to resolve. The refusal of most Arab states to accept unambiguously the legitimacy of a Jewish state, the Likud government's determination to hold on to the West Bank, Gaza, and Golan Heights, superpower and inter-Arab rivalries, and the inevitable instability stemming from a region in the midst of social, economic, and political change have acquired a momentum of their own, creating a multidimensional conflict difficult to disentangle, let alone resolve.

Still, the problem of the "much too promised land"—how to reconcile Israel's sovereignty and security with the national aspirations of the Palestinian people and the interests of their Arab patrons—remains the core issue. Those who question the centrality of the issue quite correctly point out that finding a homeland for the Palestinians will not guarantee a stable Middle East nor insure a speedy end to the Arab-Israeli rivalries. Nonetheless an unresolved Palestinian problem will exacerbate regional instability and guarantee an endless conflict between Israel and its Arab neighbors. That the Palestinian issue alone is not a powerful enough incentive to force Arab states into an unwanted military clash with Israel should not obscure how great an obstacle it poses to their ability to conclude a lasting peace. For reasons that will become clear, the Palestinian issue is still an extraordinarily volatile and resilient factor in Middle East politics—fundamentally affecting the way the Arab states, Palestin-

**The views expressed in this article are the author's and do not reflect the views of the Department of State or any other government agency.

ians, and Israelis look at themselves and each other. It is no coincidence that the most recent Arab-Israeli war, precipitated by Israel's June 1982 invasion of Lebanon, was at heart a conflict between Israel and the PLO, the institutional embodiment of Palestinian nationalism. Nor it is surprising that the area's latest peace initiative—the Reagan plan of September 1982—foundered on a combination of Israel's opposition to a Palestinian homeland and Jordan's refusal to move without formal PLO support. Thus, after half a century, what to do about the Palestinians continues to affect how the Arabs and Israelis make war and peace.

That the Palestinian problem should prove so intractable is hardly surprising. The issues involved go much deeper than those of a legal or territorial dispute over competing claims and boundaries. They are now embedded in the national consciousness and identities of Israelis, Palestinians, and Arabs. Not only do Palestinians and Israelis refuse to accept the legitimacy of each other's claims, but their conflict has become inextricably and dangerously linked to the domestic and foreign policies of most Arab regimes.

To make matters worse, the Palestinian problem is overlaid with both the kind of deeply emotional, religious, and ideological issues (Jerusalem, holy places, divine right, and "national destiny") and vital geostrategic concerns (oil, bases, superpower rivalry) that do not always produce rational and logical reactions by locals and outsiders. All of this is occurring in the context of a highly unstable region in which the parties are armed not only with the most deadly weaponry money can buy but with passions and hatreds that distort images of their adversaries.

This peculiar entanglement has given the Palestinian problem a number of unique but interconnected dimensions, three of which provide the focus of this chapter: first, the relationship between Israelis and Palestinians; second, the dynamics between Arab states and the Palestinians; and third, the unique nature of the Palestinian experience. This is not to ignore the importance of the conflict's international and external dimensions, but the heart of the problem is regional and must ultimately be resolved by the peoples of the area. Without an appreciation of each of these internal dimensions and the way each influences the others, it is impossible to understand the full context of the problem. Indeed, any solution to what has become one of the most complex problems in international politics, if indeed one is possible, will have to take into account the complexities of each dimension and resolve key contradictions and conflicts within and between them.

THE HISTORICAL SETTING

Nowhere are the complexities of these three dimensions better reflected than in the development of the Palestinian national movement and its impact on Arab-Israeli and inter-Arab politics. Although the political and organizational dimension of the Palestinian experience is but one aspect of their story, it serves as a useful window through which to view larger issues, specifically to examine the Palestinian relationship with the Arab states, their historical conflict with political Zionism and Israel, and developments within their own communities. These historical themes reveal a striking continuity.

For the majority of Arabic-speaking inhabitants of Ottoman controlled Palestine there was little sense of a defined national identity before the twentieth century. The idea of *Filastin* had a religious, cultural, geographic significance during these early years,[1] but for the majority of the area's inhabitants—poor Muslim farmers—identity was fixed along family, religious, and regional lines. Although the Christian Arab minority was more susceptible to the secular, national ideas of their western coreligionists, the Muslim community remained traditional and wary of change. Until the collapse of the Ottoman Empire and the British occupation of Palestine, most Muslims, despite the growing repressiveness of Turkish policies, remained loyal to the sultan in Istanbul.[2]

It was neither the policies of the Ottomans nor of the Europeans, however, that were responsible for laying the foundations of a separate Palestinian national identity. Although heavily influenced by emerging Arab nationalist ideology, particularly in Syria, Arabs in Palestine—Muslim and Christians alike—were profoundly influenced by the rise of political Zionism and increasing Jewish immigration and land purchases. Fearful that a Zionist movement, supported by Britain as the new mandatory power for Palestine, would transform the entire area, Arab politicians and intellectuals intensified their efforts to lay specific claims to Palestine based on the continuity of Arab settlement and their majority status there.[3] French suppression of the emerging Arab nationalist movement in Syria further reinforced a sense of Palestinian particularism.

Throughout the 1920s and 1930s, the Arabs of Palestine tried to close ranks, organize politically against the Zionists, and persuade the British to discontinue their support for a Jewish homeland. Hampered by divisions within their ranks, their leadership's refusal to cooperate with the mandatory government, and the Zionists' success in building strong political, social, and economic institutions, Palestinian Arabs failed to develop an effective strategy to combat either the British or the Jews. Although increasing radicalization of Palestinian activity—culminating in the general strike and revolt of 1936-39—accelerated Britain's retreat from the idea of a partitioned Palestine,[4] temporarily galvanized nationalist leadership, and forced the Jews, the British, and the Arab states to take Palestinians more seriously, Britain's suppression of the revolt, the bitterness it left among those Palestinians who participated and those who did not, left the Palestinian community divided, weakened, and without effective leadership, and more dependent on Arab support.[5]

It was at this precise moment that the Jewish community, galvanized by the Nazi campaign to exterminate European Jewry and Britain's refusal to open the doors to Jewish refugees, intensified its efforts to push at home and abroad for the idea of a national homeland. By 1946 elements of the Jewish underground in Palestine were organized for a possible showdown with Arabs and openly attacking British military and civilian targets in an effort to get them to withdraw. Meanwhile, Zionists abroad actively campaigned for a Jewish state—a campaign that led to the U.N. November 1947 plan to partition Palestine into a Jewish and an Arab state. The Arabs of Palestine, dependent on Arab states whose interests were not their own, lacking pragmatic and authoritative leadership, and insistent on rejecting any compromise that they believed legitimized the injustice they sought to prevent, would have no part of the partition plan. In May 1948 Zionists established their state. Five Arab armies moved to oppose it. This campaign, spearheaded by Egypt and Transjordan, and undertaken with Arab national, rather than Palestinian, interests in mind, would have disastrous implications for the local Palestinian population.

Caught up in the chaos of civil war and the Arab invasion, without effective leadership, their institutions in disarray, and terrified by reports of massacres of Arab villages like Deir Yassin, thousands of Palestinians fled their homelands to seek refuge in Arab-controlled areas or in neighboring states. Of the approximately 1.3 million Palestinians residing in Palestine in 1947, fewer than half remained in their original homes by 1949. These refugees became dependent on international support and the goodwill of Arab regimes that were often contemptuous and suspicious of their new guests.

With the refugees scattered in a dozen Arab countries and Palestinian leadership discredited and in confusion, the initiative on the Palestine question passed to the Arab states, where it had effectively been since the end of the Arab revolt. Egypt's decision to sponsor an all-Palestine government in Gaza in 1948 and Abdallah's efforts to convince Palestinians that the interests of Palestine would be best served by cooperating with the Hashemites could not mask the reality that the Palestine issue had become a captive of inter-Arab politics and the interests of particular Arab regimes. Although the emotional power of the Palestine issue at the popular level paradoxically held Arab regimes hostage as well (indeed, Abdallah was murdered in 1951 by a young Palestinian outraged by his pragmatic and moderate policies), Arab regimes were successful in directing, coopting, or suppressing independent Palestinian political activity. Throughout the 1950s Palestinians identified with pan-Arab causes and movements and continued to look to the Arab states to take the lead against Israel.

During these years, Palestinian refugees did not lose their identity or attachment to their land. On the contrary, the trauma of the dispersal and the ambivalent, if not hostile, reception accorded them by their Arab hosts reinforced their separate status as Palestinians. In their art, literature, and poetry the attachment to *Filastin* remained strong.[6] Durability of clan and family structure solidified their sense of community and reinforced attachment to the land.

It was from the Diaspora Palestinians—the most alienated and embittered communities—that a new national leadership would emerge. By the early 1960s, particularly with the collapse of the Egyptian-Syrian unity scheme, it was becoming clear to a younger generation of Palestinians that the pan-Arab crusade to liberate Palestine was more a convenient slogan than a practical objective. Nor was this younger generation content, as their parents had been, to simply reminisce and dream about orange groves in Jaffa and olive trees in Jerusalem. Whether the ideology emphasized a more ideological pan-Arab element or Marxist perspective, as later advocated by George Habash and the Popular Front for the Liberation of Palestine (PFLP) or a simpler nationalism espoused by Yasir Arafat's Fatah organization, the emphasis was on Palestinians taking independent and militant action to regain their homeland,[7] and right injustices. Their goal was to seek mass support among Palestinians and enlist the aid of Arab regimes and public opinion.

The emergence of independent Palestinian groups like Fatah and the Arab Nationalist Movement (ANM), however, could not mask their weakness and dependence on Arab support. These groups still lacked broad support either among Palestinians or the Arab masses. Given the volatility of the Palestine issue in the Arab "street" and the ever present danger that Palestinian guerillas might trigger an unwanted war with Israel through uncontrolled attacks, Arab regimes tried to control the pace and focus of Palestinian political activity. Moreover, dedication to the Palestinian cause was an important tool in the ongoing contest for influence and power within the inter-Arab system. Nasser's bid to make Egypt the center of pan-Arab nationalist sentiment and heart of the Arab world invariably made him a strong, although strict patron of the Palestinian cause. Nasser wanted to demonstrate his commitment to the Palestinians, yet keep them subordinate to Egypt's own interests. Almost ten years after Egypt had sponsored the Goverment of All Palestine, Nasser established the Palestine National Union in Gaza. There Palestinians were encouraged to maintain their identity and to set up a Palestinian legislative council. Nasser also supported fedayeen raids against Israel when it suited Egypt's interests and sought to control them when it did not.[8]

Abdallah of Jordan also sought to insure that the Palestinian issue presented no threat to his larger plans for influence in the Arab world or on the West Bank. Having formally annexed the West Bank in 1950, Abdallah sought through a combination of integration, cooptation, and local alliance with West Bank elites to convince Palestinians that their cause would be best served by close alignment with Amman.[9]

Out of this complex environment of inter-Arab rivalries and rising Palestinian frustration and activism came the PLO—created in 1964 largely as a result of Nasser's bid to check growing Syrian influence over Fatah and to better manage the Palestinian issue. The PLO deferred to Egypt's interests and was headed by Ahmad Shukairy, a pro-Egyptian Palestinian attorney. Nonetheless, it reflected the growing importance the Arab states were forced to accord the Palestinian issue, demonstrated an increasing political awareness among Palestinians, and created the framework and institutions for the contemporary Palestinian national movement[10]—a Palestine National Congress (PNC) and Executive Committee; a charter; and a Palestine Liberation Army (PLA). Moreover, it accelerated the efforts of those independent Palestinian groups, particularly Fatah, to create a more broadly based movement that derived its legitimacy not from Arab regimes but from popular appeal. Six months after the PLO's first congress in east Jerusalem, Fatah launched its first military operation against Israel.

Israel's devastating defeat of the Arab armies in June 1967 had a profound impact on the Palestinian national movement and shaped its strategy and tactics for the next decade. In the years before the war the Palestinians had lacked a convincing and inspiring ideology and a popular base of support. The magnitude of the Arab defeat not only discredited

Arab military power and political ideology but created an ideological and political vacuum that Palestinian guerillas tried to fill. The Palestinian fedayeen, with their romantic bold call for armed struggle, and the increasing frequency of operations in the first few years after the Arab defeat seemed to offer a psychological lift to disillusioned Arab publics and Palestinian refugees.

The growing prestige of the Palestinian resistance movement was reflected in the decline of the Shukairy-led PLO and the rise of Fatah and other smaller groups. Fatah's clash with a much larger Israeli force at Karameh, Jordan, in March 1968 dramatically raised its popularity and created new myths and symbols. These became invaluable as Fatah, by 1969 under Arafat's lead, began to lay claim to leadership of the newly reconstituted PLO.

Fatah's successes, however, should not mask the obstacles that the Palestinian resistance movement continued to face—dangerous dependence on Arab support, lack of unity, and vulnerability to Israel's military power. By 1970 the Israelis were striking at Palestinian bases in Jordan and Lebanon, further complicating the PLO's relations with its Arab hosts.[11]

Nowhere were the problems afflicting the Palestinians more clearly reflected than in the Jordanian crisis of September 1970—a bloody confrontation with the Jordinian authorities that led to the end of the Palestinians' independent political and military base in Jordan. The crisis, triggered by the PFLP's hijacking of four international airliners to Jordan, was an effort to undermine the Jordanian regime and sabotage Nasser's and Hussein's tentative acceptance of a U.S.-sponsored initiative to end the Egyptian-Israeli war of attrition. The crisis demonstrated how little control the PLO as an umbrella organization could exert over its constituent groups and revealed the limited nature of PLO support in Jordan and among Arab regimes. No Arab state could afford to associate itself with a Palestinian effort to topple an established Arab regime.[12] The Arab support that did materialize—Syrian PLA units and Egyptian mediation efforts—came too late to save the Palestinians from their worst defeat since 1948. The sight of Palestinian fedayeen fleeing across Jordan into Israel to escape the king's Bedouin forces dramatically demonstrated the extent of the debacle.[13]

Events in Jordan left the Palestinian movement divided, embittered, and with a host of organizational problems.[14] Without a clear sense of direction, with no base of operations yet firmly established in Lebanon, Palestinians found themselves more vulnerable and dependent on Arab support. Fatah, eager to avoid an open conflict with Arab states, turned to a more clandestine strategy of terrorism against Israel, Arab, European, and U.S. targets. The Black September Organization—a cover for Fatah's terrorist arm—was designed to demonstrate that Palestinians were still a factor to be reckoned with and to hold the organization together by providing an outlet for those demanding militant action.

Once again it was a Middle East war that triggered an important shift in PLO tactics. The October 1973 conflict and Arab oil embargo opened up new opportunities for Palestinian political gains. The war had restored Arab self-respect and inflated Arab pride, but it also generated a new pragmatism based on Israel's military superiority, the potential dangers of another war, and the internal problems that beset most of the Arab regimes.[15]

The war forced the PLO, specifically Fatah, to adjust its thinking. Not only had a "limited" war seemed to advance Egypt's interests; it had created new risks and opportunities. The flurry of postwar U.S. diplomatic activity and the convening of the Geneva conference in December 1973 convinced Arafat that unless the PLO formulated its own political response to the post-October situation, it might well be shut out of negotiations. Palestinian fears were heightened by Jordan's long-standing interest in regaining the West Bank and U.S. efforts to induce King Hussein to enter into negotiations with Israel.

In response to these changing circumstances the PLO began to formulate a strategy designed to outflank King Hussein, consolidate Arab support, and cultivate a moderate image abroad. In order to strengthen its role in any political negotiations, Fatah succeeded in selling the idea of establishing a "national authority" on any part of Palestine "liberated" from Israel. This ambiguous concept was intended to give the PLO flexibility in the political arena and sell its phased program as a tactical imperative without compromising its right to struggle to regain the rest of Palestine. Moreover, in November 1974 at the Arab Summit in Rabat, the Arab states granted the PLO the status of sole legitimate representative of the Palestinian people, denying King Hussein Arab support on this issue. That month the PLO scored its greatest diplomatic coup with Arafat's address before the U.N. General Assembly.

The PLO's success abroad, however, was not matched by a strong position in the region. The next six years witnessed a dramatic fluctuation in its fortunes, as Israel and key Arab states narrowed its room to maneuver politically and militarily. Civil war in Lebanon in 1975-76 brought new conflict with the Lebanese and Syrians, whose occupation of Lebanon made the PLO more dependent on Damascus. Moreover, Sadat's decision to seek an accommodation with Israel threatened to take the most powerful Arab state off the confrontation line with Israel, further increasing the PLO's dependence on the Syrians.

Finally, the emergence of Begin's Likud government resulted in a series of Israeli policies designed to strike at the PLO militarily and root out its influence on the West Bank and Gaza. The first Israeli invasion of Lebanon in March 1978, following the worst PLO terrorist attack in Israel's history, indicated that the Begin government was prepared to use large-scale military force to deal with the PLO in Lebanon. Four years later it moved into Lebanon again in an effort to crush the PLO as a military and political force.

THE PALESTINIAN-ISRAELI DIMENSION: THE POLITICS OF MUTUAL DENIAL

It might easily be said that after more than half a century of conflict between Jews and Palestinian Arabs, the basic problem remains strikingly the same: how to reconcile the conflicting claims of two peoples to the same territory. That the development of the Palestinian national move-- ment was slower than that of political Zionism or that the initiative on the Palestinian problem quickly became enmeshed in inter-Arab politics should not obscure the basic character of the conflict. By the 1920s the conflict in Palestine pitted two national movements—political Zionism and a nascent Palestine nationalism—against one another and challenged both to organize politically, secure external support, and prepare for conflict against the other.

The two movements seemed locked into an adversarial relationship almost from the beginning. Although there were personal contacts between Zionists and Palestinian Arabs and even some efforts at cooperation, there were few serious efforts to reach an accommodation at the political level. By the 1930s both movements viewed their conflict increasingly in military terms, as the conflict turned to large-scale violence. Radicals on each side denied the legitimacy of the other's national claims, although in accepting both the 1937 and 1947 partition plans, the mainstream Zionist leadership had reluctantly accepted the need to compromise.

The establishment of Israel, the first Arab-Israeli war, and the dispersal of hundreds of thousands of Palestinians foreclosed the possibility of any accommodation between Israelis and Palestinian Arabs and created a legacy of hatred and bitterness. The Palestinian issue was now inextricably linked to the conflict between the Arab states and Israel. Moreover, the events of the 1940s created traumas for each community that would shape its view of itself and its adversary and elevate a dispute over territory to a matter of survival and national identity.

For the Israelis, indeed for world Jewry, the Nazi success in exterminating six out of every seven European Jews and the lack of international efforts to stop it or provide havens for refugees generated a determination to establish and defend a Jewish state, whatever the cost. For most, the Arabs' inability to accept the legitimacy of that idea and their all-out campaign to stop it represented a more localized effort to finish what the Nazis had started. The back-to-back experiences of the Holocaust and the war of independence, coming within three years of one another, inevitably resulted in a fundamental hostility and distrust toward the Arabs and generated a tendency to dismiss the claims of Palestinians and their Arab neighbors.

After 1948 an Israeli consensus on the Palestinian dimension of the problem quickly crystallized. The Palestinians were not viewed as a national group with specific claims to statehood, but as refugees to be supported by the international dole or resettled within the Arab world. Indeed, for many the dispersal of the Palestinians and Jordan's integration of the West Bank had solved the Palestinian problem. The Israeli view that the Arab states were cynically manipulating the Palestinian issue in their support of the fedayeen, and growing Palestinian guerilla and terrorist activity reinforced Israeli belief that Palestinians were simply tools of the larger Arab campaign to destroy Israel. Palestinians were seen as refugees and terrorists, but not as potential political interlocutors.

The emergence of a more independent PLO leadership, the growing international interest and support for the Palestinian cause, and Israel's occupation of the West Bank and Gaza forced many Israelis to recognize that there was indeed a Palestinian problem that required resolution. In the years after the October 1973 war, a wide range of options were discussed—limited autonomy, Jordanian Palestinian confederation—but with no Palestinian or Arab interlocutor, and no military or political force strong enough to force or even induce Israel to withdraw, there were no immediate pressures for concessions. On the contrary, for a variety of strategic, ideological, and political reasons, there was growing determination to keep the West Bank. Despite the ruling labor government's preference for some kind of settlement with Jordan, few with the exception of the extreme Left favored the repartition of Palestine to create an independent Palestinian state.

Since 1977 the Likud government has departed from Labor's vague formulations about solving the Palestinian problem within a Jordanian framework and has taken steps to ensure that Israel will not lose physical control over the West Bank. Although in agreeing to the Camp David framework, which uses the term "legitimate rights of the Palestinians," the Begin government paradoxically went further in accepting a formulation that could be interpreted as being more forthcoming on the question of Palestinian autonomy than any of its predecessors, it chooses to interpret that autonomy along the narrowest of lines. The Israeli government, spurred by ideological considerations and apparently supported by a popular consensus, does not grant any legitimacy to the idea of any independent Palestinian national claim to the West Bank and Gaza.

For Palestinians, the establishment of Israel and displacement of refugees created a legacy of bitterness and new social, economic, and political realities that would have a profound impact on the way they looked at Israel, the Arab world, and themselves. Unlike European Jewry, Palestinians were not confronted with physical extinction but threatened by the loss of their identity and the obliteration of an entire way of life in Palestine. Thousands of refugees and their children became alienated, embittered, and dependent on Arab regimes that treated them with a mixture of suspicion and contempt. Deprived of their agrarian-based livelihood, many lived in camps and shantytowns. Even those who succeeded through education in a wide variety of professional fields remained without a real political identity—marginal to the societies in which they lived.[16]

Out of this environment came a militant and radical Palestinian national leadership determined not only to regain their land and self-respect but to right the wrongs and correct the injustices their people had suffered.[17] Creating a new source of identity and a national movement for a displaced, fragmented, and dispirited community required an ideology that was maximalist, revolutionary, and romantic in quality, to motivate a younger generation to regain their self-respect and pride and direct their energies against Israel as well as those Arab states and international forces that had betrayed the Palestinian cause.

This revolutionary fervor—a spirit conspicuously absent from those West Bank Palestinians who came under Jordanian and then Israeli control and those living within Israel proper—was reflected in their view of Israel and the maximalist nature of their objectives. In part, this was a response to the problem of maintaining grass-roots support in an alienated and radicalized community that had little more to lose. But it also reflected an unwillingless to compromise and an inability to show tactical flexibility to advance their cause if it meant abandoning principles. There was from the beginning an atmosphere of unreality about the movement. Regardless of the odds against them and the paucity of their resources in the early years, the Palestinian resistance movement espoused the liberation of all Palestine and the elimination of the Jewish state. Rarely had the ideology of one national movement been so centered around the extinction of the other. Indeed, of the 33 articles that now compose the PLO's National Covenant, at least half imply that Israel has no right to exist.[18]

By the mid 1970s, the PLO's leadership, primarily under Fatah's direction, began to show signs of flexibility in its approach toward a negotiated solution. The change in tactics resulted from a number of factors. The post-1973 war situation created new political realities that the PLO wanted to exploit and King Hussein seemed interested in a U.S.-brokered West Bank settlement. At the 12th session of the PNC in 1974 and again in 1977 resolutions were adopted that seemed to lay the groundwork for Palestinian acceptance of a state on the West Bank and Gaza, should the prospects for negotiation arise. As the PLO made a determined effort to improve its international image, it appeared as if the Palestinians had grasped what the Zionists had realized 50 years earlier—political compromise was crucial to the success of a small movement dependent on the support of larger powers for its success.

Whether the PLO's policies were tactical or reflected a fundamental change in strategy is difficult to determine. In any event it was too little a change too late. Divided within their own ranks and dependent on key Arab states, which were prepared to block a political deal that they did not approve, the PLO was unwilling or unable to commit itself unambiguously to a negotiated settlement. Moreover, Israel, hardened by 30 years of radical rhetoric and terrorist activity, intensely suspicious of the PLO's new tactics and opposed to an independent Palestinian state, saw little reason to provide it with incentives to moderate its attitudes. Indeed, after 30 years, the Palestinians had succeeded in playing their revolutionary and radical roles only too well and had convinced most Israelis that moderate gestures and political compromise were for their effect on Western opinion and were merely part of the PLO's campaign of *marhaliyya*—the liberation of Palestine in stages.

It was no coincidence that the Palestinian-Israeli conflict, based as it was on the mutual denial of the other's national claims, should have assumed the character of a political and military struggle. In this historical contest Palestinians have dealt with political Zionism and the state of Israel from a position of weakness.[19] The idea of armed struggle has been a key ingredient in Palestinian ideology and strategy since the 1950s. Indispensable as it has been in mobilizing Palestinian ranks and gaining credibility within the Arab world, it has never been an effective weapon against Israel. While guerilla and terrorist activities make the PLO a factor in the Middle East equation, they were never able to further Palestinian goals by forcing Israel to cede territory or to effect a shift in the political/military balance that would have resulted in an effective Arab war coalition or great-power support capable of forcing Israel to meet Palestinian demands. The PLO's capability to shell and rocket northern Israel—its most effective military weapon to date—produced an Israeli invasion of Lebanon that has weakened the PLO militarily and politically.

Equally important is the effect that the PLO's armed struggle has had upon Israel. Far from sapping Israel's morale and engaging the Israelis in a war of attrition, Palestinian guerilla and terrorist activity has only increased its determination to deal with the Palestinian problem in military terms and created enormous obstacles to any political accommodation. The PLO's hope that the Israeli occupation of the West Bank and Gaza could be used to stimulate a popular uprising similar to that in Algeria or Vietnam was quickly dashed by superior Israeli security procedures and the unwillingness of the local population to support such a campaign.

On the contrary, the armed struggle, although no doubt essential to the PLO in the early years, has cost the Palestinians dearly. Cross-border raids from PLO sanctuaries in Arab host countries were met with costly Israeli retaliation and embroiled the PLO in bloody confrontations with Jordan and Lebanon. The PLO's military activities in Lebanon have made the resistance movement dangerously dependent on the Syrians and given Damascus powerful leverage in Palestinian politics. Indeed, the frequency of PLO attacks on Israeli troops in Lebanon during the past year could easily backfire, triggering an Israeli-Syrian confrontation that could eliminate any remaining freedom of action that the PLO now enjoys. Finally, the PLO's history of involvement in international terrorism has created a nightmarish public relations problem that continues to haunt the PLO to this day.

Politically, the Palestinians have fared much better against Israel. From a marginal organization entirely dependent on Arab support, the

PLO has emerged as a key player, recognized by most Palestinians, Arab states, and much of the international community as the legitimate representation of the Palestinians. Supported by the Arab world, the PLO has had remarkable success in impressing the international community with the importance of the Palestinian issue and the centrality of its own role in any solution. It has some form of diplomatic recognition in more countries than those that recognize Israel.

Gains on the international stage, however, are not effective unless they are translated into concrete political leverage and influence. Lacking reliable great-power support and dependent on allies whose interests were not always their own, the PLO has had difficulty in competing with Israel—a modern Westernized state, which until relatively recently was a master of effective public relations. Despite the assistance the PLO receives from the Soviet Union and the support it enjoys in Asia, Europe, and Africa, it lacks the kind of durable relationship with a superpower that Israel enjoys with the United States. If Palestinians are to have any chance of achieving a homeland, they will have to gain the active support of the United States—the only power with the influence and credibility necessary to broker any settlement.

The PLO has already scored impressive political gains in its struggle with Israel on the West Bank and Gaza. It has, for reasons that will become clear later, acquired a veto power over Palestinian or Jordanian participation in negotiations with Israel. But even in the "West Bank connection" the limits of the PLO's ability to sustain an effective military and political opposition to the Israeli occupation become evident. There were, to be sure, periods of severe violence in the occupied territories, but these have been cyclical and in response to local issues—land expropriation, university closings, and dismissal of mayors. The PLO played a key role in orchestrating these demonstrations. Nonetheless, physically separated from the territories and faced with superior Israeli military power and a very pragmatic local population, it could not direct a broad-based opposition to Israel's policies on the West Bank. In over a decade and a half of Israeli occupation, the Palestinians inside and outside the territories have failed to make the costs of the occupation too high for Israel to bear. For the foreseeable future there is little that suggests a change in this situation.

The PLO's inability to thwart Israeli policies on the West Bank, however, should not obscure the influence it has acquired there. Although the PLO inspires rather than directs nationalist activities in the area, since the mid 1970s it has emerged as the single most dynamic expression of Palestinian nationalism for the local inhabitants. Through a unique combination of respect and intimidation it has acquired powerful leverage in preventing Arabs on the West Bank from entering into negotiations directly with Israel or Jordan over the future of the territories.

In some respects the PLO rules by default. Over the years, both Jordan and Israel for their own reasons have tried to block the emergence of a broad-based respected local leadership reflecting nationalist sentiments. Although the social, economic, and political changes resulting from Israel's occupation of the West bank paradoxically facilitated the emergence of such a leadership, subsequent Labor and Likud policies made it impossible for it to develop. Had either Jordan or Israel agreed to allow a credible West Bank leadership to emerge or made concessions on Palestinian national aspirations, it might have been possible to weaken the PLO's influence. Indeed the PLO leadership has always been concerned about the rise of an independent West Bank elite that might be prepared to strike a deal at its expense. Should King Hussein, with Arab support, step forward to negotiate with Israel and the PLO still refuse to participate, West Bank notables would probably join the negotiations in an effort to cut the best deal they could.

THE PALESTINIAN-ARAB DIMENSION: THE POLITICS OF DEPENDENCE

The "Arabization" of the Palestinian problem is one of its most important and least understood dimensions. The involvement of the Arab states in the *qadiyat Filastini* (the Palestinian cause) has shaped the Palestinian view of Israel and the development of Palestinian national politics in profound ways. Palestinians themselves recognize the importance of Arab support but have an ambivalent and conflicted view of the Arab role. Arab states fill PLO coffers, facilitate transfer of most of its military equipment, and plead its case in world capitals. What gives the Palestinian issue its durability and makes it so volatile a factor in Middle East politics is the Arab commitment to the idea of Palestine. Nonetheless, this support has come at an enormous price. Although the Palestinians have also acquired considerable leverage within the inter-Arab system, they are no match for established and powerful regimes determined to insure that their own national interests are protected.[20]

Any discussion of the Arab dimension of the Palestinian problem must begin with an effort to assess the nature of the relationship between the Palestinians and the Arab states. Some have suggested it is entirely cynical—based on Arab efforts to use the Palestinian issue as a weapon against Israel and against each other. Others have argued that the Arab commitment is primarily moral and ideological, stemming from the unique nature of the pan-Arab system. The relationship, however, is not one-dimensional and exists on different levels, encompassing elements of ideology, moral commitment, and pragmatic politics. Moreover, each Arab state, particularly those with large Palestinian populations and vital stakes in the outcome of the conflict with Israel, has its own agenda and interests with respect to the Palestinian problem, in addition to the demands and constraints of inter-Arab politics.

First, the idea of Palestine and the plight of the Palestinian people have enormous emotional appeal at the popular level. This popular commitment is based on a variety of factors, but is rooted in the common feeling that the injustices and suffering of the Palestinian people are a blow and humiliation to the "Arab nation" as a whole.[21] However illusory the concept of pan-Arabism has become on a practical level, the idea of a common identity—shared victories and failures—persists. That in Arab eyes those responsible for the plight of the Palestinians are Israeli Jews, supported by a Christian West, excites emotions in a traditional Muslim society and reinforces feelings of vulnerability and weakness. That a collection of infidels established a Western-oriented state, occupied the third holiest city in Islam, and resisted for 30 years the combined efforts of the Arab nation to regain Palestine is a source of humiliation for both secular and religious thinkers. In this respect the Palestinian issue runs the political spectrum and elicits support from Arab nationalists, fundamentalists, and Marxists alike—providing each with an opportunity to demonstrate its pan-Arab, Islamic, and revolutionary credentials and frequently to attack established regimes that it opposes.

The ideological component of the Palestine issue, however, coexists with other less idealistic motives and political realities. Most Arab regimes, even those that espouse revolutionary ideologies, are essentially status quo powers. As the romantic ideas of pan-Arabism have been tempered by the sobering realities of state development and military weakness vis-à-vis Israel, the attention to "national" interests has grown stronger.[22] Although this narrowing of interests and pragmatism has also affected the Palestinian national movement, the PLO remains committed to a fundamental and risky change in the political and geographic status quo—the establishment of an independent state. Thus, status quo powers are faced with the persistent efforts of a national movement, some of whose groups espouse radical social and economic changes, to create new realities, or at a minimum, carry on a military struggle against Israel that could easily jeopardize their particular interests.[23]

It is not that most Arab regimes are theoretically opposed to Palestinian goals; most support the principles of self-determination and a Palestinian state. Still, Arab regimes, particularly Syria and Jordan, want to insure that in accomplishing its goals the PLO is respectful and in some cases subordinate to their interests. None of the states that share common borders with Israel will allow the PLO to drag them into an untimely or unwanted war. Nor will some of the PLO's key supporters, particularly Syria, allow the Palestinians to participate in a settlement that ignores their interests. It is no coincidence that with the exception of Egypt, the remaining Arab states that border Israel—Jordan, Syria, and Lebanon— have had bitter military conflicts with the PLO.

Equally important, the Palestinian issue has become deeply entrenched in the domestic and foreign politics of most Arab states. Regimes with large Palestinian populations—Jordan, Syria, Lebanon, and Kuwait— cannot ignore the power that the Palestinian issue can generate in the street. Most of these regimes are already struggling with the problem of political legitimacy and cannot allow a well-organized pro-Palestinian constituency—foreign or domestic—to outflank them on this issue.

Moreover, conservative Arab states that have close ties with the West, particularly the United States, feel particularly vulnerable on the Palestinian issue. Already sensitive to charges of cooperation with the United States, Israel's primary ally, they cannot afford to be lax in championing the Palestinian cause. They are also fearful of Palestinian terrorist attacks and use large financial contributions as insurance policies to mollify radical elements. On the other hand, radical Arab states, particularly Syria, Iraq, and Libya, have used the Palestinian issue to validate their pan-Arab credentials and to wage political war against one another.

The volatility of the Palestinian issue in inter-Arab politics has had a powerful impact in preventing movement toward a settlement. Although it has been a unique source of unity for the Arab world, it has also been a source of bitter controversy. In an Arab world divided between the "moderate" states for which a negotiated settlement is a top priority (Egypt, Jordan, Saudi Arabia, Lebanon) and the "radical" states, which are in no hurry to settle (Iraq, Syria, and Libya), the Palestinian issue becomes a useful tool for radicals to protect their interests and preserve their influence in the inter-Arab arena. The moderates, forced to coopt radical rivals and too weak to strike off on their own, adopt a lowest-common-denominator approach that guarantees political paralysis and at best produces ambiguous summit communiques on key issues such as nonrecognition of Israel. For a variety of reasons, Arab hardliners, supported by Palestinian radicals, are given excessive leverage in determining the Arab consensus on the style and substance of a negotiated settlement.

That the Arab states have an emotional, ideological, and political stake in the Palestinian issue does not mean that they are willing or able to launch an all-out campaign on its behalf. The avowed support for the Palestinians and the PLO that characterizes government-sponsored press releases and summit communiques simply does not square with Arab actions. For Egypt, Syria, Jordan, and Lebanon—the states most vitally affected by the conflict with Israel—the primary challenge, particularly after 1973, has been how to protect and advance their own interests and still discharge their commitment to the Palestinian cause.

Although other Arab states (Saudi Arabia, Algeria, Iraq, Libya) have played an important role in the Palestinian issue, these four states have had a much greater impact on the Palestinians and figured most prominently in their strategy and tactics. Three of these states—Egypt, Syria, and Jordan—have historically competed for influence over the Palestinian movement and have tried with varying degrees of success to insure that the PLO remained responsive to their interests. The fourth state—Lebanon—provided the PLO with its main base of operations for more than a decade.

Throughout the 1950s and 1960s Egypt, as the largest and most powerful Arab state, was a source of moral and ideological support for Palestinian leaders. Although the Egyptians tried to keep tight control over the emerging Palestinian national movement, Nasser's pan-Arab policies, his militant attitude toward Israel, and support for the fedayeen operations from Gaza was a source of inspiration for many Palestinians. By the late 1950s, Nasser's picture had replaced that of Haj al-Amin al-Husayni in many Palestinian homes.[24]

With the collapse of Egyptian-Syrian unity plans, Cairo's heavy-handed pressure on the PLO, and Israel's crushing defeat of an Egyptian-led war coalition in 1967, Palestinians began to adopt a more independent line, as it became clear that Nasser was unable or unwilling to carry on the struggle against Israel. Egypt's acceptance of the Rogers plan in 1970 indicated that there were potentially fundamental differences with the PLO over tactics and strategy.

After the October 1973 war, Sadat's decision to seek a negotiated settlement with Israel brought PLO-Egyptian relations to an all-time low. Despite efforts by the mainstream Palestinian leadership to maintain contacts with Sadat and his successor, Hosni Mubarak, any meaningful Egyptian-Palestinian rapprochement will be difficult, because of Cairo's commitment to a policy of accommodation with Israel. If the PLO hopes to use Egypt's resources to further its political goals it must tacitly endorse the reality of Egypt's decision to end its confrontation with Israel—a price the Palestinian resistance movement is not yet prepared to pay.

Nowhere is the ambivalence that characterizes Palestinian-Arab relations better reflected than in the PLO's ties with Syria. Since the 1960s the Syrians have been the most consistent supporters of a militant Palestinian nationalism, providing material and moral support. Damascus's Baathist ideology, its hardline view of Israel, and its tendency to see the Palestinian cause as part of the larger Arab (Syrian) struggle have encouraged the Syrians to play a major role in Palestinian politics.

This involvement, however, has come at an enormous price. Syria's efforts to insure that Palestinian goals remain compatible with, if not subordinate to, its national interests have brought successive Syrian regimes into direct conflict with the PLO. Syria's own Palestinian groups and its influence in Lebanon have given it powerful leverage in Palestinian politics. Since the late 1970s, Damascus, feeling increasingly isolated within the Arab world, has tried to insure that Arafat does not pursue policies that jeopardize its interests. Toward this end, the Syrians pressured the PLO to boycott the 1980 Arab Summit in Amman, (the first such gathering the PLO missed since it was created), threatened to cut off PLO arms shipments in Lebanon, tried to disrupt the Palestinian-Jordanian dialogue, and backed anti-Arafat rebels in Lebanon's Bekaa Valley in 1983. The Israeli invasion of Lebanon, which ended the PLO's independent base of operations, has made the Palestinian national movement more dependent than ever on Syria's support—a fact that will further restrict the PLO's room to maneuver.

The Palestinian-Jordanian relationship has also been characterized by cooperation and competition. Jordan was the only Arab state to grant Palestinian refugees citizenship and to try to equalize their social and economic status vis-à-vis Jordanians. Nonetheless, Amman tried to suppress independent political activity on the East Bank and coopt it on the West Bank. Like his grandfather Abdallah, King Hussein saw an independent Palestinian national movement as a dangerous threat to Hashemite rule on the East Bank and its continuing influence on the

West Bank. In September 1970, he crushed the fedayeen challenge to his authority.

Over the years Hussein and the mainstream Palestinian leadership have tried for tactical reasons to work out a modus vivendi. For the Palestinians, Jordan has always been of critical importance. The largest single community of Palestinians reside there. Moreover, the PLO, recognizing the importance of Jordan in American and Israeli thinking on a West Bank settlement, have tried to block any unilaterial Jordanian initiative. The PLO's military defeat in Lebanon and the U.S. interest in the Jordanian option, evidenced by the Reagan Plan of September 1982, will again focus attention on the Jordanian-Palestinian link. Nonetheless, Palestinian, Syrian, and Israeli opposition to the Reagan initiative will make any workable PLO-Jordanian deal a precarious one at best.

Although there has been a large Palestinian community in Lebanon since 1949, it was not until the early 1970s that the Palestinian resistance movement sought to establish its main base of operations there. Lebanon offered a large and sympathetic Palestinian population, a base to organize politically and militarily, and a weak central government unable to prevent the emergence of an independent statelike infrastructure. The relationship was not mutually advantageous. The influx of thousands of Palestinians upset an already precarious communal/sectarian balance, initiated a major rivalry with the Maronite Christians, and facilitated a growing Israeli and Syrian intervention in Lebanese affairs. Although many Lebanese were initially sympathetic to the plight of the Palestinians, they were not enthusiastic about allowing them to carry on their national struggle at Lebanese expense. After a bloody civil war, Syrian occupation, and two Israeli invasions, the Lebanese-Palestinian relationship remains explosive and precarious. The PLO's expulsion from West Beirut in August 1982 has not resolved the problem of Palestinian attacks from the Bekaa or the debate over what to do about the 400,000 Palestinian civilians that remain in the country.

For Palestinians—political activists, fedayeen, and refugees alike—the dilemma of the Arabization of the Palestinian problem is clear. The success of their national movement, indeed the wellbeing of their communities throughout the Arab world, depend in large measure on continued Arab support. Yet they have frequently clashed with these regimes, most dramatically in September of 1970 and June of 1976, but also on a variety of less sensational political issues. On the one hand, most Arab states will not abandon their commitment to the "idea" of Palestine for a number of domestic, ideological, and security reasons. On the other hand, they have not allowed this idea to conflict with the "reality" of their particular national interests. Egypt's commitment to Palestinian rights did not stop Sadat from negotiating a settlement with Israel. Nor did Syria's pro-Palestinian credentials prevent the Assad regime from sitting out the 1978 Israeli invasion of Lebanon and giving only limited support during the second.

Without an independent base the Palestinian national movement is more vulnerable to the changing interests of its Arab allies and adversaries than ever before. A political strategy designed to get the Palestinians into a negotiated settlement will require the active support of conservative Arab states—Jordan, Egypt, and Saudi Arabia—and would necessitate a tempering of Palestinian expectations, virtually guaranteeing dissension within Palestinian ranks. The continuation of the armed struggle, on the other hand, will insure that the Palestinians remain dependent on Syria—a fact that has already seriously reduced Arafat's room to maneuver. Indeed, after almost a century Palestinians remain locked in the perilous world of inter-Arab politics in which their national movement was born. Reconciling their own interests with those of Arab regimes that do not fully support their goals will remain a difficult if not insurmountable challenge.

THE PALESTINIAN-PALESTINIAN DIMENSION: THE SEARCH FOR AUTHORITY AND UNITY

The structure of Palestinian society is inextricably linked to the political development of the Palestinian national movement. How Palestinians have related to Palestinians has played a key role in defining their relationship with the Arab states and their role in the struggle against Israel. Almost half a century before the establishment of the PLO, the leaders of the Palestinian Arab community were already trying to cope with the divisions and diffusion of authority that characterized their society and politics. The social structure of Palestinian Arab society under Ottoman rule was highly stratified. Divisions persisted between Muslims and Christians, landowners and peasants, town and village, and among family clans. Despite the strengths of the village and family networks, Arab society in Palestine, as elsewhere in the Arab world, lacked a single center of authority. Even anti-Zionism, which increased the political awareness and unity of the Palestinian Arab community, could not overcome the traditional cleavages that divided the community.[25]

The divisive nature of Palestinian political life was perpetuated and exacerbated by the first Arab-Israeli war. The dispersal of more than half of the Palestinian community from their homes and the collapse of their institutions caused further fragmentation and upheaval. The physical dispersal of one community into at least four major blocs had a profound impact on the development of the Palestinian national movement.

Only in Jordan, where an estimated 600,000 Palestinians registered as refugees in 1949, did the government make any effort to integrate them into the local society and economy. Jordan formally annexed the West Bank in 1950 and sought to coopt traditional Palestinian leadership, and thwart any radical independent Palestinian challenge. Palestinians were granted citizenship and passports and were not required to have work permits in order to find employment. There was political discrimination, to be sure, but Palestinians came to occupy a vital role in Jordanian business and bureaucracy. Those refugees who arrived in 1948, while maintaining their Palestinian identity, have supported the monarchy and have developed real interests in the stability of the Hashemite kingdom.

The Hashemites have had less success on the West Bank—losing considerable ground to Israel and the PLO after the loss of the territory in the 1967 war. Nonetheless, family and village ties between East and West Bank Palestinians and Jordan's presence and influence there for 19 years still gives the Hashemites considerable leverage, and King Hussein would like to increase it further. King Hussein has long been concerned about the emergence of a more radical Palestinian nationalist movement that he cannot control and that could compete with the Hashemites for the loyalty of Jordan's Palestinian community, now the largest single Palestinian community and a majority of the Jordanian population. Reintegrating the West Bank into Jordan, even if it were possible, would double Jordan's Palestinian population and create major social, economic, and politican problems. Still, the survival of the Hashemite kingdom may come to depend on Jordan's ability to influence and shape the outcome of any political settlement on the West Bank.

The Palestinian experience in Lebanon reveals the extreme sides of the Palestinian Diaspora. On one hand, there were those Palestinians who acquired citizenship and played a key role in Lebanon's business, banking, professional, and academic sectors. For the majority, however, the Lebanese sojourn was harsh. Unlike Jordan, Lebanon's almost 200,000 refugees in 1948-49 (now estimated at 400,000-500,000) were excluded from Lebanese society. Lebanese authorities, particularly the Maronites, concerned that Palestinians would upset an already precariously balanced political system and threaten their power base, clashed with the PLO. The Palestinians were the catalyst that triggered Lebanon's 1975 civil war and brought Israeli and Syrian intervention in Lebanese affairs.

The withdrawal of the PLO from Beirut and southern Lebanon in 1982 left the Palestinian community in a more precarious position than ever before. The Lebanese government will not integrate the majority nor guarantee their security; the multinational force will not remain in place forever; and the withdrawal of Isareli forces from southern Lebanon will strip away any remaining security that the refugees have there. Thus the Palestinians will remain vulnerable to their Lebanese and non-Lebanese allies alike.

The Palestinian community in Syria, which now numbers some 250,000, enjoyed a much greater degree of physical security. The refugees were granted equal rights with Syrian citizens and widespread access to jobs and schools. Unlike Lebanon, Palestinians in Syria served in government and in the army, although there were restrictions on travel and political activity.[26] Moreover, successive Syrian regimes, intensely nationalist and convinced of the importance of the Syrian role in the Palestinian cause and the region, intervened heavily in Palestinian politics, creating their own PLO-affiliated group, Saiqa, and supporting a variety of others. Palestinians have been forced to deal with the anomaly that Damascus has been a consistent supporter of militant Palestinian nationalism and yet one of its most formidable adversaries. The tension inherent in this relationship is likely to intensify as Palestinians, now without an independent base, become more dependent on the Syrians for support.

The experience of Palestinian Arabs who remained in their homes, either in Israel proper or on the Jordanian-occupied West Bank, varied considerably, depending on the policies of their new hosts. In Gaza, occupied by Egypt in 1948 and by Israel in 1967, Palestinians have remained in a kind of twilight zone. In 1949 Gaza's 350,000 Palestinian refugees lived in overcrowded and disadvantaged conditions, although after 1967 employment opportunities in Israel increased social and economic mobility. Nonetheless, Gazan society is still highly stratified, with a few prominent families like the Shawa clan dominating its economic and political life. Although some local leaders found it necessary to cooperate with the military authorities, Gaza remained a hotbed of Palestinian nationalism and until the early 1970s presented the Israelis with a significant security problem.

Palestinians on the West Bank fared much better. Although Jordanian policy focused on keeping the area dependent and subservient to the

East Bank, the local population was granted Jordanian citizenship, passports, and the economic benefits bestowed on those traditional elites that chose to cooperate with the Hashemites.

The Israeli occupation of the West Bank in 1967 brought changes that would transform the social, political, and economic life of the area. Although the Israelis encouraged the Jordanian-West Bank connection in an effort to preserve stability and counter radical elements, the diminution of Jordanian influence damaged the prestige of the traditional elite. The rise of the PLO after 1973 further discredited this group, although they retained their role as contact between the military authorities and the local population. Moreover, the economic opportunities of the occupation paradoxically allowed middle-class elements to acquire resources independent of the large landowning families and to increase their political prestige.[27] These new groups were more nationalist and identified with the PLO. Their increasing radicalization was reflected in the 1976 municipal elections that brought to power a new group of elected mayors, also more closely identified with the PLO. The Likud government's hardline security procedures and settlement policies further accelerated this process.[28]

The growing radicalization of many on the West Bank, however, could not change certain realities about the political situation there. First, most West Bankers are essentially conservative and pragmatic, interested in local economic and social concerns. Many have cooperated with both the Jordanians and the Israelis, and while supportive of the PLO as the most dynamic expression of Palestinian nationalism, will not sacrifice their local interests on its behalf. Although they will not under present conditions support any Israeli-sponsored autonomy framework for the occupied territories, they have been unable and unwilling to mount a military or political campaign to make the costs of the occupation too high for Israel to bear.

Second, West Bank society, however united in opposition to Israeli rule, is still divided along family, religious, and regional lines—cleavages that have presented real obstacles to the emergence of a unified nationalist leadership. Both the Jordanians and Israelis have tried to exploit these differences and play on the economic self-interest of the local population. Finally, as supportive as Arabs on the West Bank are of nationalist policies, the PLO does not have a guaranteed lock on their loyalties. They were not caught up in the process of physical displacement, like many of the Palestinians on the coastal plain, but remained on the land with strong ties to their families, clans, and towns. Moreover, most of the current leadership of the PLO was not drawn from the West Bank, has not been in Palestine for almost 40 years, and in some respects has different interests altogether. The PLO has quite correctly been concerned about challenges to its leadership in the occupied territories, whether it is from the Israelis, Jordanians, Communists, or fundamentalists. Should an Israeli or Jordanian government policy emerge that offers real concessions toward satisfying Palestinian national aspirations and the PLO fail to respond, those on the West Bank, however divided, might look to a local leadership that could.

Perhaps most unique are the experiences of those Palestinian Arabs who remained in their homes and came to reside within the borders of the new Jewish state. This community, now numbering some 650,000 (about 16 percent of the entire Israeli population), enjoyed the social and economic benefits of their status as Israeli citizens. They have been politically active, voting in higher proportions than Jewish Israelis,[29] although they have had a difficult time organizing and exploiting the political system. These Palestinians have historically tended to identify with Communist party candidates, although the Labor Party has attracted some support.

While theoretically granted equal status under the law, Israel's Arab population suffers from de facto social and economic discrimination, and at the professional level, a lack of employment opportunities commensurate with their status and training. Over the years they have expressed these grievances, particularly on the issue of land expropriation, increasing nationalist sentiment and closer identification with the PLO.[30] Although Palestinian Arabs living in Israel have developed a stake in the state—a desire for prosperity, full rights, strong family and village ties—increasing contact with the West Bank and the rising prestige of the PLO have increased their national feelings as Palestinians. Regardless of their quiescence in the past, the presence of a fast-growing and increasingly politicized Arab community in Israel will present yet another hurdle along the road toward a solution of the Palestinian problem.

Although the experiences of Palestinians living in the Diaspora varied considerably, common trends emerged that would affect the political attitudes of the Palestinian community as a whole. Socially and economically the most dramatic change was the loss of land and the end to a primarily agrarian-based society. Transplanted to a refugee camp/shantytown environment, Palestinians found themselves dependent on the international dole and Arab support and deprived of the land that had given them economic means and social status. Many were forced to develop new skills and through education and sheer determination became some of the most successful professionals in the Arab world.

The dislocation and dispersal of much of the pre-1948 Palestinian community had important political and psychological effects that would shape the development of the national movement. Although the divisions within Palestinian society and their dependence on Arab support had their roots in the pre-1948 period, both circumstances were exacerbated by their refugee experience. First, the dispersal of the Palestinian refugees made it extremely difficult to establish a legitimate and authoritative political center capable of coordinating an independent and unified national movement. In part, this resulted from the obvious logistical problems of trying to organize a unified movement whose constituencies were not only located in a dozen different places but hosted by Arab regimes determined to control their military and political activities.

Equally important, the divisions that existed in pre-1948 Palestinian society were strengthened in the Diaspora. To a large extent the refugee camps and shantytowns were organized along family and village lines, with the traditional clan or *hamula* playing a major role. Religious differences were also important. Palestinians from Christian backgrounds gravitated toward secular and supra national ideologies in an effort to equalize their status in a world dominated by Muslims. Similarily, Muslims made use of Islamic symbols and values to lend greater legitimacy to their cause and attract widespread support. Survival of family, religious, and village loyalties served to provide an important reference during difficult years, but it retarded the emergence of a strongly unified leadership.

Although the PLO, primarily Fatah, has had considerable success in forming new loyalties, the Palestinian national movement is today still riddled with the organizational and ideological differences that have consistently undermined its policies. Palestinians may pride themselves on the democratic nature of the movement and institutions, but these internal debates have taken the form of struggles over resources and a fight for legitimate political power that have often led to political paralysis. Fatah is the acknowledged heart of the PLO, but it has to contend with opposition from smaller groups and from within its own ranks. Palestinian dependence on Arab regimes that have their own priorities further exacerbates this problem.

The nature of the Palestinian experience since 1948 has generated an intransigent and maximalist ethic among the PLO leadership and refugees, which has undermined the movement's ability to function in an environ-

ment that requires tactical flexibility and outright compromise for success. In the early years, adherence to a radical line was perhaps basic to
mobilizing mass support among young and dispirited Palestinians. Radicalization, however, quickly became more than a tactic and ultimately
shaped the movement's view of reality. This perspective was underscored
by the assumption that time was not on Israel's side and that it would
be premature and unwise to compromise and to accept the historical
injustice of a Jewish state. Even the PLO's mainstream leadership, which
by the early 1970s was beginning to see the recklessness of such a policy,
was prepared to tacitly permit these attitudes to jeopardize their initiatives.
But the evolution of Arafat's apparent willingness to settle for a West
Bank/Gaza state, rather than all of Palestine, was too little too late.
Without reciprocal gestures and incentives from Israel or the United
States, the PLO never had an opportunity to move beyond ambiguous
declarations at Palestine National Council (PNC) meetings. Today its
structure and dependence on Arab states that see little urgency for a
settlement with Israel have straitjacketed its ability to take the lead in a
negotiated settlement or even respond to outside initiatives.

Finally, the realities of the Diaspora resulted in an inevitable and
dangerous dependency on Arab allies and adversaries. Some were more
committed to the idea of Palestine than others but all were determined
not to allow the reality of Palestine to interfere with their own national
interests. Palestinians were challenged to harness Arab power, yet to
formulate a strategy free from Arab tutelage. The PLO has not yet
succeeded in this endeavor. Although in some respects the Arab states
have become hostages to an unresolved Palestine problem, they continue
to have the upper hand. No Arab state would permit a Palestinian leadership to settle independently with Israel unless its own interests were
satisfied. Indeed, two Arab states—Egypt and Lebanon—have not allowed
the Palestinian issues to prevent them from signing formal agreements
with Israel that go well beyond simple armistice accords. Moreover, no
Arab state will allow the PLO to drag it into an unwanted and untimely
war with Israel or to pursue political initiatives contrary to their interests.

* * *

The complexity of the Palestine problem—the contradictions and
tensions that characterize each of the three dimensions discussed above—
suggests that it may never be resolved to the satisfaction of Israel, the
Palestinians, and the Arab states. No solution will be possible until Pal-

estinians and Israelis recognize the reality of each other's claims and the necessity of translating this recognition into a territorial solution that protects their security and distinct national identity. Yet before such a dialogue could even begin, certain requirements would have to be met in each of the other dimensions that compromise the problem. Palestinians would have to unify their ranks and agree on a strategy that would require decisive action and flexibility. And a modus vivendi between Palestinians and key Arab states, particularly Syria and Jordan, would be required to insure that Arab interests were protected. Without the participation of these states there can be no lasting solution.

There is little chance that all of these conditions could be met simultaneously in a region as volatile and unpredictable as the Middle East. One has only to look at the impact of the Reagan plan of September 1982 to understand how difficult it will be to pursue any comprehensive initiative. Moreover, regional factors would have to coincide favorably with an international environment in which the United States and the Soviet Union would cooperate rather than compete on Arab-Israeli issues. Indeed, one of the ironies of the conflict is that only a comprehensive settlement will guarantee a lasting solution, yet meeting the conditions for such an approach may well be impossible.

Events since the 1982 Israeli invasion of Lebanon have made the prospects of any settlement much more remote. Tensions within the Israeli-Palestinian dimension are as acute as ever. The Israeli invasion has created yet another legacy of bitterness and hatred. Heavy Palestine civilian casualties, the massacres at Sabra and Shatila, and the Ansar prison camp in southern Lebanon created a new set of martyrs and symbols for Palestinians that will make any accommodation with Israel much harder. Continuing Palestinian attacks against Israeli forces in Lebanon will insure that the Israeli government and public alike continue to view the Palestinian problem in military terms. This perception will hamper the efforts of those on both sides who want to shift the problem and its solution to a political rather than a military dimension.

Nor do developments in the second dimension—the relationship between the Arab states and the Palestinians—augur well for the future. Although Arab states like Jordan and Saudi Arabia are impressed with the importance of finding an equitable solution to the Palestinian problem and fear a radicalized PLO in the wake of the Israeli invasion, they are both unable and unwilling to take the necessary steps to break the diplomatic logjam. Correctly convinced that the Likud government is not prepared for meaningful concessions on this issue and too weak to initiate policies that depart from the Arab consensus, these regimes look at the United States to take the lead in pressing Israel. Nor, despite their political or financial leverage with the PLO, do they have the influence required to bring the Palestinians to the negotiating table.

The weakness of those Arab states that attach great importance to a speedy resolution of the Palestinian problem has created ample opportunities for other Arab regimes that are in no hurry to reach a solution. Nowhere is this more clearly reflected than in Syrian policy toward the PLO. Damascus sees its influence over the Palestinian national movement as its primary bargaining card in protecting its interests in larger Arab-Israeli issues and blocking any settlement of which it does not approve. Already isolated within the Arab world, convinced that Israel will never return the Golan Heights, and fearful of the political and strategic consequences of the Israeli-Lebanese withdrawal agreement, Syrian President Assad is determined to insure that Yasir Arafat respects Syrian concerns. Syrian support for Fatah rebels and the expulsion of Arafat from Damascus is only a small indication of how far Assad may be prepared to go.

The new realities created by the Israeli invasion of Lebanon have facilitated the Syrian campaign. With no independent base of operations and with his political strategy in disarray, Arafat has less leverage than ever with which to counter Damascus. As long as the PLO continues to follow a strategy of "armed struggle," it will have no choice but to depend on Syrian support—the only Arab state bordering Israel that still professes a willingness to carry on the confrontation. Moreover, Arafat will require Syrian support to maintain contacts with Palestinian refugees and fighters in Lebanon. All of this suggests that unless Arafat can find a way to neutralize Syrian pressure, Assad will have greater control over formulation of the PLO's political strategy.

Finally, developments within the Palestinian dimension underscore the divisiveness and inflexibility that still paralyze the PLO. Recent events do not hold much promise for the PLO or for the Palestinian community in Lebanon. Intense opposition to the Reagan plan, the Hussein-Arafat negotiations, and the grass-roots rebellion within Fatah reveal a national movement bitterly divided over how best to cope with the future. With no visible political strategy and no realistic military option the PLO will continue to suffer the constraints that have hampered it over the years. Moreover, Palestinians in Lebanon are now more vulnerable than ever to their adversaries in that country, while West Bank Palestinians, without leadership and direction, have little choice but to defer to the realities of de facto Israeli annexation. Although continuing disarray within the

PLO might push the people of the West Bank to look after their own interests and consider participating in a Jordanian-Israeli solution for their area, they would have to be convinced that such a settlement provided real gains toward a national independent Palestinian entity.

If no settlement of the Palestinian problem acceptable to Palestinans, Israel, and the Arab world is likely, what then are the long-term consequences of no solution? First, it must be made clear what a solution will not do. The Middle East is replete with problems—economic, social, and political modernization, inter-Arab rivalries, superpower involvement—that are not inspired primarily by Arab-Israeli issues and will not be solved by a solution to the Palestinian problem, however perfect it might be. Nor would a solution magically protect U.S. and Western interests or, for that matter, guarantee a speedy end to Arab-Israeli rivalries. Indeed there are some solutions to the problems that could easily create rather than defuse tensions.

Nonetheless, failure to resolve this problem will make any long-term accommodation impossible and exacerbate a number of internal problems with which both Israel and the Arabs have to deal. It is true that most Arab states are weary of the Palestinian issue, fearful of another round with the Israelis, and eager to exchange the uncertainties of a no-war, no-peace situation for a more stable environment. And it is difficult to conceive of a situation in which the Palestine issue could unify Arab ranks and force the current leaders of Jordan, Syria, and Iraq into a war coalition against Israel. Still, it will prevent them from concluding formal peace agreements. Egypt had both the incentive and the power to conclude and implement a peace treaty with Israel. No other Arab state has both. Given the area's history, the present condition of no war/no peace will ultimately deteriorate into a much less stable situation. Changes in regimes, particularly if they are along radical nationalist or fundamentalist lines, could bring to power governments motivated less by pragmatic considerations and in the case of Jordan and Saudi Arabia, less friendly to the United States. Despite the compelling logic and rationale of Egypt's commitment to accommodation with Israel, there are no magic guarantees for the indefinite continuation of the peace treaty. Egypt has an array of economic, social, and political problems, which could result in new leadership less committed to the policies of Sadat and Mubarak. Here again, the Palestine issue may not provide the catalyst for another war with Israel, but it will become a powerful weapon in the hands of those who have no interest in peace.

Moreover, an unresolved Palestine problem could act as a destabilizing factor in states with large Palestinian populations. Although Palestinians in Jordan are remarkably well integrated and tend to support the Hashemites, the fact that they constitute a majority of the population and retain a distinct national identity of their own does not bode well for long-term stability. The refugees who arrived in 1967 are not as "Jordanianized" and are more supportive of nationalistic PLO policies. King Hussein is legitimately concerned that without a settlement he will be less able to manage this Jordanian-Palestinian link and that external and internal pressures for more power will grow. The view that Jordan is already a Palestinian state in everything but name—a view popular in some quarters in Israel and elsewhere—has already convinced Hussein that many are contemplating a solution at Hashemite expense. He doubtless believes that Israel will over time, encourage if not force West Bank Palestinians to leave and that Jordan will be forced to assimilate a large and discontented Palestinian population. Such a development would probably shift the demographic and political balance against East Bank Jordanians and could lead to the end of Hashemite rule.

In Lebanon, where Palestinians constitute an estimated 400,000 to 500,000, the problem may be more immediate. The presence of thousands of Palestinian refugees who are not integrated into Lebanese society and will not be allowed the opportunity, will continue to strain an already precariously balanced political system and continue to provide the pretext for Israeli and Syrian intervention. Given the weakness of central authority, the political grievances and sectarian rivalries, it is likely that discontented Palestinians will provide a large pool of willing recruits for those Lebanese groups that are determined to challenge the authority of the state.

Finally, the consequences of an unresolved Palestinian problem will have profound long-range implications for Israel. It will guarantee a continued state of tension and help push the region toward another Arab-Israeli war. This will in turn assure the necessity of massive economic and military assistance from abroad and guarantee a continued dangerous dependence on the United States. What effect these factors will have on the social and psychological makeup of a people already burdened by the legacy of five wars in 30 years is difficult to determine.

Moreover, if Israel seeks to solve the Palestinian issue internally, either by formal annexation or an imposed autonomy arrangement, it would mean a fundamental change in the character of political Zionism and the idea of a Jewish state. Demographic trends—increasing Jewish emigration, decreasing immigration, and a higher Arab birth rate—suggest that over time Israel will be faced with an Arab majority. Some believe that this is a manageable problem, cite increasing Arab emigration, and suggest that Palestinians can either be coopted or forced to leave. Nonetheless, the prospect that a Jewish state with even half of its population composed of discontented Sunni Muslims could survive is highly problematic. In the unlikely event that a formal annexation brought with it a campaign to grant Palestinian Arabs equal civil rights with Jews, the political power would shift in favor of the Arabs.

Finally, the effects of governing the West Bank and Gaza will, despite some of the positive social and economic effects of Israeli rule, have an injurious effect on the occupied and occupier. Although there is no reason to expect any change in this situation, relations will continue to be characterized by bitterness, hatred, and sporadic violence. Moreover, increasing land expropriation—perhaps the single most volatile issue in the West Bank—could generate more revolutionary attitudes among the young, and together with increasing Islamic fundamentalist feeling, produce future generations that are willing, whatever the odds, to defy Israeli occupation authorities.

To Israelis, the moral and ethical implications of the occupation present real dilemmas. For a people that knows all too well the pain and humiliation of minority status and prides itself on its tradition of social justice and compassion, governing people against their will can only change their view of their state and society. Although for many, events in the occupied territories can be separated from everyday life in Israel, this will not be possible as the link with the West Bank grows stronger and the two communities remain separate. There is likely to be growing disillusionment, particularly among young Israelis who have to do military service in the West Bank, and increasing tension and difficulties for those who live near heavily populated Arab areas.

Thus the Palestinian dilemma will affect the nature of the Arab-Israeli conflict for years to come. As long as the Arab states remain even marginally committed to the Palestinian cause and refuse to negotiate with Israel until Palestinian national aspirations are fulfilled, the conflict will continue at some level. The durability of the Palestinian issue will be reinforced by the religious, economic, and strategic importance of the Middle East and the continuing interest of both superpowers and a variety of other important states, who for their own reasons will be forced to become involved in this issue. Above all, the hopes, passions, and fears of the Arabs, Israelis, and Palestinians will guarantee that the issue remains a volatile one, as each group continues its search for dignity, national identity, and security—a search that seems destined to lead to continued conflict rather than reconciliation and peace.

NOTES

1. Yehoshua Porath, *The Emergence of the Palestinian-Arab National Movement, 1918-1929* (London: Frank Cass, 1974), p. 16; see also Neville J. Mandel, *The Arabs and Zionism Before World War I* (Berkeley: University of California Press, 1976), pp. 1-31. Also Adnan Abu Ghazaleh, "Arab Cultural Nationalism in Palestine During the British Mandate," *Journal of Palestine Studies*, (Spring 1972), pp. 37-38.

2. Ann Mosley Lesch, *Arab Politics in Palestine 1917-1939* (Ithaca: Cornell University Press, 1979): 25.

3. Porath, pp. 40-41.

4. Lesch, P. 226; W.F. Abboushi, "The Road to Rebellion: Arab Palestine in the 1930s," *Journal of Palestine Studies*, 6 (Spring 1977): 23-46. See Yehoshua Porath, *The Palestine Arab National Movement: From Riots to Rebellion 1929-1939* (London: Frank Cass, 1974).

5. William B. Quandt, Fuad Jabber, and Ann Mosley Lesch, *The Politics of Palestinian Nationalism*, Berkeley: University of California Press, 1973), pp. 34-37; Barry Rubin, *The Arab States and the Palestine Conflict* (Syracuse: Syracuse University Press, 1981), pp. 99-116.

6. A. L. Tibawi, "Visions of the Return: The Palestine Arab Refugees in Arabic Poetry and Art," *Middle East Journal*, 17 (Autumn 1963): 507-26. See also Yehoshafat Harkabi, "The Palestinians in the Fifties and Their Awakening as Reflected in Their Literature," in *Palestine Arab Politics*, ed. Moshe Maoz (Jerusalem: Academic Press, 1975), pp. 52-54.

7. Hisham Sharabi, "Liberation or Settlement," *Journal of Palestine Studies*, 2 (Winter 1973): 33-48. See his study, *Palestinian Guerillas: Their Credibility and Effectiveness* (Washington, D.C.: Georgetown University; Supplementary Papers, 1970).

8. Avi Shlaim, "Historical Perspective: Egypt and the Fedayeen, 1953-1956," *Middle East International* No. 84 (June 1978): 24-26.

9. Shaul Mishal, *West Bank East Bank* (New Haven: Yale University Press, 1978), pp. 111-20.

10. Issa al-Shuaibi, "The Development of Palestinian Entity—Consciousness," Part II, *Journal of Palestine Studies* 9 (Winter 1980): 50-51.

11. Bard O'Neill, *Armed Struggle in Palestine* (Boulder: Westview Press, 1978), pp. 74-89.

12. Fouad Ajami, *The Arab Predicament* (Cambridge: Cambridge University Press, 1981), pp. 144-46.

13. Michael Hudson, "The Palestinian Resistance Movement Since 1967," in *The Middle East: Quest for An American Policy*, ed. Willard A. Beling (Albany: SUNY Press, 1973), p. 172.

14. Aaron David Miller, *The PLO and the Politics of Survival* (New York: Praeger Publishers, 1983), p. 31.

15. Ajami, The Arab Predicament, p. 150.

16. Ann Mosley Lesch, "Palestinian Politics and the Future of Arab-Israeli Relations," in World Politics and the Arab-Israeli Conflict, ed. Robert O. Freedman (New York: Pergemon Press, 1979), p. 220. See also Fawaz Turki, The Disinherited (New York: Monthly Review Press, 1972), pp. 51-52.

17. Harkabi, "The Palestinians in the Fifties," pp. 52-56.

18. Yehoshafat Harkabi, The Palestinian Covenant and Its Meaning (London: Valentine Mitchell, 1979), p. 11.

19. See Gabriel Ben-Dor "Nationalism Without Sovereignty and Nationalism with Multiple Sovereignties: The Palestinians and Inter-Arab Relations," in The Palestinians and the Middle East Conflict, ed. Gabriel Ben-Dor (Ramat Gan, Israel: Turtledove Publishers, 1978), p. 158.

20. Gabriel Ben-Dor, "The Institutionalization of Palestinian Nationalism 1967-1973," in From June to October: The Middle East Between 1967 and 1973, eds. Itamar Rabinovich and Haim Shaked (New Brunswick: Transaction Books, 1978), pp. 254-60.

21. See Walid Khalidi, "Thinking the Unthinkable: A Sovereign Palestinian State," Foreign Affairs 56 (July 1978): 696-98.

22. Fouad Ajami, "The End of Pan Arabism," Foreign Affairs 57 (Winter 1978-79): 355-73.

23. Walid Kazziha, Palestine in the Arab Dilemma (London: Croom Helm, 1979), pp. 35-38.

24. Don Peretz, Evan M. Wilson, and Richard J. Ward, A Palestine Entity (Washington, D.C.: Middle East Institute, 1979), p. 35.

25. Donna Robinson Divine, "The Dialectics of Palestinian Politics," in Palestinian Society and Politics, ed. Joel Migdal (Princeton: Princeton University Press, 1980), pp. 219-29. See also Rosemary Sayigh, Palestinians: From Peasants to Revolutionaries (London: Zed Press, 1979), pp. 40-53.

26. Lesch, "Palestinian Politics and the Future of Arab-Israeli Relations," p. 220; see also Sayigh, From Peasants to Revolutionaries, p. 111.

27. Mark A. Heller, "Politics and Social Change in the West Bank Since 1967," in Palestinian Society and Politics, ed. Joel Migdal (Princeton: Princeton University Press, 1980), pp. 185-211.

28. See Ann Mosley Lesch, Political Perceptions of the Palestinians on the West Bank and the Gaza Strip (Washington, D.C.: Middle East Institute, 1980.)

29. Ian Lustick, Arabs in the Jewish State (Austin: University of Texas, 1980), p. 4.

30. See Mark. A Heller, A Palestinian State: The Implications for Israel (Cambridge: Harvard University Press, 1983), p. 107. See also Mark A. Tessler, "Israel's Arabs and the Palestinian Problem," Middle East Journal 31 (Summer 1977): 313-29; and John E. Hoffman and Benjamin Beit-Hallahmi, "The Palestinian Identity and Israel's Arabs", in The Palestinians and the Middle East Conflict, ed. Gabriel Ben-Dor, pp. 215-22.

6

Continuity and Change:
An Overview

Haim Shaked

While the Arab-Israeli conflict is by no means the only generator of tension in the Middle East, it has certainly been very prominent on the short list of major causes for trouble in the region for a long time. The significance of this conflict in the regional texture of events and processes, and the great importance of the region within the international system, have warranted the continued attention of the world's statesmen and general public alike. Its almost periodical explosion, or escalation into violence, has maintained the conflict's high rating among the issues that are considered by the media matters of major, constant public interest. Indeed, it is hard to find in modern history another conflict anywhere in the world that has maintained such prominence for so many years. Unfortunately, however, this interest has not contributed to a better understanding of the conflict and its protagonists' motives and actions. For a number of reasons, the conflict has been a rich source of sensational headlines and stories, while its crux has eluded not only the better part of the initiated general public but also quite a few self-styled expert analysts.

First, its longevity has created a stratified structure of complex factors and interactions. Scholarly studies as well as media commentaries tend to concentrate their analysis monographically on one period or a single issue, or on the most recent and most easily accessible layer: that of today's news.

Second, an extraordinary or remarkable event in the conflict causes a surge of instant attention to the event itself, rather than to its background and context or to the historical processes that created it. These events figure very prominently as international focuses of concentrated attention, but only for a relatively short period of time—usually the duration of the event and its immediate aftermath. The nature of the modern media and their quest—usually at short notice—for instant coverage of such events and commentary have contributed to a great deal of stereotyping and inaccuracy. The need of the media, particularly television, to encapsulate reportage and explanation into extremely brief exposures, with one eye always kept on fierce competition over ratings or sales, has added a sizable measure of sensationalism and oversimplification. Both, combined with ignorance or biases, have over many years profoundly confused or distorted the Arab-Israeli conflict.

Third, since this conflict is a living dispute, with great political, military, and economic life-or-death implications for many nations and powers, it gave birth to an elaborate, sophisticated propaganda effort, sustained by many intererst groups and supported by considerable, if not enormous, financial resources. Consequently, those who are interested in tracing the sources of this conflict and its evolution are inundated by deliberate lies, sophisticated disinformation, and, worse, half-truths.

A fourth cause of great misunderstanding is the fact that the Arab-Israeli conflict takes place in a region whose culture and languages are different from those common to the Western world. It is too often the case that references outside the region to the conflict do not really penetrate its inner core, due to the analyst's inability to use primary documents and sources and to properly understand the anxieties, motives, actions, and reactions common to the societies that take part in it. Worse yet, in many cases the very terminology used by the antagonists is alien to the uninitiated observer, particularly if the latter has to rely on translations, excerpts, and selections. This is further complicated when Western models and standards are applied to the analysis of Middle East political systems and structures.

The aim of this chapter is not to provide a detailed survey or summary of the history of the Arab-Israeli conflict. Each of the other chapters in this book covers in detail one of its major aspects or dimensions and analyzes the principal events and processes relevant to its main theme. Nor is it the intention here to predict specific events that may occur or to draw plausible scenarios. Rather, the objective is to provide an overview of the conflict in its historical perspective. With special attention to processes of continuity and change, the discussion concentrates on the main characteristics and stages of the dispute, the main causes of its escalation and deescalation, and its agenda in the middle of the 1980s. Hopefully, the analysis should contribute to a better understanding c´ the processes that gradually turn its future into the present, and the present into the past.

THE MAIN CHARACTERISTICS OF THE CONFLICT

From a distance, the Arab-Israeli conflict might be perceived as a concoction of complicated issues that the most recent Israeli-Arab war has created. At the time of this writing, it would seem that the overwhelming majority of analyses published in professional journals and in the daily media tend to concentrate on the results of the latest Israeli-Palestinian war, which was fought in Lebanon in the summer of 1982. At times, the analysis is traced back to the situation created by the previous major war, launched by Egypt and Syria against Israel in 1973. In a surprising number of cases, however, the analysis tends to skip that war, and also the war of attrition waged by Egypt against Israel in 1969-70, and to commence its investigation with the 1967 war, fought by Israel against Egypt, Syria, and Jordan. It is there that history begins for most contemporary allusions to the conflict, either because of the belief (shared by many) that the war represents a watershed in the history of the Arab-Israeli clash, or because that is a convenient starting point for critical or anti-Israeli argumentation, for it represents Israeli expansionism. More meticulous analysts do refer to the 1956 Sinai War, launched by Great Britain, France, and Israel against Egypt. And there are those who take one additional step backwards, and begin the unhappy story with the 1948-49 war. Some of the latter point out that this war was launched by seven Arab states, which invaded Palestine against Israel (and in their parlance it is normally referred to as the War of Independence or War of Liberation). Others call it the (Arab) Holocaust, and claim that the Arab armies intervened in Palestine as a salvage operation aimed at rescuing the Palestinian Arabs from the throes of lethal Jewish attacks. Yet, even this relatively early dating is inaccurate, for the Arab-Israeli conflict did not begin in 1947-48 and is much more than three and a half decades old. Its historical beginning lies deeper than the Arab rebellion in Palestine in 1936-39, or the Arab acts of violence against Jews in Palestine in 1929 or even as early as 1921. It began even earlier than the 1917 Balfour Declaration, which promised the creation of a national Jewish home, or the McMahon-Hussein correspondence about future Arab independence negotiated toward the end of the First World War. The true historical beginning of the Arab-Israeli conflict is in 1882—the year that saw the start of a secular, national immigration movement of Jews from Europe to a part of the world that was then under Ottoman control (and only a number of decades later would become officially and politically known as Palestine). From that time onward, two nascent national movements—Zionism and Arab nationalism—would be pitched against each other in a long, painful battle.

The dating of the origin of the Arab-Israeli conflict is meaningful, because it exposes the first major characteristic of the conflict: its unusual longevity as compared with other modern conflicts. The Arab-Israeli conflict is a modern version of a "hundred-year war." Its long duration has a twofold significance. It indicates the existence of a set of nourishing causes of unusual vitality. Also, it means that the very length of the conflict has an incremental value, which becomes a factor it itself. The long, cumulative experience of the parties to this conflict and their "living group memory," which is guided or misguided by this experience, make a decisive contribution to the survival of mutual suspicions and the emergence of new anxieties. In the case of the Arab-Israeli conflict, this is further aggravated because the suspicions on both sides are nourished by historical experiences of great glory and even greater frustrations, the origins of which go back much further than one century. The roots of the modern national myth of Israeli-Jewish society and its attachment to the land of Israel are traceable to the biblical patriarch Abraham, or to Moses, or to King David, while the sources of the modern national myth of Arab society are rooted in the stories of Abraham's son, Ishmael, Muhammad, and Saladin. Moreover, a 1,300-year-long, complex relationship of the cultural-religious worlds of Judaism and Islam, each with its self-image and interpretation of the other, which is superimposed on the modern Arab-Israeli conflict, adds yet another problematic ingredient to this old struggle.

The Arab-Israeli conflict possesses not only unusual historical depth; it is also notoriously violent. From its outset, its history is strewn with small- and large-scale, limited and comprehensive acts of violence and counterviolence. These had a tremendous impact on the antagonists, even when relatively few people were wounded or killed and when damage to property was limited. The 1929 "events" (as they were called by the Jews) of Hebron, in which Jews were killed, or the cases of Deir Yassin in 1948 and Kaft Qassim in 1956, in which Arabs were killed, are good examples in point. Notwithstanding the many differences between these events, all share a significant common denominator: while the loss of life in each of them was relatively small in numbers, their symbolic impact on communal memories was long-lasting. There are analysts who contend that this syndrome of violence shows a peculiar rhythm. Considering the dates of the objectively or subjectively defined major outbursts—1921,

1929, 1936-39, 1947-49, 1956, 1967, 1969-70, 1973, and 1982—it is easily discernible that meaningful acts of hostility erupted between Jews and Arabs approximately once every decade. The implied question is whether it is the pronounced acts of violence or the relatively long periods of non-violent coexistence between eruptions that is the more typical of this relationship. An optimistic attitude will, of course, accentuate the latter. A more pessimistic approach will underscore the former. In any case, it is quite clear that the use of force as a means to resolve disputed issues is a major attribute of the Arab-Israeli conflict.

The very term "Arab-Israeli conflict" is grossly misleading with regard to the number of *dramatis personae*. At its face value, the term imparts a parity between two parties: Israel on the one hand and the Arabs on the other. In fact, the conflict is polypartite, with the chief actors being Israel on the one side and numerous Arab political entities on the other. Thus the Arab-Israeli conflict incorporates a dispute between the Jewish society in Palestine, turned into the state of Israel, and Palestinian Arab society now located in mandatory Palestine, Jordan, and other places in the Arab world where Palestinians reside temporarily or semipermanently. Simultaneously, there exists a state of war between Israel and her neighbors (normally referred to as the "confrontation states"): Syria, Jordan, and until recently, Egypt and Lebanon. Other Arab states, which do not share a contiguous boundary with Israel, also take part in the conflict: Iraq, Libya, Saudi Arabia, Sudan, Tunisia, Algeria, Morocco, and all the Persian Gulf states. The remaining members of the Arab League and a number of Islamic countries (such as Pakistan, or Iran since the rise of Khomeini in 1979) have also been involved on the Arab side. This long list is not exhaustive, for there are other states, non-Arab and non-Islamic, that have significantly participated in the conflict. Of primary importance among the latter are, of course, the major powers—Great Britain and France, and subsequently the superpowers—the USSR and the United States. A number of countries in Europe, Asia (Japan), Africa (Uganda, Ethiopia), and even Central America (Cuba) should also figure on this list. Naturally, the level and intensity of each of these countries' involvement, as well as the precise nature of its participation—direct or indirect—vary from one case to the other and at different times.

The kaleidoscopic nature of the Arab-Israeli conflict is tied in with another of its features: it is a multiissue, or multidimensional conflict. The attitudes and policies of each of the participating parties are molded by its own system of internal forces and pressures and by its interests. These, in turn, influence that party's grievances and ambitions, and the means it uses in order to remedy or improve them. Furthermore, as the interests change over time, so do the policies designed to take care of them.

The Arab-Israeli conflict is not only long, internecine, polypartied, and multidimensional. It is also many-sided. It is not merely a collection of bilateral disputes between Israel and each of its antagonists but also a multilateral dispute between Israel and the whole Arab world. Consequently, when an Arab country makes a move that is only indirectly related to Israel, but may affect the delicate regional balance of power, it has a connected-vessels effect on the balance of power within the Israeli-Arab system. Instances in recent years were Egypt's intervention in the Yemeni civil war in the 1960s, Syria's abortive intervention in the Jordanian-Palestinian war of 1970 and later in the Lebanese civil war of 1975-76, and the Iraq-Iran war of the early 1980s. Similarly, Israel's occupation of territories adjacent to its own boundaries (Sinai for a short while after 1956 and more than a decade after 1967, as well as the West Bank, the Golan Heights, and the Gaza Strip in 1967), her presence in Lebanon in 1982-83, or her involvement in faraway places (such as Kurdistan and the southern Sudan in the 1960s) acquired a general importance that transcended the specific impact of such an Israeli move on the particular Arab state that was the object of Israel's action. Inter-Arab coalitions and treaties or, conversely, the "Arab World's cold war," its division into camps, which was characteristic of the 1950s and 1960s, and the fragmentation of the Arab world in the 1970's has a major influence on the nature of the Arab-Israeli conflict, as the latter, in turn, affected the shaping of inter-Arab relations. An additional dimension is the continuous deep involvement in the conflict of the major powers and then the superpowers, as part of their global competition for influence and control. It turned the dispute from a local or regional issue into an international affair. The penetration of Britain and France into the Middle East in the nineteenth and early twentieth centuries, their struggle for presence there, and the means they employed in order to secure and then protect their acquired influence had a tremendous and mostly negative impact on the Arab-Israeli conflict in its formative years (from 1882 to the late 1940s). The rather quick and disorderly withdrawal of Britain from the region following the Second World War also has an adverse effect on the situation. Rather than bring about a resolution of the problem, it seriously aggravated it and eventually led to the first major war between Jews and Arabs over Palestine in 1948-49. The subsequent penetration of the USSR and the United States into the region and their dealings with the immediate parties to the conflict have also had a major impact on its evolution since 1948-49. The Middle East has been a very important geopolitical and geostrategic component of the East-West axis of confrontation. The importance of the region within this framework, and the significance of the Arab-Israeli conflict within this region—a significance that exceeds the limits of specific time and place— have contributed to the fact that, unlike many other regional conflicts, the Arab-Israeli one has retained for a long time its elevated position on the international agenda.

It follows that the Arab-Israeli conflict is more than just a chronically inflamed relationship between Israel and its environment. Over the years, the above-mentioned attributes have influenced the very nature of those involved societies for whom this conflict is of primary importance, as well as the contours of intraregional and even international relations. Moreover, during the decade of 1973-83, the struggle came to be identified in international public opinion as a central factor contributing to the spiraling prices of the most important single source of world energy—oil. Even if the objective truth may be profoundly different, the fact remains that for a long time many nations subjected their policies and action to the assumption that the prices of a very sensitive commodity such as oil were fully linked to developments in the Arab-Israeli conflict. Furthermore, since violent eruptions in the Middle East threatened to boil over and spread to areas outside the region, they forced the superpowers to take positions concerning their protégés. Therefore, the superpowers found themselves quite often in undesirable confrontational situations and on a timetable that was not planned, let alone controlled, by them. A good example in point is the state of alert announced for the United States military forces toward the end of the October War of 1973 and the significant Russian military movements that occurred simultaneously.

What is the Arab-Israeli conflict all about? As in the case of the participants, so, too, with regard to the major bone of contention—the elements are neither easily definable nor are they static. At different times and in changing circumstances the main grievances that constitute the conflict assume different faces. At the time of writing, the innocent observer might conclude that the main, if not the only, issue is Israel's problematic presence in Lebanon, and her policy of setting up settlements in territories it occupied as a result of the 1967 war. Before the war in Lebanon in 1982, the main issue seemed to be Israel's withdrawal from the territories it had occupied in 1967, and the viability and desirability of the creation of an independent, PLO-led Palestinian state. Any examination of references to the Arab-Israeli conflict and its resolution made from 1967 will yield a surprising conclusion: most of them almost completely ignore the fact that the Arab-Israeli conflict raged in the Middle East well before the June 1967 war and that this war was, in fact, a consequence of the conflict and not its cause. A close investigation of the period that preceded 1967 would also demonstrate that the central issue was constantly changing its appearance. Toward the end of the 1950s and during the early 1960s the immediate issue was the allocation and use of meager regional water resources. Many specialists predicted a comprehensive Arab-Israeli war (which never came about) over Israel's large-scale diversion of water from the Jordan River to its Negev desert. The early 1950s, on the other hand, were replete with Arab statements about "a second round," that is, another major all-Arab war which was to be conducted against Israel in an attempt to rectify the consequences of the 1948-49 war and open the way for a return of Palestinian refugees to Palestine. In the 1940s, center stage was occupied by another theme: a fierce struggle between Jews and Arabs over the question of the rights and wrongs of the establishment of an independent, sovereign Jewish state in Palestine. Intertwined with it was another, more veteran issue, which had loomed large since the early 1930s: the right of Jews to immigrate to and settle in Palestine and to create their permanent, sovereign state there. The supporters regarded such a program as a legitimate fulfillment of the aspirations of a persecuted (Jewish) people, whose historical attachment to the Land of Israel withstood time itself. The opposers saw in the same program a dispossession of an innocent (Arab-Palestinian) people by alien intruders. Indeed, throughout all stages in the evolution of the Arab-Israeli conflict, the main issue was the question of Arab-Israeli coexistence. Beneath the concrete and tactical questions, which kept changing their appearances, there was one underlying issue all along: who would win in the head-on collision of two national movements, likened to an irrestible force trying to move an immovable object. The main theater of this struggle has been the territory known either as the Land of Israel or Palestine. The movements were Zionism versus Arab nationalism in general, or its Palestinian offshoot in particular. The problem was, can a *modus vivendi* between the two be worked out, or is their basic relationship one of mutual exclusivity? Thus, the issue at stake was by far larger and more complex than the size of Israel or this or that political-military move by the Arabs. The fateful confrontation between Arabism and Zionism has been intertwined with questions that relate to the interpretation by each side of its history and national mission. There were two additional complications: first, the location of this confrontation—at the very heart of a crossroads of international influences; and second, its timing—during the height of a crisis precipitated by the impact of the penetration of Europe into the Middle East, the collision between cultures (known as the process of Westernization and modernization) that ensued, the subsequent struggle of the region's people for independence, and the existential problems they experienced after they attained their formal or practical political independence.

For many years experts have been arguing back and forth the question of core versus periphery in the Arab-Israeli conflict. There are those who claim that the Palestinian problem is the heart of the conflict—for this is where it all began—and that all the rest is nothing but "soft" or "hard" margins. Others have charged that while it is true that, historically speaking, the Arab-Israeli conflict commenced with the violent struggle between Jews and Arabs within Palestine and over its fate, its Palestinian component has become, over time, just one of many facets. Furthermore, they claim, it is no longer the most important one. The difference between these two approaches is not merely technical, and the conclusions to be drawn from each stand very far apart. The first view implies that the main remedy depends primarily on the satisfaction of Palestinian aspirations. The second predicates a resolution on a much more comprehensive and fundamental change in the conflict's environment. While the two are not mutually exclusive, each is related to the angle of observation—and it is perceived differently in different places and times.

The mutual common denominator of all involved national movements—Zionist, Arab, or Palestinian—is the centrality of the conflict and its omnipresence in their respective lives. The Zionist movement and the state of Israel equate it with a continuous threat and an ongoing, widespread attempt to delegitimize their very existence. From an Israeli point of view, the conflict is not a "normal" one, for it does not really relate to concrete disputes such as the size of Israel, its policy, or *modus operandi*. As perceived from Jerusalem, the enemy is out to annihilate the sovereignty and independence of the state of Israel, irrespective of this state's actions. From a Palestinian point of view, the conflict is equally not "normal," because it does not take place between two entities that have identical status and power, but between a militarily powerful, independent state and a dispersed people fighting for its rights, wrested from it by a cruel history, treacherous helpers, and a sophisticated enemy. From an all-Arab perspective, Israel is equated with the world's powers of evil—imperialism and colonialism—which have severely harmed the

Arab nation's struggle to regain its lost glory. From the point of view of each confrontation state, and depending on the outlook of its regime and proximity to or distance from Israel, the latter is an enemy for reasons and in ways that are not identical with those of its other sister states. In each and all cases, one party's attitude to the other is based not only on sober considerations of *real politik* and political or military strategy but also on primordial anxieties and burdensome fears, which stem from sad experiences of many generations, deep-seated suspicions, or serious crises. In recent years a religious, mythical dimension, which was always latent in the two parties' attitudes, has come to the fore and should be added to this list. Each of the parties is also fully convinced of its full, if not absolute, justice and the antagonist's total injustice. Each is inclined to accuse the other of a decisive contribution to the emergence of the conflict and its endless festering.

A closer examination, however, will also expose significant differences among the parties. Israel believes that it fights, in a hostile environment, for its very life. Its legitimacy is not to be doubted at all and is not a matter for negotiation. At the base of Israel's policy since 1948 has been an obsession with security, centered on the concept that Israel fights to maintain the status quo, that is, against the Arab desire to obliterate the existence of a sovereign, independent Jewish state. For many years, even when Israel fired the first shot in an Arab-Israeli war, the Israeli perception and justification resided in the concept of a preventive war. Until 1977—when the Likud government won the elections in Israel, the occupation (or, as it was referred to officially, "administration") of the territories taken in 1967 was regarded as an added guarantee of Israel's security, yet a negotiable asset about which a compromise should eventually be reached. Since the mid-1930s the Jewish Yishuv in Palestine and then in Israel saw themselves pitched not only against the Palestinian Arabs but against the whole Arab world, which, split as it was among various political trends and forces, was united in its enmity to Israel. No one in Israel felt that the human misery of the Palestinian refugees should be ignored. Very few Israelis ever argued that the resolution of the conflict was not an urgent matter or that it could be solved without an adequate satisfaction of Palestinian wishes. But many Israelis regarded the solution of the Palestinian constituent as an integral part of a more comprehensive solution rather than its substitute. In Israeli eyes, the Palestinian problem is primarily an Arab problem and it is the Arab world, not Israel, that has the primary responsibility to come to grips with it and to devise a proper solution to it. Moreover, there has been an Israeli consensus that even if the Palestinians were satisfied with a this-or-that plan or proposed solution, they were not in a position to deliver the rest of the Arab world to the negotiation table. Thus, the Israeli logic went on, since there can be no solution that will satisfy all Palestinian factions without considerable weakening of Israel's might, and since a weakened Israel would still face a hostile Arab world, the whole scheme would turn into a stage in the attempted annihilation of Israel.

The majority of the Israeli public and its political mainstream never denied the right of peaceful existence of any Arab political entity. As many Israelis saw it, this included the Palestinians, who had their own state—Jordan. On the other hand, the Arab world—at least since the establishment of the state of Israel—fought for the nullification of the status quo, that is, toward the cessation of Israel's existence as a sovereign polity or, in the initial stage, for the return to the status quo ante. After the 1948-49 war it seemed that if Israel were to agree to go back to the boundaries drawn up in the 1947 U.N. partition plan (which had been accepted by the Jewish population and rejected by the Arab population of Palestine), and would readmit the Palestinian refugees, the Arab world would regard this as a return to the status quo ante. Twenty years later, after 1967, it seemed that if Israel were to agree to go back to the June 4, 1967 (or 1948-49) boundaries, the Arab world would be willing to regard this as a proper return to the status quo ante. Until Israel's peace treaty in Egypt it was unclear what would follow such a return to "square one"—a termination of the conflict or the implication of the Arab "stages" or "salami" plan.

For many years Arab spokesmen stated that Israel should be dealt with in a number of moves: first a return to the pre-June 1967 boundaries and then the reopening of the "1948 file." They were not willing to consider full peace in return for an Israeli withdrawal, unless it was followed by "the full restoration of Palestinian rights"—at best an ambiguous request. Israel, on her part, argued that the wars she fought with the Arabs had been imposed on her and that each of them created a new situation, from which direct negotiations for peace should start without any preconditions. The Arabs retorted that Israel, under cover of a war of defense, was actually an illegitimate entity that was aggressive and expansionist to boot—a cancer or dagger in the heart of the Arab world. Each party saw its adversary as the incarnation of evil, but while the Arab countries had one Israel to contend with, Israel confronted a multistate Arab system, whose various independent components represented enmity resulting from different reasons and in different forms. Each of the antagonists searched for the Archimedes point that could be used to improve its position vis-à-vis the enemy. Simultaneously, each party developed an elaborate system of attitudes and arguments designed to justify its own policies and negate the other side's moves. Gradually, and to some extent as a result of the lengthy period of time in which the adversaries were totally separated from each other by war and closed boundaries, their willingness and ability to understand each other diminished significantly. This, in turn, created more misunderstanding and disagreement. As in a Greek tragedy, a situation evolved in which all participants were right (at least in their own eyes), but at the conclusion of the play the stage was filled with dead bodies.

THE EVOLUTION OF THE CONFLICT

Like any living political situation, the Arab-Israeli conflict is dynamic and changes constantly, while some of its constituents become fixed elements that can be discerned at any given moment. It is therefore easy to allude mistakenly to the Arab-Israeli conflict through its specific agenda at a certain time, and thereby lose sight of its change over time. It is equally misleading to diagnose its elements of continuity without due regard to its constant change. In both cases, the analytical and practical conclusions would be grossly off the mark.

The element of continuity consists of two subelements: the environmental and the substantial. From its inception, and throughout its whole history, the conflict was affected by the condition of its environment: the international, regional, and inter-Arab systems, the ideological framework, and the domestic situation within each of the involved local political entities. The international involvement in the Middle East was characterized, during most of the modern history of the region, by fierce competition rather than agreement concerning spheres of influence (the only notable exception being the relatively brief division of the region between Great Britain and France in the period between the First and the Second World War). This competition, naturally, was not devoid of intrigue, and its resolution was not always in the interest of all outside powers. As a matter of fact, the conflict was frequently utilized by one power to strengthen itself and weaken the other. Thus, the USSR used the Arab-Israeli dispute in its encroachment upon the Middle East in the late 1940s, by supporting Israel against the Arabs, and since the mid-1950s, by supporting the Arabs against Israel. The United States took advantage of the October 1973 war to buttress its positions and launch a major thrust aimed at supplanting the USSR.

The regional and inter-Arab system was characterized, for most of the time, by polarization, fragmentation, and change of the leadership and rallying cause of the different camps. As long, however, as the main battle cry of the Arab world was its unification (pan-Arabism), and even after unification ceased to be an operational program, the inter-Arab system found it much easier to rally around opposition to Israel than to agree on any positive plan of action. The predominant ideological trend in the region was and remains nationalism, supported by strong elements of political messianism or religious myth, or both. Until the attainment of independence in the aftermath of the Second World War, each political entity experienced intensive internal strife. Following independence, most of the newly established states went through convulsions of instability, expressed often by coups d'état and revolutions. All of these, and accelerated processes of complex economic, technological, and societal change, which collided with religious-cultural, political, and social traditions, created great and constant turbulence in the region. The Arab-Israeli conflict was one of its "eyes."

The Arab-Israeli conflict, albeit not the only source of tension in the region, occupied a prominent place in this environment. The element of continuity in the conflict's substance was also salient. It consisted of mutual hatred and suspicion; of Israel's constant feeling that it was braving an ocean of animosity endangering its existence; and of the feeling of the majority of the Arabs most of the time that Israel's very existence constituted an affront to their welfare. All of these and the pattern of recurrent small- or large-scale violence marked the conflict 50 years ago and still characterize it today.

But there is another side to this coin—that of constant, at times profound change in the nature of each of these factors. For the purpose of a brief discussion of the changes that occurred in the nature of Arab-Israeli conflict and its environment, five periods in its evolution may be discerned: 1882-1917; 1917-1948/49; 1948/49-1967; 1967-1982; and 1982-.

1882-1917

The period of 1882-1917, which begins with the initially minuscule project of a modern, national Jewish settlement in the ancient Land of Israel, might best be titled the emergence of the Arab-Israeli conflict. It saw the creation of the basic preconditions for the lengthy encounter between Jews and Arabs; more or less concurrently, the two new forces of Zionism and Arabism arrived on the historical stage. From now on, the Jewish-Muslim relationship, as it was defined for centuries under the rule of a succession of Islamic empires, is redefined in new terms—Zionism versus Arabism—and the difference between the old and the new terminology was not just semantic. During this period, there were no independent Arab states; therefore the conflict is devoid of an inter-Arab context. On the other hand, the major powers are busy with intrigue and they scramble for the pieces of the collapsing Ottoman Empire. The as yet amorphous Arab-Israeli conflict does not play an active role but the stage is set for its appearance. Thus, at the end of this period, with the termination of the First World War and on the eve of the establishment of the mandatory system, the antagonists are poised, with conflicting promises made by Great Britain in their possession. Even at this embryonic stage, their budding interests can hardly be reconciled.

1917-1948/49

The second period begins with the Balfour Declaration and concludes with the establishment of the state of Israel. The crux of the conflict, now almost fully developed, is the struggle and counterstruggle concerning the establishment of a Jewish state within the boundaries of mandatory Palestine. Interestingly, the period commences with the temporary cooperation between the leader of Zionism, Chaim Weizmann, and the leader of Arabism, the Hashemite Faysal. This convergence of interests culminates in the Weizmann-Faysal agreement signed in 1919, only to remain an unimplemented piece of paper. Soon the paths of the two movements part, and after the completion, in the early 1920s, of the postwar rearrangement of the region, including the severance by the British of Transjordan from mandatory Palestine, the main theme of the Arab-Jewish relationship turns into a struggle for the control of Palestine west of the River Jordan. The relatively small, weak, but fast-growing Jewish Yishuv attempts to change the status quo and to create demographic, organizational, economic, military, and political facts through a well-thought-out plan of land purchases and settlements. Simultaneously, the Arab population's protest and opposition mounts and expresses itself in growing violence against the Jews and the British. As far as the major-power involvement is concerned, for most of this period the issue is not one of interpower competition but of an inability of the one power that is supposed to be in control—Great Britain—to resolve the issue satisfactorily. Confronted by the growing tension in Palestine, Britain often plays a two-faced role, which further aggravates the situation.

Four major changes distinguish the second period from the previous one. First, from an embryonic state the conflict is by now become full-bodied. By the mid-1940s the main issues, the argumentation, modus operandi, and involved camps are clearly set. Second, from the mid-1930s, as a result of certain developments that are outside the scope of this analysis and not without Great Britain's machination, the struggle for Palestine is gradually expropriated from the hands of the Palestinian Arabs and becomes a political pawn in the hands of the fledgling Arab states and, ipso facto, of inter-Arab relations. This change is clearly exemplified by the invasion of Palestine by the armies of seven Arab states, the day after the termination of the British mandate for Palestine and the announcement of the establishment of the state of Israel on May 15, 1948. Third, toward the end of this period, Britain (and France) began to withdraw from the region, as part of the global processes of decolonization precipitated by the Second World War. Their departure creates a power vacuum and an opportunity immediately seized upon by the Soviet Union as part of her traditional quest for a say in the Middle East. Fourth, by the middle of the period, the struggle for independence in different parts of the Middle East is strengthened and accelerated. Toward the end of the period, most Arab states and newly formed Jewish state are in place, whereas the Palestinian Arabs suffer a devastating blow. Not only do they lose the 1948-49 war—when it is over they find themselves split under Jordanian, Egyptian, Israeli, Syrian, and Lebanese authorities, many of them refugees in their own milieu, and all of them pulverized socially and politically.

1948/49-1967

The third period commences with the aftermath of a major war between Israel and all of its close and some of its distant neighbors, and concludes with a war between Israel and three out of its four immediate neighbors. In both cases the wars terminate with cease-fire and armistice agreements and not—as is customary in world affairs—with the capitulation of one of the parties or the exhaustion of both and with peace arrangements and treaties. Thus, each of the two wars carries—more than is usual with most wars—the seeds of the next war. The crux of the conflict is, throughout this period, the general (but not completely unified) Arab attempt to launch a campaign for the *reconquista* of Palestine, and the successful attempt by Israel to maintain the status quo, that is, to successfully defend the main achievement of the Zionist movement in 1948.

The main antagonists now are not Israel and the Palestinians but Israel and the Arab states, while the Palestinians are relegated to the role of refugees and dispossessed. The Arab struggle against Israel is expressed in a combination of political and economic boycott, as well as diplomatic and military pressures. In the military sphere, the Arab world endorses armed infiltration of Palestinian *Fidaiyyun* into Israel, tries to create military alliances for cooperation, and undertakes an extensive modernization of its fighting capacity. Israel's struggle against the Arabs is exemplified by attempts to repel the infiltration through specific military reprisals and major wars (1956 and, in fact, also 1967). On the diplomatic and economic fronts, Israel's answer to the imposition of isolation is the leapfrogging into the non-Arab countries of the Middle East (chiefly Iran and Turkey), Africa (mainly Ethiopia and its neighbors), and south-east Asia.

Throughout this period, Israel regards itself as a state-in-siege, defending itself from an external threat, but ever ready to negotiate peace. The Arab image of Israel is the opposite of Israel's self-image. To the Arabs, Israel comes more and more to represent their nemesis. This process is enhanced by waves of domestic instability, which most Arab countries experience in the late 1940s and early 1950s. These convulsions are not limited merely to the usurpation of power within the ruling elite or oligarchy, but express deep seated socioeconomic changes and revolutionary programs aimed at changing the face of society and government. Consequently, the involvement of the revolutionary regimes in the Arab-Israeli conflict assumes a crusader's zest. Within the inter-Arab system the polarization grows between the competing Arab camps—the "progressives" and the "reactionaries," as they came to be known in the region. In the rivalry for the leadership of the Arab world Gamal Abdel Nasser's Egypt assumes an indeniable seniority and its spirit, as far as regional policies are concerned, is imbued with a deep, messianic fervor of militant pan-Arabism, whose banner is the unification of the Arab world. Due to its political importance, military capability, and ideological fervor, Egypt becomes the rallying point for the Arab struggle against Israel.

Simultaneously, great changes take place in the sphere of international affairs. Britain and France completely leave the Middle East and

North Africa, while their successors—the USSR and the United States—find themselves in active competition for footholds and influence in the vacated areas. By the end of this period the more aggressive and resolute of the two—the USSR which in the meantime has turned away from Israel and supports the Arabs—seems to enjoy a preponderance over its chief adversary. More importantly, unlike the arrangement between Britain and France, which divided the region between them during the better part of the twentieth century, the USSR and the United States never clearly define their respective areas of influence. Their disagreements, deepening involvement in the region, and the gradual rise of its importance to each of them further contribute to the destabilization of the region.

1967-1982

The fourth period in the history of the Arab-Israeli conflict opens with a devastating, surprising Israeli victory over Egypt, Syria, and Jordan. It terminates with a war that, unlike those of 1948-49, 1967, and 1973 and similar to the war of 1956, was initiated by Israel. The occupation of the whole of Sinai, the Golan Heights, the West Bank, and the Gaza Strip by Israel in 1967 had a profound effect. While until 1967 the central issue was the question of Palestine (which never became a primary national issue for any Arab state), as of 1967 the question of loss of territory becomes nationally paramount for three major Arab protagonists in the conflict. In this period, the agenda contains not merely the return of Palestine to the Palestinians but also the return of Sinai to Egypt, the Golan Heights to Syria, and the West Bank (including East Jerusalem) and possibly also the Gaza Strip to Jordan or the Palestinians. Moreover, after a generation in which the Palestinians themselves did not play a major role, they now gradually reemerge as an active political-military factor. Also, as a result of a combination of a number of factors, including the routing of the regular armies of Egypt, Syria, and Jordan by Israel, the militant PLO organization comes to play a central role in the power interplay that constitutes the Arab-Israeli conflict. This entity—revolutionary in its program and terrorist in its operation—signifies in many ways the delayed-reaction syndrome in the development of the Arab national movement as a "super movement" of pluralistic national movements: Jordanian, Iraqi, Egyptian, Syrian, and so forth.

The forces that now wrestle in the Arab world include the Palestinians (who are trying to regain the mastership of their own destiny, which they lost in the 1930s), and each of the other countries (which continue to try to subsume the Palestinian interests to their own national interests). While the Arab states do not forsake their interest in the Palestine question and are even willing to give prominence to the PLO, they are unwilling to bend their own interest to conform with the real needs of the Palestinians. Thus, an inherent disagreement evolves within the Arab world as to the priorities of the Arab struggle against Israel: should it concentrate on the 1967 or the 1948 "file"? And if on both, what is the preferable order of priorities? The 1973 war, initiated by Egypt and Syria, is an example of putting the priority on the 1967 file. The Rabat 1974 Arab Summit recognition of the PLO as the sole legitimate spokesman of the Palestinians is an illustration of an attempt to make headway with the 1948 file.

As far as Israel is concerned, this period also sees dramatic change. The results of the 1967 war create in Israel a feeling of strength and invincibility, shaken only by another war—that of 1973. More importantly, the occupation in 1967 of territories, in particular the West Bank, contributed to the awakening of an Israeli messianism, which grows gradually and affects the downfall of the Labor alliance and the rise of the Likud party to power in the 1977 elections (referred to in Israel as the overturn). For the first time in the history of the conflict, the concepts of "Greater Syria" (which since 1975-76 could add to its credit the virtual occupation of Lebanon) and "Greater Jordan" (whose king never really gave up his claim to the West Bank, conquered by his grandfather) meet the concept of "Greater Israel" (by now the program of the political party in power).

Simultaneously, the 1970s produce a number of profound circumstantial changes that have an impact on the conflict. The domestic scene in most Arab countries acquires a higher measure of stability than has been the case since independence. The system of inter-Arab relations becomes more fragmented than ever before. Instead of polarization between two camps, the Arab world now becomes multipolar. The messianic pan-Arabist ideology is replaced by a political pragmatism and by a localized type of nationalism that was always latent in Arab nationalism. On the international level, the competition between the superpowers continues as ever, but a series of sophisticated moves made by an unusual U.S. secretary of state provides the United States with greater prominence in the affairs of the region. The United States, whose basic interest in the Middle East is to promote stability and the resolution of the Arab-Israeli conflict, emerges as the only international arbiter between Israelis and Arabs.

All of the above, as well as the growing realization in the Arab world— particularly in the light of the military results of the 1973 war— that Israel cannot be eliminated by military force, and a number of specific other causes that are outside the scope of this analysis, create a new constellation in the conflict. Coupled with talented and imaginative leadership, this new constellation triggers Egypt's and Israel's direct negotiations in 1977. These produce after protracted and very complicated negotiations and not without a deep, highest-level U.S. involvement, the Israeli-Egyptian peace treaty of 1979. The treaty embodies three crucial elements. First, its structure separates the Israeli-Egyptian issues from the Israeli-Palestinian issues. Second, Egypt fully and unequivocally recognizes Israel's legitimacy and agrees to full normalization. Third, Israel fully returns the Sinai, that is, the Egyptian territory it has occupied in 1967. Thus is eliminated the concrete national Egyptian bone of contention in its dispute with Israel. To a certain extent, Egypt's removal from the circle of active conflict with Israel refocuses attention on the question of Palestine. Jordan's unwillingness throughout the whole period to reassume active responsibility for the Palestinian issue, the creation of a Palestinian mini confrontation state in Lebanon after the crushing of the Palestinian fighting units in Jordan in September 1970, and Syria's attempt to step into the vacancy created by Egypt's withdrawal from all Arab leadership—all these contributed to the reemergence of the Palestinian aspect of the Arab-Israeli conflict and its acquisition of new prominence.

1982-?

Mistakenly, the 1982 war has been titled the Lebanese war. More accurately, it should be called the Israeli-Palestinian war in Lebanon. From an Israeli point of view, it is the second Israeli involvement, since 1948-49, in a major war with the Palestinians. From a Palestinian point of view, it is their fourth embroilment in large-scale warfare, preceded by the 1936-39 rebellion in Palestine, the 1948-49 war with the Jews, and the 1970 war with Jordan. The internecine nature of the first engagement weakened them considerably. The second ended with a great debacle. The third terminated with their explusion and loss of a military base in Jordan. The fourth results in an evacuation and loss of military base in Lebanon. All entailed terrible bloodshed.

While it is too early, at the time of writing, to evaluate the full consequences of the 1982 war in Lebanon and all its implications for the Arab-Israeli conflict, it would seem that this war opened a new phase in the conflict's history. It may have moved the pendulum from a point in the confrontation which, since the mid-1970s, has come to focus primarily on Israeli-Palestinian issues, to a point where the dispute is again pitched between Israel and Arab states, predominantly Syria and Jordan. Thus, while the 1948 Palestine file has by no means been closed as a result of the 1982 war, the emphasis has seemingly shifted again to the other end of the spectrum. Some other trends that were discernible toward the end of the fourth period have been enhanced in this, the fifth. It was fully realized that the key to the solution of the Arab-Israeli conflict, as far as superpower involvement is concerned, is in the hands of the United States, not the USSR. Also, it became clear that the Arab states are unwilling to sacrifice any of their vital interests for the sake of the Palestinians, beyond paying lip service to their cause, the level of which also seemed to subside in comparison with their outspokenness since the mid-1930s. Thus, the inter-Arab system completed an almost 180-degree turn. Moreover, unlike the self-image and outside perception of an all-Arab strength that dominated the 1970s, due to the successful hiking of oil prices and accumulation of great petrodollar wealth between 1973 and 1981, the beginning of the 1980s saw an all-Arab weakening, due to the global decline in oil consumption and the drop in oil prices. On the other hand, while Israel remained an intolerable thorn in the side of the Arab world, it gradually also came to be regarded as an existing fact, with relatively mighty military capabilities and political wherewithal, which could not be completely isolated. Apparently, the Fahd plan of 1981 and the acceptance of its main principles in the Fez Arab Summit of 1982 symbolized this budding realization. Israel, for its part, continued to adhere to the main conditions for its dealings with any Arab state that would be forthcoming: a willingness to enter into direct negotiations, on the basis of the Camp David accords of 1978, with no preconditions.

Yet, side by side with this element of continuity, a significant change seemed to be creeping into the Israeli position: the thought that in the aftermath of the Israeli-Egyptian peace treaty, perhaps the resolution of the conflict was no longer a matter of urgency. Rather, this logic went on, a hasty move might deny Israel certain cards, or time, required for the implementation of a policy designed—in Israel's thinking—to buttress its defense of its security interests on the West Bank. In contrast with many hysterical analyses, it would seem that the pace of these discernible changes in both the Arab world and Israel has been quite slow. For the Arab world the Fez resolution was still far removed from a willingness to make peace with Israel, even if this would be a "cold peace" like the one between Egypt and Israel. As for Israel, it would seem that its national consensus was still far removed from a willingness to relegate peace with Israel's neighbors to a secondary place in the list of top Zionist desiderata. A truthful peace challenge, it was argued, would still generate within Israel irresistible domestic pressures to compromise for its own sake.

CAUSES OF ESCALATION

An analysis of the evolution of the Arab-Israeli conflict, its permanent features, and the changes that occurred in its course demonstrates the futility of any attempt to define an all-inclusive formula that will explain its eruptions, periods of relative quiet, and causes of escalation or moderation. Yet, it is possible to isolate a number of elements that contribute more in one direction than in another. The process by which such factors are isolated is, of course, not an exact science. Moreover, some of these factors may appear in reality in contradictory forms. While some may contribute under certain circumstances to escalation, they may contribute to moderation under different circumstances. Among the many factors that in the past contributed to escalation, the following are worth listing:

Domestic instability, internal problems, and national frustration. Shaky regimes sometimes externalize their problems by conducting an adventurous foreign policy. In the case of the Arab states such policies were frequently directed against each other rather than against Israel. But even in such cases as the abortive Syrian military intervention in the Palestinian-Jordanian war in 1970, the Arab-Israeli conflict was indirectly affected. The accumulation of national frustrations has also contributed to escalation. While it is impossible to define a boiling point for such frustrations, there is no doubt that they have played an important role.

Radicalism. Radical-revolutionary ideologies, of leftist-socialist inclinations or rightist or fundamentalist outlooks, have contributed to escalation. An example of the first type is the Baath ideology and its implementation in Syria and Iraq. The Khomeini revolution in Iran is of the second type. Qaddafi's regime is a strange combination of both.

A self-image of excessive strength, no-choice feelings, or a military-solution concept. Situations in which one party operated from a subjective presumption of excessive strength—militarily, politically, or economically (or some of the above)—and, conversely, the feelings of "no choice" when confronted by the adversary's moves, tended to raise the probability of escalation in the conflict. During its history, a number of military-solution concepts appeared: attempts to annihilate the enemy or at least break its military capability; to change the geopolitical situation and the balance of power; to "unfreeze" a political stalemate by controlled or limited hostilities; and the use of terror and antiterror activities as leverage for political pressure.

The arms race and the acquisition of sophisticated weaponry. In the course of the last 30 years, the Middle East turned into a grand arsenal, overequipped with highly sophisticated arms systems. The appearance of such systems in a conflict-ridden region adds to the temptation to use military power as part of political action or even as a substitute for it. In this context, the possible nuclearization of the Middle East assumes special significance. One school of thought believes that the introduction of nuclear weapons on the Israeli as well as the Arab side, would create a "balance of terror" and a system of conventional arrangements that would at least deescalate the conflict or even resolve it. Another school believes that the introduction of nuclear weapons into the Middle East will inevitably lead to Armageddon—as a result of irresponsible behavior, or the temptatin to launch a quick and decisive "buttons war." Paradoxically, attempts to preempt and prevent the introduction of nuclear weapons into the area may themselves lead to escalation, as the Israeli raid of the Iraqi nuclear reactor Osirak in 1981 amply illustrated.

Inter-Arab polarization and the powers' intrigue. As has already been established, the state of inter-Arab relations and the involvement of outside powers meaningfully impact the Arab-Israeli conflict and its temperature. Competition for influence, seniority, or hegemony within each of these two systems has had considerable unsettling consequences for the conflict. Radical-revolutionary governments frequently enjoyed the support—including military support—of the Soviet Union, whose basic interests in the region have benefited from the continued existence of an Israeli-Arab conflict simmering "on a small fire." Moderate, conservative governments normally enjoyed the support, including that in the military sphere, of the United States, whose basic interests are better served by the relaxation of the Arab-Israeli conflict and its termination. The inability, or unwillingness, of the two superpowers to divide the region among themselves by creating clearly defined zones of influence, and their recurrent attempts to undermine each other's footholds there, have further contributed to escalation.

CAUSES OF RELAXATION

Obviously, the converse of the above list contributes to relaxation of the conflict. But, some additional contributing factors should be noted:

The time factor. While the longevity of the conflict has been cited above as an indicator of great vitality, which lowers the probability of the conflict's easy dissipation, the time element has an additional significance that contributes in the opposite direction: a new generation is growing up in the Middle East. This new generation has been born or educated under conditions in which the existence of Israel has been a feature of the environment. It is difficult to assess whether and how this factor contributes to the willingness to reach an agreement, but it would seem that, generally speaking, it has a positive effect.

Pragmatism and "metal fatigue". While the first two decades following the Second World War were marked in the region by the ascendancy of radical-revolutionary attitudes, the last two decades have been characterized by growing pragmatism. The latter attitude regards reality as a given situation that has to be accepted and, at best, manipulated, rather than overturned. Instead of programs for the redivision and reallocation of society's economic resources, which characterized the revolutionary regimes of the Middle East in the 1950s and 1960s, a new concept has surfaced, which emphasizes modernization, industrialization, and raising the standard of living of the population as its main objectives. The "bourgeoisization" of Arab society and the realization that Israeli-Arab wars are getting to be more and more costly without a commensurate growth in their effectiveness, as well as what might be termed "metal fatigue" resulting from a long involvement in a violent conflict, also contribute toward moderation.

Inability to subdue the enemy. After a long series of small and large military engagements, the Arabs have realized that they cannot break Israel's military might. Possibly this was the biggest single lesson from the 1973 war, in which two Arab states enjoyed the advantages of full surprise and a coordinated pincers move. It is also clear to Israel that while it is capable of reaching a decisive victory on the battleground, it cannot conquer the enemy's country or subdue its adversary to the point where Israel could dictate conditions from a position of victor vis-à-vis vanquished. This does not mean that the antagonists will not plan and use a hostile act in order to improve their positions or serve their geopolitical interests. Indeed, the latest war of 1982 was precisely of this ilk. It also saw, for the first time, Israeli soldiers beseiging and entering an Arab capital. The general impact of the inability to force the enemy to capitulate totally and to dictate conditions contributes, in the long run, to further moderation.

Domestic stability and the fragmentation of inter-Arab relations. The relative domestic stability that as compared with the constant upheaval of the 1950s, was a new feature of the Arab world in the 1970s and the fragmentation of inter-Arab relations in the same decade have also contributed to the relaxation of the conflict.

The Israeli-Egyptian peace. A detailed analysis of the factors that brought about the Egyptian-Israeli peace treaty, the substance of the arrangement, and its specific consequences are outside the scope of this chapter. It is important, however, to note that in the history of the Arab-Israeli conflict this peace, albeit fragile and problematic, has constituted the greatest single positive breakthrough. The process that led to this peace and the agreement itself embody a number of principles that are crucial for any future Arab-Israeli arrangement. It was reached voluntarily by the chief antagonists and through direct negotiations between them. It contained two crucial elements: first, the satisfaction of Israel's main aspirations—full recognition, normalization, and the renouncement of force as a means to resolve international disputes; and the fulfillment of Egypt's main aspirations—the return of the Sinai in its entirety to the fold of Egyptian sovereignty, without making it appear to be a separate Israeli-Egyptian peace, at least initially. Second, it was effected through a deep involvement of a superpower, but by the provision of auspices rather than by outside imposition. The fact that this peace has survived the vicissitudes of a number of turbulent years in the volatile Middle East and the abrupt departure in 1981 of one of its chief architects—the late President Sadat—is significant in that it has helped alleviate many of the doubts of skeptics in Israel. Even if the Israeli-Egyptian peace cannot yet be regarded as a solid fixture of the Middle East scene, and although it has created some dangerous frustrations in both Egypt and Israel, as long as it holds it radically alters the dynamics of the Arab-Israeli conflict. The Arab world without Egypt cannot possibly conduct an all-out, protracted war on Israel. The Israeli-Egyptian peace therefore encourages Arab moderation. Also, it provides a moderate counter to the position of the "rejectionists" within the Arab world. The "middle" thus becomes a moderate posture. On the other hand, Israel's serious doubt about the possibility of breaking out of the vicious circle of constant war with its neighbors is also gradually assuaged by this situation. While ostensibly it gives Israel a freer hand to act against the Arab world (as the Arab opposition to Egypt has claimed), in reality it also imposes major constraints on Israel's politicostrategic conduct, for it has to consider a possible adverse effect on its peace with Egypt. The main question with regard to this peace, which remains unanswered, is whether it is doomed to turn into a historical episode like the Faysal-Weizmann agreement of 1919, remembered only by historians of the past, or whether it is destined to be a harbinger of developments that future historians will regard as the watershed in the evolution of the Arab-Israeli conflict.

PERSPECTIVES ON THE FUTURE

Can a solution be devised for the Arab-Israeli conflict? Is the attainment of a just and durable peace between Israel and the Arabs at all possible? The underlying question, unanswered for many years, is twofold. First, have all or at least some of Israel's major adversaries genuinely reached a conclusion that Israel is an existing fact that ought to be recognized and negotiated with? Second, what is the proper order of treatment, or the condition sine qua non? A full, explicit and unconditioned recognition by the relevant Arab states of Israel's right to exist in peace with secure and recognized boundaries, or a similarly clear Israeli announcement of its willingness to compromise on her positions concerning the territories and Palestinian statehood?

The questions cannot be properly addressed, as many analysts and mediators have tried to do, unless a major feature of the conflict's reality is borne in mind. It has a built-in structural asymmetry: Israel's perception of having to cope with a number of mortal enemies at any given time, and her suspicion that reaching agreement with one of them will not necessarily deliver the other adversaries to the negotiating table. Moreover, in Israeli eyes all arrangements are reversible and while they require that Israel divest itself of tangible security assets, the Arab counterpart is actually giving up abstract trump cards and is making paper commitments that can be annulled with relative ease, particularly if a change of regime occurs. To the Arabs Israel is a formidable military enemy that threatens them. Its Achilles heel is its legitimacy. They therefore regard recognition as the only negotiating asset that, as they see it, should not be thrown in at the beginning of negotiations. This discrepancy in mutual perception is one of the features of the chicken-and-egg situation that has been so characteristic of the Arab-Israeli conflict.

Against this backdrop it might be useful to list briefly a number of general conditions that are required if constructive progress toward a gradual resolution of the Arab-Israeli conflict is to be made. First, trivial as it may sound, it is essential that the relevant parties share a vital interest in the promotion of peace. While a few leaders and governments will agree to that, they do not always wish to attach an urgency to an arrangement, because of the required compromises and concessions. Second, the solution or formula cannot be imposed by force by an external or local actor. Time and again it has been demonstrated that, at best, a war can serve as a catalyst for progress, not as a substitute for diplomacy. The 1973 and possibly also the 1982 wars are good cases in point. Third, a "polyparticipatory forum" is not the most appropriate framework for negotiations. The Arab-Israeli Geneva conference of 1974, under the auspices of the two superpowers, became a debating forum that led nowhere. Rather, the 1974-75 agreements between Israel, Egypt, and Syria and later the Camp David Egyptian-Israeli accords of 1978, as well as the 1982 Lebanese-Israeli agreement for normalization and withdrawal of all foreign forces, were all worked out on a bilateral level with the active mediation of one superpower. Fourth, the cumulative experience with agreements in the realm of the Arab-Israeli conflict demonstrates that an arrangement should be sought over concrete bilateral matters relating to the parties directly involved. One of the weaknesses of the Camp David construction is the involvement of two parties (Jordan and the Palestinians) that were not participatory to the negotiation process, nor could any of the three participating parties deliver them. Similarly, the May 1983 Lebanese-Israeli agreement suffers from an inherent weakness with regard to a third party—Syria. Fifth, the initiative for an arrangement should emanate from within, rather than from outside the region. Military and/or economic assistance and political arm-twisting by a superpower or external guarantees of the arrangement can help but not substitute for the dealings between the concerned local parties. Sixth, the negotiations between the relevant parties must be direct. "Shuttle diplomacy" may at best produce results on a technical-tactical level such as disengagement or delineation of cease-fire lines. It cannot produce the kind of breakthrough that the Begin-Sadat Summits or the Israeli-Lebanese high-level committees produced. Seventh, while each of the participating parties may, of course, air its outlook, attitudes, policies, and demands in the process of the negotiations, these cannot be predicated on preconditions to which the other party does not wish to accede. Eighth, an agreement reached must be founded on principles and formulas agreed upon by previously successful negotiations with the same party or with other parties. It must also create a new situation, as if adding a new brick to the construction of arrangement. Thus, the Camp David accords incorporated important elements of the U.N. Security Council resolutions 242 (of 1967) and 338 (of 1973). But it also created a new floor for more progress. On the other hand, the Israeli-Lebanese agreement demonstrates that it would be a mistake to assume that one model of an agreement can be copied and applied to all situations at all times. Differences in circumstances and interests dictate variety and flexibility rather than uniformity and rigidity in the models for arrangement. Ninth, for negotiations to conclude successfully and, more importantly, for the agreement reached through them to hold and be implemented, the arrangement must provide enough satisfaction of each party's aspirations so that if the agreement is not adhered to, the parties would lose more than they might gain.

During the many years of the Arab-Israeli conflict, hundreds if not thousands of proposals and plans have been devised in an attempt to induce peace between Israel and the Arabs. Some deal with the solution

of specific issues such as Jerusalem, Arab or Jewish refugees, demilitarization, and international guarantees. Others (such as the Brookings plan
of 1975) are comprehensive and purport to deal with all the major issues
of the conflict. Their common denominator is the fundamental require-
ment that the involved parties undergo a profound attitudinal change and
develop a willingness to move together toward an arrangement, rather
than continue to walk the war path. In this connection the following
question normally surfaces: should the next major move concentrate on
the Palestine problem hoping that any progress will improve the chances
for peace between Israel and the Arab world, or should the bilateral
relationship between Israel and her immediate neighbors be treated first,
thus creating conditions that will be more conducive to progress along
the Palestinian track? The answer to this question seems to change with
time and circumstances. It would seem that Israel's vital interest, as
defined by the Israeli government, is to deal first with the Arab states.
The Palestinian interest is the mirror image of Israel's and the relevant
Arab states seem to be outspoken on the priority of Palestinian matters,
but undecided when it comes to commitment and action. A basic element in Israel's national assessment is that the Palestinian component is
secondary. The Arab world behaves as if the Palestinian component were
primary, but will not explicitly announce that its resolution will ipso facto
mean the end of conflict between them and Israel. Any attempt to cope
with the intricacies of the Arab-Israeli conflict that does not consider the
need to satisfy enough Palestinian aspirations ignores the necessary
condition for meaningful progress. Any attempt, on the other hand, to
propose drastic moves for the fulfillment of Palestinian aspirations that
does not consider the simultaneous need to reassure Israel with regard
to the elimination of enmity with the rest of the Arab world, is similarly
doomed.

Finally, the question of the time element has to be considered. One
aspect of the Middle East debate about the future of the Arab-Israeli
conflict concerns the question of whether time is on the side of Israel or
the Arabs. This question, of course, is meaningless unless discussed in
terms of how each side uses that period of time at its disposal. Analyzed
in historical perspective, it would seem that Israel has put time to better
use as far as the consolidation of military wherewithal and the enhancement of its national cohesion are concerned, while the Arabs have used
time better as far as the undermining of Israel's international status is concerned. During the first hundred years or so of the Arab-Israeli conflict,
the Arab world acted on the assumption that in the long run and irre-

spective of the result of all wars with Israel, time was on its side. The imagery of Israel as a repetition of the Crusaders' state, which succumbed to Islamic military pressure after a number of generations, during which it occupied Jerusalem, was very popular in the Arab world. The notion that eventually the Arabs would win one decisive battle and erase Israel from the Middle East map nourished a notion that an arrangement with Israel was not only urgently required, but might represent a historical aberration. For Israel, time was of the essence, and great urgency was attached—at least psychologically—to the need to find an appropriate solution that would terminate Israel's war with its environment. In recent years, and possibly as a result of the accelerated Israeli settlement policy of the West Bank, the attitude to time seems to have been reversed. It is on the Arab side, and particularly among the Palestinian inhabitants of the West Bank, that a feeling of great urgency about an arrangement, before Israel establishes completely irreversible facts on the ground, has emerged. As the second century of the Arab-Israeli conflict begins, this dramatic change—intangible as it is—may be of great consequence.

A superficial observation of the history of the Arab-Israeli conflict and the headlines it constantly contributes to the world's media would warrant a conclusion that, inevitably, it will turn from a hundred-year war into an eternal war. A closer analysis, which considers the elements of change as well as regional undercurrents, raises a possibility that partial solutions and arrangements may yet be reached and eventually crystallize into a new and peaceful situation. On balance, it is quite possible that spectacular acts of violence and major hostilities will recur in the region, or that regression will set into spheres in which a modicum of agreement has already been reached. A comprehensive historical perspective, however, should consider not only major wars but also breakthroughs for peace. If the line is drawn here, it provides cause for reserved optimism, for it suggests that at some time in the 1970s the Arab-Israeli conflict may have changed course from erratic escalation to gradual resolution. Israel's growing might, which enabled its government to follow a policy of rigidity combined with flexibility, and profound changes in the Arab world, which enable a significant part thereof to follow a policy of flexibility combined with rigidity, have been the most important instruments of the gradual transformation of the Arab-Israeli conflict. Assuming that conflicts are not resolved but gradually dissipate, the question for the coming years is whether enough imagination and perseverance will be mustered by all involved parties to help raise the threshold of war and improve the chances for peace, simultaneously. The answer to this question lies primarily in the hands of the chief local antagonists.

Selected and Annotated Bibliography
CHAPTER 1: GENESIS

For studies of Arab nationalism, see Zeine N. Zeine, *The Emergence of Arab Nationalism*, 3rd ed. (Delmar, N.Y., 1973); Sylvia Haim, *Arab Nationalism: An Anthology* (Berkeley, 1962); and Albert Hourani, *Arabic Thought in the Liberal Age, 1798-1939* (London, 1939). The best book on traditional Arab social structure is Reuben Levy, *The Social Structure of Islam* (London, 1957). The best brief essay on Arab history and culture is still Bernard Lewis, *The Arabs in History* (New York, 1966). The best short treatment of the response of Arab civilization to the West is Bernard Lewis, *The Middle East and the West* (Bloomington, 1964). For a historical study on the relations between Jews and Arabs, see S. D. Goitein, *Jews and Arabs: Their Contacts Through the Ages*, 3rd ed. (New York, 1974), and Abraham I. Katsch *Judaism in Islam*, 3rd ed. (New York, 1980). Source material on Arab nationalism can be found in John J. Donohue and John L. Esposito, *Islam in Transition: Muslim Perspectives* pts. I and II (New York, 1983); and Kemal H. Karpat, ed. *Political and Social Thought in the Contemporary Middle East*, pts. II and V (New York, 1982).

Historical studies on the history, politics and sociology of Palestinian society include Joel S. Migdal, ed. *Palestinian Society and Politics* (Princeton, 1980); Ann Mosley Lesch, *Arab Politics in Palestine, 1917-1939* (Ithaca, 1979); and especially the two-volume work by Yehoshua Porath, *The Emergence of the Palestinian Arab National Movement* (London, 1974 and 1979).

Studies on Zionist history and ideology and the early history of Israel include Howard M. Sachar, *A History of Israel: From the Rise of Zionism to Our Time* (New York, 1979); Walter Laqueur, *A History of Zionism* (New York, 1972); Sholomo Avineri, *The Making of Modern Zionism* (New York, 1981); and David Vital, *Zionism: The Formative Years* (Oxford; 1982). The best short essay on Zionism, with accompanying source materials, is Arthur Hertzberg, *The Zionist Idea* (New York, 1969).

For histories and analyses of aspects of the mandate period, and especially the period leading up to partition, see Christopher Sykes, *Crossroads to Israel: 1917-1948* (London, 1965); J.C. Hurewitz, *The Struggle for Palestine* (New York, 1950); J. Bowyer Bell, *The Long War: Israel and the Arabs Since 1946* (Englewood cliffs, N.J., 1969); Michael J. Cohen, *Palestine: Retreat From the Mandate: The Making of British Policy, 1936-1945* (New York, 1978); and Barry Rubin, *The Arab States and the Palestine Conflict* (Syracuse, 1981).

Finally, for a compendium of very useful maps, see Martin Gilbert, *The Arab-Israeli Conflict: Its History in Maps*, 2nd ed. (London, 1976).

CHAPTER 2:
SEVEN WARS AND ONE PEACE TREATY

A number of studies provide comparative perspectives on two or more of the wars. Perhaps the most ambitious is Chaim Herzog, *The Arab-Israeli Wars: War and Peace in the Middle East from the War of Independence Through Lebanon* (New York, 1982). See also, Yair Evron, *The Middle East: Nations, Superpowers, and Wars* (New York, 1973); and Nadav Safran, *From War to War: The Arab-Israeli Confrontation, 1948-1967* (New York, 1969).

The 1948-1949 war(s) is treated in Jon Kimche and David Kimche, *Both Sides of the Hill: Britain and the Palestine War* (London, 1960); Natanel Lorch, *The Edge of the Sword: Israel's War of Independence* (New York, 1961); Edgar O'Ballance, *The Arab-Israeli War, 1948* (London, 1956); Dominique Lapierre and Larry Collins, *O Jerusalem* (New York, 1972). King Abdullah of Jordan, *Memoirs* (New York, 1950), and Abba Eban, *An Autobiography* (New York, 1977), add a personal touch.

Earl Berger, *The Covenant and the Sword* (London, 1965) expertly covers Arab-Israeli relations in the period from 1948 to 1956.

There is a considerable literature on the 1956 war, as well as on the subsequent ones. A French perspective is provided by General André Beaufré, *The Suez Expedition* (New York, 1969). Anthony Eden, *Full Circle* (London, 1960) offers a rationale for British policy. Hugh Thomas, *Suez* (London, 1970), and Anthony Nutting, *Nasser* (New York, 1972) do not let Eden off the hook. Herman Finer, *Dulles Over Suez* (Chicago, 1964) criticizes U.S. policy; and Kennett Love, *Suez: The Twice Fought War* (New York, 1969) offers a massive critique of Israeli policy. Moshe Dayan, *Diary of the Sinai Campaign* (New York, 1965) offers an insider's account of the military aspects.

The 1967 war is treated in the following: Edgar O'Ballance, *The Third Arab-Israeli War* (Hamden, Conn., 1972); Walter Z. Laqueur, *The Road to War* (London, 1969); Shabtai Teveth, *The Tanks of Tammuz* (London, 1969) who tells of the Israeli assault on the Golan Heights; David Kimche and Dan Bawley, *The Six Day War* (New York, 1968).

An Egyptian perspective on the war of attrition and the 1973 war is treated in Mohamed Heikal, *The Road to Ramadan* (New York, 1975). On the 1973 war, see Anwar Sadat, *In Search of Identity* (New York, 1978); Chaim Herzog, *The War of Atonement* (New York, 1975); and Galia Golan, *Yom Kippur and After* (New York, 1977).

The varied and complex diplomatic bargaining and negotiations conducted after the 1973 war receive attention from a variety of perspectives. In addition to Anwar Sadat's book, the most important Egyptian assessment is given by Ismail Fahmy, *Negotiating for Peace in the Middle East* (Baltimore, 1983). Among the numerous American books are Jimmy Carter, *Keeping Faith* (New York, 1982) and Henry Kissinger, *Years of Upheaval* (Boston,

1982). Valuable insights are contained in Moshe Dayan, *Breakthrough: A Personal Account of the Egypt-Israel Peace Negotiations* (New York, 1981); and Yitzhak Rabin, *The Rabin Memoirs* (Boston, 1979).

The war in Lebanon is discussed in Itamar Rabinovich, *The War for Lebanon, 1970-1982* (Ithaca, 1984); Jacobo Timerman, *The Longest War: Israel in Lebanon* (New York, 1982); and Walid Khalidi, *Conflict and Violence in Lebanon* (London, 1983).

CHAPTER 3:
TRANSFORMATION: EXTERNAL DETERMINANTS

Strategic issues and weapons-related problems are to be found in many journals and books. For example, *The Military Balance*, published annually by the International Institute for Strategic Studies in London, permits a systematic tracing of arms buildups in the region. The practical application of recent technologies and their effects on tactics and strategy is discussed in Seymour J. Deitchman, *New Technology and Military Power: General Purpose Military Forces For the 1980s and Beyond* (Boulder, 1979). A still useful examination of Arab options is Yehoshafat Harkabi, *Arab Strategies and Israel's Response* (New York, 1977). A model of what it is possible to do on a country-by-country basis is Anthony H. Cordesman, *Jordanian Arms and the Middle Eazst Balance* (Washington, D.C., 1983). Nuclear issues are discussed in Onkar Marwah and Ann Schultz, eds., *Nuclear Proliferation and the Near Nuclear Countries* (Cambridge, 1975); and Shai Feldman, *Israeli Nuclear Deterrence: A Strategy for the 1980s?* (New York, 1982).

For the policies of the superpowers and the superpower rivalry, see the following: Karen Dawisha, *Soviet Foreign Policy Towards Egypt* (London, 1979); Milton Leitenberg and Gabriel Sheffer, eds., *Great Power Intervention In the Middle East* (New York, 1979); William B. Quandt, *Decade of Decisions: American Policy Toward the Arab-Israeli Conflict, 1967-76* (Berkeley, 1977); Bernard Reich, *Quest for Peace: United States-Israel Relations and the Arab-Israeli Conflict* (New Bruswick, 1977); Alvin Z. Rubinstein, *Red Star on the Nile: The Soviet-Egyptian Influence Relationship Since the June War* (Princeton, 1977); Lawrence L. Whetten, *The Arab-Israel Dispute: Great Power Behavior* (London, 1976); and Yaacov Bar-Siman-Tov, *The Israeli-Egyptian War of Attrition* (New York, 1980).

The best source for information about the evolution of the Arab-Israeli conflict in the United Nations can be found in the documents and articles compiled by John Norton Moore, ed., *The Arab-Israeli Conflict: Readings and Documents* (Princeton, 1977). See also, U Thant, *View From the U.N.: The Memoirs of U Thant* (New York, 1978).

Though there has been a great deal written on the oil issue, no book examines its effect on the conflict. The Arab boycott and economic warfare against Israel is analyzed in Walter Henry Nelson and Terrence Prittie, *The Economic War Against the Jews* (New York, 1977).

The literature available in the English language on Arab perceptions of the conflict and of their dilemmas is growing, especially in contributions to periodicals such as *The Middle East Journal, Jerusalem Quarterly,* and *Middle East Affairs.* For especially perceptive accounts of what is happening in the Arab world, see Fouad Ajami, *The Arab Predicament: Arab Political Thought and Practice Since 1967* (New York, 1981); Elie Kedourie, *Islam in the Modern World* (New York, 1980); Malcolm H. Kerr, *The Arab Cold War* (New York, 1971); Hamid Enayat, *Modern Islamic Political Thought* (Austin, 1982); John W. Amos II, *Arab-Israeli Military/Political Relations: Arab Perceptions and the Politics of Escalation* (New York, 1979); A. I. Dawisha, *Egypt in the Arab World* (New York, 1976); and William R. Polk, *The Arab World,* 5th ed. (Cambridge, 1980).

The component of the Arab-Israeli conflict that involves religious and cultural tensions and differences between Arabs and Jews is very difficult to analyze politically. Attempts to foster dialogue on the subject more often than not result in discomfort rather than enlightenment and understanding. A few studies rise above partisan perspectives. Gerald Caplan, *Arab and Jew in Jerusalem: Explorations in Community Health* (Cambridge, 1982); Rafik Halabi, *The West Bank Story: An Israeli Arab's View of Both Sides of a Tangled Conflict* (New York, 1982); Albert Memmi, *Jews and Arabs* (Chicago, 1975); and Alexander Yonah, *The Role of Communications in the Middle East Conflict: Ideological and Religious Aspects* (New York, 1973).

CHAPTER 4: ISRAEL: FROM IDEOLOGY TO REALITY

Political ideology and attitude in Israel are discussed in several informative books. Among them are Alan Arian, *Ideological Change in Israel* (Cleveland, 1968); Schlomo Aronson, *Conflict and Bargaining in the Middle East* (Baltimore, 1978); Leonard Fein, *Politics in Israel* (Boston, 1967); and Robert O. Freedman, ed., *Israel in the Begin Era* (New York, 1982), the best collection to date on the post-1977 period, covering all aspects of Israeli politics. Rael Jean Isaac, *Israel Divided: Ideological Politics in the Jewish State* (Baltimore, 1976) is basically a study of extraparliamentary movements after 1967, but also a provocative overview of Israeli politics. Don Peretz in *The Government and Politics of Israel* (Boulder, 1979) gives a brief, clear introduction to the basic operation of the political system.

On electoral politics, see Jacob M. Landau, Ergun Ozbudun, and Frank

Tachau, eds., *Electoral Politics in the Middle East: Issues, Voters, and Elites* (London, 1980), especially articles by Landau on electoral issues, by Arian on voting behavior, and by Gutmann on the parliamentary elite. Howard R. Penniman, ed., *Israel at the Polls: The Knesset Elections of 1977* (Washington, 1979) presents an impressive array of articles covering all aspects of the critical 1977 elections.

Also, see Yuval Elizur and Eliahu Salpeter, *Who Rules Israel?* (New York, 1973), a portrait of Israel's traditional elite (pre-1977), described by two leading journalists; Amos Elon, *The Israelis: Founders and Sons* (New York, 1971), an arresting treatment of the generation gap and a somewhat controversial study by one of Israel's leading writers; and the authoritative analysis of the political leadership in Israel, pre-1977, by two prominent Israeli political scientists, Emanuel Gutmann and Jacob M. Landau, "The Political Elite and National Leadership in Israel," in George Lenczowski, ed., *Political Elites in the Middle East* (Washington, 1975), pp. 163-99.

Michael Brecher has published two companion volumes on Israeli foreign policy decision making: *The Foreign Policy System of Israel* (New Haven, 1972); and *Decisions in Israel's Foreign Policy* (New Haven, 1975).

Israel's social problems are discussed in Michael Curtis and Mordecai Chertoff, eds., *Israel: Social Structure and Change* (New Brunswick, 1973); in *Israeli Society* (New York, 1967), the definitive study of the subject by Israel's leading sociologist, Schmuel N. Eisenstadt; and in Russell A. Stone, *Social Change in Israel: Attitudes and Events, 1967-1979* (Praeger, 1982), a most thorough study of Israeli public opinion, based on data from the Continuing Survey of the Israeli Institute for Applied Social Research. Also see Dan Horowitz and Moshe Lissak, *Origins of the Israeli Polity: Palestine under the Mandate* (Chicago and London, 1978) for a sophisticated sociological and political study of the origin of Israeli institutions in the mandate period. Ben Halpern in *The Idea of the Jewish State*, 2d ed. (Cambridge, Mass., 1969) gives a classic overview of Zionism and the creation of the state of Israel. And Nadav Safran provides an illuminating introduction to Israel and an analysis of U.S.-Israeli relations since 1949 in *Israel: The Embattled Ally* (Cambridge, Mass., 1978).

CHAPTER 5: THE PALESTINIAN DIMENSION

History

The most comprehensive and authoritative study of the origins of the Palestinian national movement before the Second World War is Yehoshua Porath's two-volume study, *The Emergence of the Palestinian Arab National Movement, 1918-1929* (London, 1974) and *The Palestinian Arab National*

Movement: From Riots to Rebellion, 1929-1939 (London, 1977). Ann Mosley Lesch, Arab Politics in Palestine, 1917-1939: The Frustration of a Nationalist Movement (Ithaca, 1979) is an excellent and concise treatment of the same period. Neville Mandel's The Arabs and Zionism Before World War I (Berkeley, 1976) is an excellent resource for the Arab response to political Zionism before 1914.

For a concise and insightful treatment of the Arab states' reaction to the Palestinian problem before 1948, see Barry Rubin, The Arab States and the Palestine Conflict, (Syracuse, 1981). British policy toward the question of Palestine is the focus of any number of useful works, most recently Michael J. Cohen's two-volume Palestine: Retreat from the Mandate, The Making of British Policy, 1936-1945 (New York, 1981) and Palestine and the Great Powers, 1945-1948 (Princeton, 1982). Simcha Palpan's Zionism and the Palestinians (New York, 1979) provides an insightful study of Zionist attitudes. The impact of the 1948 war on the Palestinian community is examined in Jon and David Kimche's Both Sides of the Hill (London, 1969); Ibrahim Abu-Lughod's (ed.) The Transformation of Palestine (Evanston, 1971); and Nafuz Nazzal, The Palestinian Exodus from Galilee (Beirut, 1978).

The development of the PLO and contemporary Palestinian nationalism is the subject of a number of colorful works by journalists who focus on the military and political dimensions, particularly John K. Cooley, Green March, Black September, The Story of the Palestinian Arabs (London, 1973); Christopher Dobson, Black September: its short, violent history (New York, 1974); David Hirst, The Gun and the Olive Branch (London, 1977); Raid al-Rayyes and Dunia Nashas, Guerillas for Palestine (London, 1976).

Politics

The Palestinian National Movement—its ideology, organization, and politics—is the subject of a number of studies. For an interesting and concise analysis of Palestinian ideology and military strategy in the post-1967 period, see Hisham Sharabi, Palestine Guerillas: Their Credibility and Effectiveness (Washington, D.C.: 1979). For a different approach to many of the same issues, see Yehoshafat Harkabi, Fedayeen Action and Arab Strategy (London, 1968). A more comprehensive treatment of Palestinian military tactics and strategy can be found in Bard E. O'Neill, Armed Struggle in Palestine: A Political-Military Analysis (Boulder, 1978).

William B. Quandt, Faud Jabber, and Ann Mosely Lesch, The Politics of Palestinian Nationalism (Berkeley, 1973), although now dated, still provides the best introduction to the organizational and inter-Arab aspects of Palestinian nationalism. John W. Amos II, Palestinian Resistance: Organization of a Nationalist Movement (New York, 1980) offers a detailed look at PLO struggle and ideology. Aryeh Y. Yodfat and Yuval Arnon-Ohanna, PLO

Strategy and Tactics (New York, 1981) provides a more general look at the organization. Aaron David Miller, *The PLO and the Politics of Survival* (New York, 1983) analyzes the organizational inter-Arab and Israeli challenges confronting the PLO. For an eloquently argued, although polemical, view of the Palestine issue, see Edward W. Said, *The Question of Palestine* (New York, 1979).

For more specialized studies of various aspects of the Palestinian resistance movement, see Walid W. Kazziha, *Revolutionary Transformation in the Arab World; Habash and his Comrades from Nationalism to Marxism* (London, 1975) on the origins of the Marxist groups within the PLO; Kazziha's *Palestine in the Arab Dilemma* (London, 1979) for a general discussion of the Arab states and the Palestine question. Yehoshafat Harkabi, *The Palestinian Covenant and its Meaning* (London, 1979) on PLO ideology; Galia Golan, *The Soviet Union and the Palestinian Liberation Organization: An Uneasy Alliance* (New York, 1980) for the Soviet angle.

Society

A collection of essays of varying quality dealing with various aspects of Palestinian history, society, and politics can be found in Gabriel Ben-Dor (ed.) *The Palestinians and the Middle East Conflict* (Ramat Gan, 1978). For a grass-roots Palestinian perspective of the social and economic aspects of the refugee experience, see Rosemary Sayigh, *Palestinians: From Peasants to Revolutionaries* (London, 1979); see also Khalil Nakleh and Elia Zureik (eds.) *The Sociology of the Palestinians* (London, 1980). Joel S. Migdal (editor) *Palestinian Society and Politics* (Princeton, Press, 1980) also includes essays on Palestinian society and economics. Two fascinating perspectives on the refugee experience can be found in Fawaz Turki, *The Disinherited* (New York, 1972) and Abu Iyad, *My Home My Land: A Narrative of the Palestinian Struggle* (New York, 1981).

On the Palestinians in Jordan before 1967, see Shaul Mishal, *West Bank East Bank* (New Haven, 1978). For the most recent treatment of the Arabs within Israel proper, see Ian Lustick, *Arabs in the Jewish State*, (Austin, 1980). On the attitudes of West Bank and Gaza Palestinians, see Ann Mosely Lesch, *Political Perceptions of the Palestinians on the West Bank and the Gaza Strip* (Washington, D.C., 1980); Rafki Halabi, *The West Bank Story* (New York, 1982). On West Bank and Gaza economies, see Brian Van Arkadie, *Benefits and Burdens: A Report on the West Bank and Gaza Strip Economics Since 1967* (New York; 1977).

For studies of possible solutions to the Palestinian problem see Mark A. Heller, *A Palestinian State: The Implications for Israel* (Cambridge, 1983); Daniel J. Elazar, *Judea, Samaria, and Gaza: Views on the Present and Future* (Washington, D.C.: 1982); Emile A. Nakleh, *The West Bank and Gaza:*

Toward the Making of A Palestinian State (Washington, D.C.: 1979); Aryeh Shalev, *The Autonomy—Problems and Possible Solutions*, (Tel Aviv, 1980).

CHAPTER 6:
CONTINUITY AND CHANGE: AN OVERVIEW

Whither the Arab-Israeli relationship? Prescriptive suggestions for meliorating and solving the conflict abound, mostly in journal articles. A few reports and studies offering very different proposals may be cited, if only to alert the reader to the diversity that exists: David Astor and Valerie Yorke, *Peace in the Middle East* (London, 1978); William R. Brown, *The Last Crusade: A Negotiator's Middle East Handbook* (Chicago, 1980); Daniel Heradstviet, *The Arab-Israeli Conflict: Psychological Obstacle to Peace* (New York, 1979); Bernard Lewis, *History: Remembered, Recovered, Invented* (Princeton, 1975); Michael Reisman, *The Art of the Possible: Diplomatic Alternatives in the Middle East* (Princeton, 1970); Saadia Touval, *The Peace Brokers: Mediators in the Arab-Israeli Conflict, 1948-1979* (Princeton, 1982); and a report prepared by the American Friends Service Committee, *A Compassionate Peace: A Future for the Middle East* (New York, 1982).

Index

A

Abdallah, King, 21, 23, 28–29, 32, 120, 148–50
Ahdut Ha'avoda, 123, 128
Ajami, Fouad, 95
Algiers Summit, 61
Alkalai, Yehuda, 14, 15
Amer, Abdel Hakim, 49
Anglo-American Commission of Inquiry on Palestine, 35
antisemitism, 4, 76, 96–101
Arafat, Yasir, 96, 149–52, 163, 171, 173
Arab boycott, 89
Arab League, 34, 183
Arab National Movement, 149
Arabism, 160, 186–87, 191
Arab revolt of 1936, 27–28
Arabs in Israel, 169
Arens, Moshe, 74
arms race, 80, 200
Assad, Hafez, 81, 165, 173

B

Balfour Declaration, 18–19, 21, 24, 26–27, 181, 192
Ba'ath Party (Syria), 94
Baghdad Pact, 93
Begin Menachem, 65, 98, 135, 136–37, 152, 172
Beirut, 139, 164
Ben-Gurion, David, 29–32, 34, 35, 38, 47, 116, 121, 124
Ben-Yehuda, Eliezer, 17
Bevin, Ernest, 34, 37, 38
Black September Organization, 152
Britain, 9–10, 17, 31, 39, 110–16
Buber, Martin, 26

C

Camp David, 62, 137, 154, 204
Carter, Jimmy, 81
Churchill, Winston, 21, 33–34

D

Damascus, 89
Dayan, Moshe, 51, 52, 72, 125, 133, 138
Deir Yassin, 148
Democratic Movement for Change, 135

E

Egypt: 57, 92–93; in war against Israel (1948-49); in Sinai-Suez War, 46–49; in June 1967 War, 49–53; in 1973 War, 53–56; see wars
Egyptian-Israeli Treaty (March 26, 1979), 41, 196
elections in Israel, 129–37
European Community (EC) and Israel, 88–90
Exodus, 37

F

Fahd plan, 198
Fahmy, Ismael, 99
Faisal, King, 19–21; see Faysal, 100, 115
Fatah, Al, 149, 150, 251, 270
Faysal, Hashemite king, see Faisal
France, 4–5, 10, 15, 19–21, 31, 46–47, 85, 181, 183, 194

G

Galilee, 29, 74
Gaza Strip, 47, 167

About the Editor and Contributors

ALAN DOWTY is a Professor of Government and International Studies at the University of Notre Dame, where he has taught since 1975. Previous to that, he was for twelve years on the faculty of the Hebrew University, in Jerusalem, during which time he also served as Executive Director of the Leonard Davis Institute for International Relations and Chairman of the Department of International Relations.

Professor Dowty is a graduate of Shimer College and the University of Chicago, where he received his Ph.D. in 1963. He has published several dozen articles on international relations, U.S. foreign policy, and the Arab-Israeli conflict. Among his books are *The Limits of American Isolation* (New York: University Press, 1971) and *Middle East Crisis: U.S. Decision-Making in 1958, 1970, and 1973* (Berkeley: University of California Press, 1983). He is active as a consultant and commentator on Middle East policy issues, on which he has also testified before Congressional committees.

ADAM M. GARFINKLE is Coordinator of the Political Studies Program at the Foreign Policy Research Institute in Philadelphia, and holds a Ph.D. from the University of Pennsylvania. His essays on the Middle East and other subjects have appeared in *Orbis, Current History, Disarmament, Grand Strategy, Parameters, Contemporary Review,* and other journals. He is the author of *Western Europe's Middle East Diplomacy and the United States* (1983) and *'Finlandization': A Map to a Metaphor* (1978), both published by the Foreign Policy Research Institute. He is also editor of the forthcoming, *Global Perspectives on Arms Control* (New York: Praeger Publishers).

AARON DAVID MILLER is an analyst on Lebanon and the Palestinians for the Department of State's Bureau of Intelligence and Research. He has a Ph.D. in Middle East history from the University of Michigan, and is the author of books on Saudi Arabia and on the PLO. His articles have appeared in the *New York Times*, *Los Angeles Times*, *Jerusalem Quarterly*, and *Current History*.

ITAMAR RABINOVICH is Professor of History and Head of the Shiloah Center for Middle Eastern and African Studies, Tel-Aviv University. He is author of *Syria Under the Ba'th, 1963-1966* (New York: Halsted Press, 1972) and *The War for Lebanon, 1970-1982* (Ithaca: Cornell University Press, 1984). In addition, he has published widely in journals such as *Survival*, *Orbis*, and *Middle East Review*, contributed chapters to several books, and co-edited a number of studies, including *From June to October* (New Brunswick: Transaction Books, 1978) and *The United States and the Middle East* (New Brunswick: Transaction Books, 1980).

ALVIN Z. RUBINSTEIN is Professor of Political Science at the University of Pennsylvania and a Senior Fellow of the Foreign Policy Research Institute. He is the author of a number of studies, including *Soviet Policy Toward Turkey, Iran, and Afghanistan* (New York: Praeger Publishers, 1982), *Soviet Foreign Policy Since World War II: Imperial and Global* (Boston: Little Brown and Company, 1981), *Red Star on the Nile: The Soviet-Egyptian Influence Relationship Since the June War* (Princeton: Princeton University Press, 1977), and *Yugoslavia and the Nonaligned World* (Princeton: Princeton University Press, 1970).

Professor Rubinstein has received fellowships from, among others, the Rockefeller Foundation, the John Simon Guggenheim Memorial Foundation, the American Council of Learned Societies—Social Science Research Council, and the Earhart Foundation. He has been Visiting Professor at the University of Virginia, Lehigh University, University of California at Santa Barbara, and the American University in Cairo.

HAIM SHAKED earned both his B.A. and M.A. *cum laude* at the Hebrew University of Jerusalem, and his Ph.D. at the School of Oriental and African Studies of the University of London, in Middle Eastern and Islamic Studies. In 1969 he joined Tel-Aviv University. From 1973 to 1980 he served as the head of its Shiloah Center for Middle East Studies and from 1975 to 1980 also as Dean, Faculty of Humanities. He is presently Director, Middle East Studies, and Visiting Professor at the University of Miami, Florida.

Dr. Shaked is the author of the *Life of the Sudanese Mahdi*; co-editor of *From June to October: The Middle East Between 1967 and 1973*; co-editor of *The Middle East and the United States*; and numerous articles and book reviews on the modern Middle East. He is one of the founders and is currently co-editor, of the annual publication *The Middle East Contemporary Survey*, and founder and editor-in-chief of *Mideast File*.